Hollywood Remakes of Iconic British Films

Screen Serialities

Series editors: Claire Perkins and Constantine Verevis

Series advisory board: Kim Akass, Glen Creeber, Shane Denson, Jennifer Forrest, Jonathan Gray, Julie Grossman, Daniel Herbert, Carolyn Jess-Cooke, Frank Kelleter, Amanda Ann Klein, Kathleen Loock, Jason Mittell, Sean O'Sullivan, Barton Palmer, Alisa Perren, Dana Polan, Iain Robert Smith, Shannon Wells-Lassagne, Linda Williams

Screen Serialities provides a forum for introducing, analysing and theorising a broad spectrum of serial screen formats – including franchises, series, serials, sequels and remakes.

Over and above individual texts that happen to be serialised, the book series takes a guiding focus on seriality as an aesthetic and industrial principle that has shaped the narrative logic, socio-cultural function and economic identity of screen texts across more than a century of cinema, television and 'new' media.

Title in this series include:

Film Reboots
Edited by Daniel Herbert and Constantine Verevis

Reanimated: The Contemporary American Horror Remake
By Laura Mee

Gender and Seriality: Practices and Politics of Contemporary US Television
By Maria Sulimma

European Film Remakes
Edited by Eduard Cuelenaere, Gertjan Willems and Stijn Joye

Superhero Blockbusters: Seriality and Politics
By Felix Brinker

Hollywood Remakes of Iconic British Films: Class, Gender and Stardom
By Agnieszka Rasmus

Hollywood Remakes of Iconic British Films

Class, Gender and Stardom

Agnieszka Rasmus

EDINBURGH
University Press

Edinburgh University Press is one of the leading university presses in the UK. We publish academic books and journals in our selected subject areas across the humanities and social sciences, combining cutting-edge scholarship with high editorial and production values to produce academic works of lasting importance. For more information visit our website: edinburghuniversitypress.com

© Agnieszka Rasmus, 2022

Edinburgh University Press Ltd
The Tun – Holyrood Road
12(2f) Jackson's Entry
Edinburgh EH8 8PJ

First published in hardback by Edinburgh University Press 2022

Typeset in 11/13 Ehrhardt MT by
IDSUK (DataConnection) Ltd, and
printed and bound by CPI Group (UK) Ltd,
Croydon, CR0 4YY

A CIP record for this book is available from the British Library

ISBN 978 1 4744 4878 9 (hardback)
ISBN 978 1 4744 4879 6 (paperback)
ISBN 978 1 4744 4880 2 (webready PDF)
ISBN 978 1 4744 4881 9 (epub)

The right of Agnieszka Rasmus to be identified as the author of this work has been asserted in accordance with the Copyright, Designs and Patents Act 1988, and the Copyright and Related Rights Regulations 2003 (SI No. 2498).

Contents

List of Figures		vi
Acknowledgements		viii
Preface		ix
1	Remaking Iconic British Films of the 1960s and 1970s	1
2	From British Working-Class Gangsters to Hollywood Heroes: *The Italian Job* and *Get Carter*	31
3	Gender, Stars and Class Wars: *Alfie* and *Sleuth*	65
4	From Devilish Masters to Evil Dames: *Bedazzled* and *The Wicker Man*	99
5	Remaking, Cultural Exchange and Personal Legacy: *The Limey*	133
References		147
Index		159

Figures

Fig. 2.1	*The Italian Job* (1969): 'Now, what would you like?' 'Everything'	39
Fig. 2.2	*The Italian Job* (2003): 'This is a love story, actually'	41
Fig. 2.3	*Get Carter* (1971): 'Slags like your Sandra can get away with it, can't they? The Doreens of this world can't, can they?'	56
Fig. 2.4	*Get Carter* (2000): Stallone's Carter clumsily comforts his niece	57
Fig. 3.1	*Alfie* (1966): 'Going up in the world, aren't I?'	73
Fig. 3.2	*Alfie* (2004): Ruby is now the cosmetics mogul Liz	78
Fig. 3.3	*Alfie* (2004): Match made in heaven	80
Fig. 3.4	*Sleuth* (1972): 'We are from different worlds, you and me'	83
Fig. 3.5	*Sleuth* (2007): Jude Law is Michael Caine	90
Fig. 3.6	*Sleuth* (2007): Caine's iconic tough-guy image mocked	91
Fig. 4.1	*Bedazzled* (1967): 'What sort of freedom of choice did I have about where I was born and what size I was and what a bloody awful job I landed myself in?'	102
Fig. 4.2	*Bedazzled* (1967): Unlikely friendship	107
Fig. 4.3	*Bedazzled* (2000): Elliot and the sexy Devil	109
Fig. 4.4	*Bedazzled* (2000): The Devil wears Versace	113

Fig. 4.5	*The Wicker Man* (1973): Sergeant Howie meets Lord Summerisle	117
Fig. 4.6	*The Wicker Man* (1973): The perfect sacrifice	118
Fig. 4.7	*The Wicker Man* (2006): Ellen Burstyn as the queen bee of the colony	125
Fig. 4.8	*The Wicker Man* (2006): 'The drone must die'	128
Fig. 5.1	*The Limey* (1999): 'King Midas in reverse'	141
Fig. 5.2	*The Limey* (1999): 'They call him the Seeker'	143

Acknowledgements

Minor passages from Chapter 1 appeared in 'Hollywood Remakes of British Films: A Case of Cross-Pollination', in the *Journal of Adaptation in Film and Performance*, 14:1 (2021), and in '"I know where I've seen you before!": Hollywood Remakes of British Films, from DVD Box Sets to the Online Debate', in *Literatur in Wissenschaft und Unterricht*, 47:1/2 (2014). Fragments of Chapter 2 were published in a different version as '"Crossing Frontiers, Staking Out New Territories": Hollywood Remaking British Crime Locations in *Get Carter*', in J. Fabiszak et al. (eds), *Crossroads in Literature and Culture* (Springer, 2013). Elements from Chapter 3 appeared in 'Same But Different: Comparing Transgression in *Sleuth*', in Mirosława Bucholtz et al. (eds), *The Visual and the Verbal in Film, Drama, Literature and Biography* (Peter Lang, 2012).

Preface

Film remakes began to be rehabilitated by academia in the 1990s thanks to a few pioneering works such as Carolyn A. Durham's *Double Takes: Culture and Gender in French Films and Their American Remakes* (1998), or Andrew Horton and Stuart Y. McDougal's edited collection *Play it Again, Sam: Retakes on Remakes*, published the same year. Many followed suit, including two cross-cultural studies of Hollywood remakes of French films, Lucy Mazdon's *Encore Hollywood: Remaking French Cinema* (2000), and Jennifer Forrest and Leonard R. Koos's edited collection *Dead Ringers: The Remake in Theory and Practice* (2002). Constantine Verevis's *Film Remakes* (2006) cemented the discipline and showed the remake to be a textual, critical and industrial category, not unlike the film genre.

Since then, there have been numerous publications, not only on cross-cultural remakes between Hollywood, Europe and East Asia (Wee 2013; Wang 2013; Smith and Verevis 2017; Smith 2016), but also within Europe (Cuelenaere et al. 2021), proving that it is not an exclusively Hollywood phenomenon, but one of global proportions, characterised by multidirectional transnational and transmedia flows. New findings within seriality studies demonstrate that the film remake is an element of larger forces at work. For Constantine Verevis and Kathleen Loock, it is involved in processes of cultural reproduction, and the practice of remaking is 'one of several industrial and cultural activities of repetition (and variation) which range from quotation and allusion, adaptation and parody, to the process-like nature of genre and serial filmmaking' (2012: 2). It is also often discussed together with other forms of cinematic repetition, continuation and renewal, such as sequels (Jess-Cooke 2009; Jess-Cooke and Verevis 2010), trilogies (Perkins and Verevis 2012) and reboots (Herbert and Verevis 2020), with which the remake overlaps. This has led Amanda Ann

Klein and R. Barton Palmer in their edited collection of essays (2016) to use the word 'multiplicities' as an umbrella term for texts that refuse to be confined or end, such as remakes, sequels, trilogies, reboots, spin-offs and cycles.

Just like the remake, British cinema was also in many ways up until that point a subject of scorn, not only for film scholars, but also for film practitioners – as seen, for example, in François Truffaut's widely-circulated proclamation that cinema and Britain are contradictory terms, or Ben Kingsley's statement that he loves British cinema like a doctor loves his dying patient (quoted in 'British Cinema': 344). However, even if critical discussion of British cinema is still often imbued with pessimism and occasional proclamations of the end of the industry, the sheer number of academic publications that have mushroomed since the 1990s seems to prove the opposite. Not only are there numerous anthologies devoted to specific decades of British cinema production, such as the previously ignored 1970s (see Gibson and Hill 2009; Shail 2008; Harper and Smith 2012; Newland 2013; Newland 2010), but also many formerly neglected titles have been brought back to critical attention, including *Get Carter* (Hodges, 1971) (see Chibnall 2003), *The Wicker Man* (Hardy, 1973) (see Brown 2000; Smith 2010; Murray et al. 2005) and, more recently, *Deep End* (Skolimowski, 1970), which is now mentioned de rigueur in current publications (see Orr 2010; Newland 2010).

It is also not a coincidence that the growth in the number of Hollywood remakes of British films occurred at a significant moment when both the remake and British film experienced critical validation in the 1990s. This found its perfect embodiment in the phenomenon of Hollywood remakes of British films, where British cinema was no longer a contradiction in terms and the remake no longer a debased copy of some superior original. *Hollywood Remakes of Iconic British Films* combines both of these research avenues. It does so to offer a long-overdue study that looks at film remaking, Hollywood and British cinema from the unique perspective of cross-cultural exchange between two countries sharing a common language and history in film cooperation. How does this 'special' relationship affect both originals and remakes in terms of production as well as on a textual and paratextual level? Are these Hollywood makeovers a simple face-lift, or perhaps an integral part in a continued cultural dialogue? Does the remake tend to pursue similar concerns or become a point of departure for something entirely new? This book proposes answers to these questions and more.

In order to do so, *Hollywood Remakes of Iconic British Films* examines a range of cult and classic titles made at the time of Hollywood's most active involvement in domestic British film production: *Alfie* (Gilbert, 1966), *Bedazzled* (Donen, 1967), *The Italian Job* (Collinson, 1969), *Get Carter* (Hodges, 1971), *Sleuth* (Mankiewicz, 1972) and *The Wicker Man* (Hardy, 1973), which were then remade between 1999 and 2007. Set during a period of significant cultural transformation, the films' preoccupation with class and gender representation in a variety of genres comes to the fore. Each chapter discusses two originals, one from the 1960s and the other from the 1970s, connected by the presence of the same star, genre and/or similar themes to allow the reader to trace the change from the optimism of the 1960s to the despondency of the 1970s. Following this analysis, the remakes are then scrutinised to see how they rewrite the original content to adjust to contemporary trends within the industry, while also trying to make the old stories resonate with a twenty-first-century audience.

Many people have been invaluable in helping guide this project through from start to finish. In particular, I wish to thank the *Screen Serialities* series editors, Claire Perkins and Constantine Verevis, for their precious support and encouragement, from the book proposal to the final publication; Richard Strachan, for his patience and understanding as the book was delayed by two health scares, one personal and one global; and the two readers who recommended the book for publication and provided me with such useful initial feedback. I am grateful to Sam Johnson and Fiona Conn at Edinburgh University Press for taking over and assisting during the final stages as well as to freelance editor Nina Macaraig and indexer Zoe Ross. Special thanks also go to Kathleen Loock, for allowing me to attend the Berlin Seriality Workshop in 2014, and Constantine Verevis, who believed in the value of this project. I also owe a debt of gratitude to the BFI library and its staff, especially Ian O'Sullivan; Magda Cieślak, for her emotional support, many phone conversations and insightful comments on the first draft; and Michał Lachman, for relieving me of administrative duties in the final stages of completing the manuscript, alongside many other colleagues from the Department of English Studies in Drama, Theatre and Film at the Institute of English Studies in Lodz, whose support and good humour are always appreciated. The screengrabs were meticulously prepared by Filip Jesionek. Finally, the book would not have happened without my husband, Timothy Bridgman, by my side. It took his unwavering enthusiasm for my ideas, his editorial commentary and nourishing meals to keep both myself and the book on the straight and narrow. Watching these films together made it a much more rewarding and fun experience. Finally, there is our son Adam, whom I thank for his jokes that always brighten my day. This book on Anglo-American remakes has without a doubt been shaped by my personal experience of living in a cross-cultural household. I wish to dedicate it to the two people with whom I share it, Tim and Adam, with all my love.

CHAPTER I

Remaking Iconic British Films of the 1960s and 1970s

> But how often do remakes (as opposed to sequels) really succeed commercially and/or creatively? The 1960s and 1970s are now seen as something of a golden age in cinema, but retooling the iconic pictures of the era had rarely yielded dividends. (2008: 271)
>
> Michael Deeley

In 1999, *Notting Hill* (Michell, UK/US) was the highest-grossing British film and the sixteenth-highest-grossing film of the year worldwide. A feel-good romantic comedy about an unlikely union between a rather unsuccessful English bookshop keeper and a glamorous Hollywood star showed not only that opposites attract, but also that love conquers all, including geographic distance and cultural difference, not to mention bank balance. However, to the acute eye of the British critics (see James 2001: 304), the film was more than just a love story between an English underdog and an American celebrity. Under the veneer of romance lay hidden (and perhaps less optimistic) truths concerning the British film industry and its relationship with Hollywood, a love affair where a powerful mistress comes and goes as she pleases, often leaving her poor lover in a state of complete disarray, trying to pick up the pieces.

This book captures two moments of that ongoing relationship. The first, in the 1960s and early 1970s, was when the British film industry's union with Hollywood was briefly a happy one before culminating in a painful divorce. As a result of that marriage, many iconic British films were produced that represented an era characterised by revolutionary sociocultural changes in British society and displayed the impact of Hollywood's involvement in the domestic film scene. In the second moment, and in a way similar to the characters of *Notting Hill*, who rekindle their love after a painful break-up, Hollywood returned to its 1960s and 1970s British films in the new millennium. It manifested its appreciation for the older classics by giving them a total makeover, resulting in an impressive number of Hollywood remakes of iconic British films.

The present study is an attempt at analysing Hollywood remakes and their British originals in terms of constructing and articulating their shared transnational identity and their difference. To show their reciprocal relationship, it will focus on four pairs of films: *Alfie* (Gilbert, 1966; Shyer, 2004), *Bedazzled* (Donen, 1967; Ramis, 2000), *The Italian Job* (Collinson, 1969; Gray, 2003) and *Get Carter* (Hodges, 1971; Kay, 2000) with its unofficial remake, *The Limey* (Soderbergh, 1999). It will point to the existence of transnational and transcultural flows already in evidence in the original works, which are then later re-articulated in their new millennial remakes. In this way, both the original and its remake can be seen as 'a hybrid work [which] [. . .] exists betwixt and between two cultural traditions while providing a path that can be explored from both directions' (Jenkins 2006: 112). To examine such points of contact, genre conventions and casting choices will be discussed together with the ways in which the earlier class conflicts and gender representation are updated to appeal to contemporary viewers' sensibilities.

HOLLYWOOD ENGLAND

To understand the nature of Hollywood remakes of cult and classic British films, it is vital to look first at the British film industry's relationship with Hollywood before it reached its pinnacle in the 1960s, when most of the originals were made. The history of this relation is well documented and has been discussed in terms of competition, colonisation, dominion, dependency and cooperation. According to Jim Leach, '[i]ronically, of course, one of the legacies of the British Empire is that Hollywood films are made in English, with the result that there is no language barrier to protect Britain's domestic market from American competition' (2004: 15). Although Britain shares this predicament with Ireland, Australia and Canada, its film industry was from the start more closely bound to Hollywood than in those other cases, for various reasons.

One of them could be explained by the supposedly 'special relationship' between Britain and America, described as sometimes distant and at other times very close (Street 2002: 2) and 'evidenced in England's important role in American history, the popularity of British rock music and fashion' (Street 2002: 4), as well as many political alliances over the years. The concept assumes 'an intimate harmonious bond between the two nations celebrated on state occasions with suitably hyperbolic prose' (Reynolds 2006: 1). According to James E. Cronin:

The Anglo-American connection, or 'special relationship' as Churchill dubbed it [. . .] is a history filled with ambivalence, with resentment and condescension as well as pride and affection. Overall, the literature depicts an intimacy that is unusual and surely produced a predisposition to be allies rather than rivals or enemies, even if it did not prevent recurring episodes of estrangement. [. . .] It also served to predispose the two countries to take the same side in the great conflicts of the twentieth century and, especially after 1940, to work out their fates collectively. (2014: 7)

That 'special' relationship has informed and imparted itself on film business negotiations between the two countries across decades. It has sometimes even found its way onto the big screen through the depiction of Anglo-American relations, *Notting Hill* being just one of many such examples (see Brickman et al. 2021). The close contacts between the two film industries started as early as in the 1920s and have continued on and off to this day, encouraged by numerous 'Hollywood-friendly' governmental policies. These policies have effectively not only failed to protect the British domestic film industry but also encouraged Hollywood's presence, thus sealing its importance for the sustenance and health of British cinema. John Hill shows how, from the very start, the definition of a 'national' cinema for legal purposes 'was constructed in a way that would allow "transnational" involvement and investment' (2016: 709), opening the doors for American control. In fact, writing about runaway productions, the authors of *Global Hollywood 2* claim that the phenomenon of filming Hollywood films abroad started in Britain in 1927, when the government introduced legislation via a Quota Act which required that cinemas show a minimum number of local films. Hollywood studios responded by investing in local productions that became called 'quota quickies' and, due to their rushed and unpolished production values, provided no effective competition for Hollywood's imports. The Quota Act began in effect 'a long history during which UK film policy was used by Hollywood to further its interests' (Miller et al. 2006: 160).

According to Andrew Higson, '"English cinema" has for most of its existence been a part of a transnational film culture and film business', a hybrid 'caught up in a complicated transnational exchange of film and filmmakers' (2011: 4). He finds that 'from at least the 1920s there was a globalising tendency in English filmmaking and the film business' seen in the breadth and scope of productions by, for example, Michael Balcon or Herbert Wilcox, who made pictures with one eye set on conquering the international box office (2011: 4). A strategy that paid off was casting a popular American star in the lead (Betty Compson, Mae Marsh and Dorothy Gish in the 1920s) to ensure the films' transatlantic appeal (Street 2002: 20–23). In the sound era, there were also a few ways to ensure a smoother crossover into the American market for British films. Sarah Street refers to a survey of reviews of British films in *Variety* (1930–32) which suggested how British films should adapt in order to appeal to a US audience:

> to have a chance in America British films needed to communicate clear and well-recorded dialogue not necessarily in an 'Oxford' accent; include some 'known' element such as an American actor or director; ensure that comedies had transatlantic comprehension and appeal; subscribe to the technical principles of sharp, continuity editing; keep sets uncluttered and include appealing female stars who would not be 'smothered' by male actors. (2002: 47)

Mike Wayne argues that the first proper American-oriented British film was developed by Alexander Korda in the sound era, with his *Private Life of Henry VIII* (1933). Korda first earned his experience in Hungary, then Hollywood, before settling down in Britain to become one of the most important British producers. His hit set 'the model for the rest of the decade as British producers chased dollars with historical epics' (2006: 61) that would appeal domestically and stateside. He was perceived as a viable threat to Hollywood supremacy, with even the biggest Hollywood moguls worrying that he might build a Hollywood-on-the-Thames empire with links to continental Europe (Trumpbour 2007: 151). But this never materialised.

Indeed, over the decades, British titles would on occasion win over American critics and viewers, leading to British producers' attempts to repeat successful transnational formulas. Such impressive box-office pullers were not frequent enough, however, to sustain a domestic film industry in the light of its powerful competitor. After World War II, Britain was 'facing a desperate need for foreign capital – especially US dollars – to fund the purchase of essential overseas goods' (Hughs 2017: 219). In August of 1947, this led the UK Treasury to impose a 75 per cent duty on American film imports. In response, the Motion Picture Association of America (MPAA) orchestrated 'a highly effective boycott and the supply of American films for exhibition in Britain dried up' (Hughs 2017: 219). Initially, British cinema experienced a short-term boost in production but soon found itself unable to cope with the demand arising from the lack of American films (219). As Hill claims, in the 1940s and 1950s Britain had 'its own modest equivalent of the Hollywood studio system whereby two British companies, Rank and ABPC, produced films in their own studios (at Pinewood and Elstree) for distribution in their own cinemas (the Odeon and ABC chains)' (2001: 30). Yet, Alan Hughs shows that the film industry was still in a 'parlous financial and physical state' after the war and required American capital for the funding of British films (2017: 219). By early 1948, 'it was clear that British production would not be able to meet the demands of either exhibitors or audiences'. Thus, '[i]n March 1948, despite well-founded British misgivings and under terms that were far from generous to Britain, the Anglo-American Film Agreement was signed' (Hughs 2017: 219–20). The agreement stipulated that the majors

> could remit up to US$17 million in revenue that had been paid by Britain for imported American films. Balances above this were 'blocked' from repatriation to the USA although they could be used for investment in film production in Britain as well as the acquisition of (British) film rights, prints and advertising, and, significantly, the purchase of capital assets such as studios, patents and technology (although not cinemas). Additional sums equivalent to those remitted to Britain from America, in respect of payments for British films exhibited in the USA, could be removed from Britain. (Hughs 2017: 220)

Looking at Anglo-American film negotiations in the 1940s, Street observes that the 'special' relationship 'could see-saw at an incredible rate, at one moment hostile while the next, cordial and accommodating' (2002: 111).

The Anglo-American Film Agreement resulted in an influx of American films and American studios which started investing heavily in runaway productions. Consequently, between 1950 and 1959, the majors financed the production of circa 170 films, which Hughs calls 'American-financed British-made films' because they satisfied 'the statutory requirements to be counted as British films for exhibition quota purposes', while appealing 'to American consumers (often through plots and settings that emphasised tropes of English identity familiar to American audiences) as well as the British market' (2017: 220). The films navigated their content to appeal to both domestic and US viewers, by either having 'an American/Hollywood star or co-star and/ or a narrative that made an explicit reference to America/Americans that was integral to the progression of the plot' (2017: 221). Hughs writes that many reflected Britain's and America's new position in the post-war political, economic and cultural landscape and their relationship during the Cold War period. America represented 'glamour, daring and courageous audacity', while Britain (or England) stood for 'stoicism, reserve and temperate masculinity', emphasising 'both the differences in respective national personalities and the virtues of Anglo-American co-operation' (2017: 223).

The end of the 1950s saw the emergence of the British New Wave. Although not directly financed by Hollywood or financially successful at the US box office, it nonetheless achieved high critical acclaim in the US. This further incited Hollywood interest and lay the foundation for American dominance of the British film scene in the 1960s. American reviewers popularised the British

New Wave, which they, unlike home critics, perceived as fresh and unconventional (see Street 2002: 11; Walker [1974] 2005: 49–50). Despite its lack of typical Hollywood glamour, they appreciated its depiction of class inequalities, the bold treatment of adult subjects, particularly sex, and the rendition of British regional identities (Street 2002: 173–74). The films followed their protagonists, usually disgruntled young males for whom the woman represented either sexual pleasure or marital entrapment, up North, where they tried to cope with the drudgery of factory work, lack of prospects, unwanted pregnancies or illegal abortions. Despite the New Wave's predominantly regressive portrayal of women and deeply hidden misogyny, its importance in introducing new landscapes, characters and themes remains undisputed.

The rise of the movement is usually attributed to the artistic influence of the French New Wave, British documentary tradition and the Angry Young Men theatrical and literary revolution, whose figurehead, John Osborne, was in turn inspired by American authors, such as Arthur Miller and Tennessee Williams (Miller 2000: 14). As Alan Burton and Steve Chibnall notice, '[t]he new realism of the Angry Young Men in literature opened up the British novel and stage drama to fresh geographies of class and region, and screen adaptations of *Look Back in Anger* (1958), *Room at The Top* (1959), and *Saturday Night and Sunday Morning* (1960) heralded a new wave of fresh faces and mature themes for the British film' (2013: 16). More importantly, Hill claims that, '[a]t precisely the time the disappearance of class was being so loudly asserted, these films, at least, seemed to provide clear evidence to the contrary' (1995: 174). According to Jeffrey Richards, the New Wave brought to the screen 'the frustrations, limitations and aspirations of the working-class young' (1999: 216). He observes:

> British 'New Wave' cinema was born out of the social and cultural upheaval of the late 1950s, which embraced the death of the Empire, the rise of working-class affluence, the emergence of a distinctive youth culture and the revival of the intellectual left. In form, it took its lead from French 'New Wave' cinema which preferred location-shooting to studio work, natural lighting to formal lighting and a fragmented, impressionist approach to traditional linear narrative. But, in content, British 'New Wave' cinema was deeply rooted in and strongly influenced by the social-realist novels of writers like Alan Sillitoe and John Braine, the theatre work of the 'Angry Young Men' like John Osborne and the 'kitchen sink' working-class dramas that were a feature of Sydney Newman's *Armchair Theatre* on ATV. (1997: 48)

Other working-class writers included David Storey and Shelagh Delaney, who also depicted working-class life in Northern cities. Film adaptations of their works featured actors who became the figureheads of the New Wave. Albert Finney, Richard Harris, Rita Tushingham and Tom Courtenay spoke in their regional accents, and many came from a working-class background. The New Wave films opened up the door to upcoming working-class actors who could now take their training gained from 'local authority grants for drama students' and 'social realist theatre and television' (Lay 2002: 61) and apply their skills to the big screen.

However, there were also other, perhaps more surprising influences behind the emergence of the new look and the new protagonist of the British New Wave. Hughs argues that it is far too reductive to see the arrival of the British New Wave and the ensuing changes within British film outputs as a direct result of opposition to 'the dominant discourse(s) of British film and/or the influences of the "postwar settlement" evident across British social, political and economic life' (2017: 218). According to him, Robert Murphy's claim that American involvement in the British New Wave was marginal is only true regarding the movement 'as an industrial economic process' because, as 'a cultural process, the iconoclastic and hedonistic characters evident in the British new wave had direct antecedents in Americanised British films set in the North', which were made from 1948 to 1958 as a result of the above-mentioned Anglo-American Film Agreement (Hughs 2017: 232).

Thus, although in terms of finance Hollywood did not play a significant role in the creation of the first social-realist films, it nonetheless exerted a cultural impact on 'contemporary and future stylistic and thematic forms in British film' (Hughs 2017: 219). Before the British New Wave, most American-financed British-made films made between 1948 and 1958 showed 'American identity and culture as meritocratic, egalitarian and unburdened by the constricting conventions of orthodox English class hierarchies' (Hughs 2017: 224). This provided British film with a strong possible alternative. Furthermore, Hughs shows how the American-financed British-made films shot in the North of England heavily relied on Hollywood genres, especially film noir and western. Their characters of the anti-hero and the femme fatale became a staple of the Northern film landscape, which took Los Angeles as its artistic inspiration, rather than London (2017: 230). Examining Northern-set films made between 1948 and 1958, he reveals the powerful impact that Hollywood exerted on the representations of the region whose 'British' characters, stories and mise-en-scène were also to some degree 'American in tone and style' (2017: 230). That cluster of cross-culturally hybrid films became instrumental in the emergence of the British New Wave, demonstrating yet again the complex impact of the American presence on the British film scene.

SWINGING LONDON

American presence would become even more significant in the 1960s, when kitchen sink realism was replaced by the phenomenon of 'Swinging London', with Hollywood ready to cash in 'on the international popularity of British pop music and fashion' (Smith 2009: 57). By the mid-1960s, all the major Hollywood studios had set up production offices in the British capital, with their investment in British film outputs reaching 90 per cent in 1967. In fact, their involvement in British film production in the 1960s became so significant that Alexander Walker decided to title his monograph devoted to the decade *Hollywood England* (1974) (published in the United States as *Hollywood UK*). Murphy's *Sixties British Cinema* ([1992] 2008) includes a chapter called 'Hollywood's England', whose apostrophe begs the question about belonging, ownership and supremacy, while the *Historical Dictionary of British Cinema* refers to this period as 'Hollywood UK' (Burton and Chibnall 2013: 17).

Significantly, as Walker argues, Americans started contributing heavily to the domestic film industry 'at the very same time as this country [Britain] was undergoing a period of unprecedented change' ([1974] 2005: 16), which was reflected in many films of the decade. The first signs of the approaching change became noticeable with the release of *Tom Jones* in 1963 (Richardson), produced by United Artists. Its eclectic and erratic style – inspired by Pop art, direct address to the camera, slapstick comedy and frivolity – set the tone for the rest of the decade. These were, according to Richards, a far cry from the naturalism and seriousness of its predecessors, signalling 'in its subject, its style and its attitude the end of the older order against which the "New Wave" heroes had chafed' (1997: 157). The sexy and roistering *Tom Jones* became the symbol of a new world focused on consumerism and characterised, in the critic's opinion, by 'colour supplements and pirate radio, glamorous television commercials, discos and boutiques, a cult of the new and the now' (1997: 157). Of course, this world to which Richards refers was the phenomenon known as 'Swinging London', which would further incite additional Hollywood investment.

Swinging London films were very popular with the audiences, but not so with the critics (Murphy 2009: 322). Richards complains about their hedonistic self-indulgence, glitter, glamour and extravaganza replacing the 'sober realism and earnest social comment' (1997: 157) of their predecessors. However, it is difficult to agree that most of the films made between 1965 and 1970 were promoting mindless optimism, as there is a visible continuity between the New Wave and its successors in the casting choices, working-class characters and certain themes. The main difference was that now the protagonists were shown navigating their way around the colourful London cityscape rather than depressing black and white Northern landscapes. Richard Lester's *A Hard Day's Night* (1964) is a good example bridging that moment. The film features the adventures of the Beatles – four working-class Liverpudlian lads – running around London, blending New Wave aesthetics with a Swinging London vibe.

Although the majority of London's population was not swinging, 'changes were occurring which did have a fundamental effect on society and the environment' (Murphy [1992] 2008: 139). Richards mentions, amongst others, such new developments in the 1960s as the legalisation of gambling, abortion and homosexuality, the abolishment of capital punishment and theatrical censorship, the reforms to the Divorce Act, the expansion of the welfare state, slum-clearance programmes, the building of new housing, the introduction of comprehensive education, the launching of new universities and colleges, and the campaign for women's rights, resulting in the Equal Pay Act in 1970. According to him, '[l]iberalization and egalitarianism were the keynotes of public policy. This spilled over into popular culture, which was dominated by the young working class and characterized by sexual permissiveness and the free use of drugs' (1999: 203).

The focus was now on youth because, 'for the first time in history, it became fashionable to be young and working class. Looks, style and attitude rather than birth and breeding became the keys to success. Rock musicians, fashion photographers, and Pop artists were the role models of the moment' (Richards 1997: 157). The domination of the young working class in popular culture can be seen from the example of a few actors who were virtually catapulted into international stardom overnight. Michael Caine's appearance in *The Ipcress File* (Furie, 1965) as a sophisticated working-class London spy earned him his place in the 1965 'Box of Pin-Ups' created by another working-class success story, photographer David Bailey. The actor's newly-found fame allowed him to land the role as a Cockney womaniser in *Alfie* (Gilbert, 1966), 'swinging' his way around London and securing him his first Oscar nomination. Another icon of 'Swinging London' was Caine's flatmate and fellow actor, Terence Stamp, who together with Caine, Sean Connery and Albert Finney redefined British screen masculinity. Stamp, believed to be one of the most beautiful men of his decade, also features in 'Bailey's Box of Pin-Ups', alongside such 1960s icons as the Rolling Stones, the infamous Kray brothers, John Lennon and Paul McCartney. As a sign of its times, the collection focuses on male celebrities (actors, designers, musicians, professional criminals) and depicts only a handful of women (all top models), bringing home the idea of the gendered nature of the 'Swinging London' scene. The dominant position of men in the cultural landscape of the 1960s and early 1970s becomes even more evident in retrospect, since most of the period's films that have gained cult status feature male protagonists at the centre of their narratives, with women performing a more decorative function on the side.

1960s London became not only a centre of international film production, but also a worldwide cultural capital associated with the power of youth culture, newly found social mobility, the sexual revolution and promiscuity. At the same time as the film business was thriving, the British fashion industry was also earning international recognition, exemplified by Mary Quant's iconic miniskirts and Vidal Sassoon's equally iconic bob. According to Hughs, Hollywood made Britain its second home, as '[t]here was also a clear cultural imperative in place insofar as the stateside popularity of British popular culture in the 1960s – ranging from James Bond to the Beatles to Carnaby Street – endowed Britain and things British with a previously unprecedented degree of cachet in the eyes of the American consumer' (2017: 219). Jeffrey S. Miller explains that, whereas social, political and cultural links between Britain and America were particularly strong during the Kennedy presidency, given that the American leader was a proclaimed Anglophile, they were even further intensified after his assassination in 1963. America became even more receptive to British cultural imports at a time when

> cultural difference gained power during the national 'trauma' of the Kennedy assassination, when other messages and meanings lacked the cohesiveness they would have in calmer times. Internal anxiety took precedence over the anxiety of influence, further opening the door for artifacts from other cultures – in this case, the culturally proximate Britain, with which the United States shared a language (if not a complete vocabulary) and with which social, cultural, and political ties had been strengthened during the Kennedy years. With Bond, as with British popular music, fashion, and films, Americans after the death of Kennedy were willing to let 'otherness' override the 'our-own-ness' of traditional American cultural utterances. (2000: 33)

Without a doubt, the two countries' cultural exchange, mutual influences and borrowings became especially close in the 1960s, when London became the hub of international film business, with numerous American film directors making Britain their temporary or even permanent home. As John Orr observes:

> The 1960s was the seminal decade, and 1960s London is now mythical in its status as a cultural magnet for the shock of the new in music, theatre, art, fashion, scandal – and cinema. Classical Hollywood joined in, dashing across the pond and modifying the old rules in the Old World: not only Otto Preminger, but Martin Ritt, Sidney Lumet, William Wyler, Stanley Donen, Joseph Mankiewicz, Stanley Kubrick, Sam Peckinpah and the returning Hitchcock, all making their 'British' movies. With the studios seeking to breathe new life into their projects, the Hollywood invasion pushed at the weakening boundaries of censorship and classical narration with freer visual styles, more location shooting and more explicit content. (2010: 15)[1]

Likewise, working in London on 'British Hollywood films' allowed many British directors 'to join the global Hollywood production network without ever leaving Britain' (Melis 2016: 69). After directing *Alfie* (1966), Lewis Gilbert went on to direct three James Bond films considered the first proper transnational movie franchise. Others left Britain to work in the US. Among them were John Schlesinger, whose British New Wave hits launched his career in Hollywood, or John Boorman, who was picked to direct *Point Blank* (1967) with Lee Marvin for MGM after his critically acclaimed debut in 1965, *Catch Us If You Can*, featuring the Dave Clark Five, which back then compared in popularity with the Beatles. Many British actors followed a similar trajectory and became globally recognised stars – such as Caine, Connery, or Julie Christie, to name just a few. These talent flows were not reduced to Anglo-American border crossings, but were also international in nature, encouraging many European film directors, including Roman Polanski, Jerzy Skolimowski, François Truffaut and Michelangelo Antonioni to come over and respond to the Swinging London scene. Antonioni mythologised it in *Blow-Up* (1967), while Skolimowski and Polanski showed the less glamorous side of living a promiscuous London life in *Deep End* (1970) and *Repulsion* (1965), respectively, where not everyone was ready or able to 'swing', creating its own set of tensions and repercussions.

Hollywood was additionally attracted to Britain by the cheap production facilities and studio personnel (Street 2002: 170). British technical expertise 'represented very good value for money at a time when the dollar was strong against European currencies' (Smith 2010: 40). Moreover, the British government's policy, established to protect and develop its domestic film industry, yet again allowed Hollywood studios to thrive. As Street explains, '[a]s long as the technicians and casts were predominantly British, films sponsored by American companies qualified as British quota films and were entitled to subsidies from the Eady Levy, a production fund established by the British government in 1950' (2002: 169). As a result, internationalism was widespread, to the degree that 'it became increasingly challenging to identify films that had not been produced without American assistance' (169), often leading to absurd situations. For example, 'United Artists received $2.1 million, or 15 per cent of the Eady fund' (169) for such British-registered international hits as *Thunderball* (Young, 1965), which at least figures a British spy. However, the Eady also assisted such films as *Star Wars* (Lucas, 1977) and *Superman* (Donner, 1978), which qualified for the subsidy under the guidelines of the Department of Trade and Industry. Shot in Pinewood studio with the help of a local crew, they were considered British productions, even though they were far from being culturally British.

Yet, one must not forget that, while in the 1960s Britain dominated and dictated tastes in popular culture, its international success and prominence were often fostered by American funding and sometimes even inspired by America's own cultural output. The 1960s were the time of an unprecedented cultural exchange between the US and UK, giving birth to one of the most popular film franchises of all time: the James Bond series. The Bond series serves as a good example of the special Anglo-American relationship, not only in terms of production, but also on the narrative level, as the two countries often team up to protect the Western world from Eastern enemies. The success of The Beatles and The Rolling Stones, whose music was inspired by Afro-American artists, epitomises well the nature of cross-cultural flows between the two countries at the time. Stevie Wonder commented: 'When I think of the Sixties, I think of two things: I think of Motown, and I think of the Beatles. Those are the major influences [. . .] we all really influenced each other' (quoted in Hamilton 2016: 121). Jack Hamilton describes this as a 'vibrant, complex, and productive transatlantic relationship', seeing the Beatles and Motown Records not as 'leading protagonists in two separate stories – that of white music and black music in the 1960s, specifically', but as 'friends across the sea' (2016: 124). Similarly, the 1960s saw the production of many classic British films whose existence was a product of 'the vibrant, complex, and productive transatlantic relationship' between the two film industries.

The period of a happy marriage between the two film industries did not last long, however. As Street opines, '[d]espite the success of many British films in America, at the end of the decade *The Economist* reported a crisis in Hollywood that had a serious impact on film production in Britain' (2002: 189). This left British producers 'without a strong infrastructure of commercial or state support for indigenous production' (Street 2002: 171). The majors incurred massive losses between 1969 and 1971 (see Horwath et al. 2004) and 'were forced to retrench and restructure in the wake of the recession' (Street 2002:190), exacerbated by the oil shock of 1973–74. Moreover, as Richards argues, 'the bubble of 'Swinging London burst when a clutch of grossly self-indulgent and hopelessly uncommercial films failed at the box office' (1999: 217). Audiences for British films were also diminishing due to the growing popularity and availability of colour television (Newland 2013: 3). Finally, Hollywood no longer had to look up to Britain for popular and youth-oriented subjects, since it now had found its own, as represented by such key films of the decade as *Bonnie and Clyde* (Penn, 1967), *The Graduate* (Nichols, 1967), *Midnight Cowboy* (Schlesinger, 1969) and *Easy Rider* (Hopper, 1969) (Murphy [1992] 2008: 275). Hollywood left at the same time as a new Conservative government was elected, the Beatles split up and the 1960s generation woke up 'from the dream world to a cold dawn and a long hangover' (Richards 1997: 167). This created a feeling of disappointment that many 1970s films responded to with gusto. As Richards concludes:

> With the 70s came the cinema's exposure to reality. London stopped swinging. The butterfly culture of the 1960s flew away. The cold, harsh

light of reality broke in on the tinsel world. The British film industry collapsed, and the historians reached for their pens to chart its rise and fall. (1999: 217)

ICONIC BRITISH FILMS IN THE 1960S AND 1970S

Before the divorce, however, many iconic British films managed to get released. Paramount funded the UK production of *Alfie*, a 'Swinging London' film, securing five Oscar nominations. *Bedazzled*, a UK/US co-production, was produced and directed by Stanley Donen, a regular American visitor to the UK; the film tapped into the popularity of the 'Swinging London' scene, offering a biting satire on the period. Paramount was also behind the making of *The Italian Job*, a UK/US co-production made two years later, when the collapse of 'Hollywood England' was already on the cards and the studios were getting ready to abandon ship. In the middle of the production, producer Michael Deeley was told that he now had to report directly to Los Angeles, as Paramount's London offices were shutting down. While the film about a bunch of eccentric British criminals and their cocky Cockney leader stealing gold from the Italian Mafia smacks of the bravado and optimism of the early 1960s, the ending with its characters trapped on a bus on the edge of an Alpine rock seems to be an indication of the uncertainty to come. *Get Carter*, a UK/US co-production, was produced by MGM 'just before the closure of the company's Boreham Wood Studios and British operations. If the announcement had come two months earlier, *Get Carter* might never have been made' (Chibnall 2003: 21). *Sleuth* was directed by another American visitor and Hollywood veteran, Joseph L. Mankiewicz, and produced by Palomar Pictures International, a subsidiary of American Broadcasting Companies, Inc. Palomar Pictures International later produced *Stepford Wives* (Forbes, 1974). The BFI claims that *Sleuth* is a UK film, while the IMDb identifies it as a UK/US co-production, showing how difficult designating a film by its country of origin was during the 'Hollywood UK' years. *The Wicker Man*'s relationship to Hollywood finance is more complex and involves a rather unsuccessful distribution deal with Warner Bros. Produced in 1973, at a time when the British film industry was plunged into a massive crisis after Hollywood's withdrawal, it serves as a painful reminder of the frailty of the British film industry without the support of its powerful overseas lover.

Despite these films' strong British identity – as they all depict local themes, stories and characters – tapping into the Zeitgeist of the decade, the films' fate upon initial release was to no small degree determined by the British film industry's complex relations with the majors. Recent publications (see Chibnall 2003; Deeley 2008; Field 2001; Smith 2010; Brown 2000) reveal the extent of

Hollywood's involvement in their production and distribution, from approving the choice of actors to altering the films' endings or designing promotional materials. Some ideas suggested by the studios were resisted, giving us reason to deliberate: Would Jack Carter have become the icon of 'Lad culture' – a movement embracing old-fashioned machismo, which emerged in the 1990s – had there been a sequel, as pushed for by the studio? Would *The Italian Job* be considered a cult British picture, had it starred Robert Redford instead of Caine, as Paramount suggested? And would English football fans now be singing 'The Self-Preservation Society' on the terraces, a song starting with the chant 'England! England!' inspired by Caine's Cockney rhyming slang, had it not been featured on *The Italian Job* soundtrack composed by Quincy Jones? Hollywood's more intrusive involvement in these 'British'[2] films could have led to different, perhaps more or less happy, conclusions. The fact remains, however, that its financial assistance led to the creation of what is now considered the golden era of British cinema.[3]

All the titles contain cross-cultural elements as the result of years of exposure to British films in the US, as well as the American presence in the British film scene. These elements show the effects of decades of transatlantic crossings in action and prove the existence of 'a shared transnational identity' that is 'understood and absorbed by audiences on both sides of the Atlantic' (Street 2002: 2). Another term relevant here is 'cross-pollination', which Kenneth Chan uses when discussing the complicated network of influences between Hollywood and Chinese cinema (2017: 87–102). To that effect, the British originals feature American actresses in crucial or cameo roles – such as Shelley Winters in *Alfie*, Maggie Blye in *The Italian Job* and Raquel Welch in *Bedazzled*. Their presence in the film may be insignificant but still dominates promotional materials. Some are directed by renowned Hollywood directors – Mankiewicz directed *Sleuth* and Donen *Bedazzled*. A successful American composer, Jones, scored *The Italian Job*. The iconography of the ultimate American film genres, western and noir, is writ large all over *Get Carter*, confirming Michael Allen's observation that the traffic between Hollywood and other cinemas is never just one-directional (2003: 85). All make use of local and regional accents and authentic locations, which were so appealing to American critics at the beginning of the British New Wave. At the same time, however, they feature male characters who operate more along the lines of Hollywood leading men – despite, or should we say because of, their working-class identity – such as Caine in all of his iconic roles. Thus, while the films remain 'different' and nationally specific, efforts were made to render them 'transferable' and 'comprehensible' (Street 2002: 2) stateside, pointing to the existence of transnational and transcultural flows already in evidence in the original works.

Now looking back at these films, it is hard to bemoan the negative effects of Hollywood's involvement in the British film industry. The era may have ended with Hollywood shutting down its UK offices, but the result of that fruitful, though admittedly not always easy, collaboration is an impressive number of now-classic films. It should, therefore, be of no surprise that it is to *Alfie*, *Bedazzled*, *The Italian Job*, *Get Carter*, *The Wicker Man* and *Sleuth*, among other films from the era, that Hollywood would return three decades later in search of success. The reasons for the rekindling of that interest are complex, however, and involve technological and sociocultural developments which will be discussed below.

REMAKES AT THE START OF THE DIGITAL ERA

Hollywood's propensity for remaking is well known. It has always looked for ideas elsewhere, attempting to capitalise on the success of undiscovered originals or updating old classics. For instance, writing about Hollywood remakes in the 1950s, Michael Druxman notices that each new technological invention resulted in redoing classic films from the past to adapt them to new screen techniques, be it sound, colour or different screen aspect (1975: 15–18). Similarly, the development of digital technology in the 1990s prompted the remaking of titles whose visuals could be further enhanced by CGI. Costas Constandinides discusses this phenomenon in terms of 'post-celluloid adaptation' involving 'the transition and transformation of media content from an old media form to a new media form' (2010: 4). Remakes, therefore, represent nothing new, as their presence has always punctuated crucial moments in cinema's technological development. What is new, however, is their unprecedented visibility, which can be seen in Leo Braudy's proclamation made in 1998 that '[o]ur time is particularly heavy in remakes' (1998: 332). Nevertheless, the reasons behind the proliferation of Hollywood remakes of British films from the mid-1990s onwards are not necessarily CGI-related alone.

Digital technology in the 1990s has had an equal, if not more significant, impact on the distribution and reception channels that have contributed to remakes' increased visibility and awareness of the existence of their predecessors. All of the remakes discussed here were released during an important transitional phase marked by two main events. The first was the arrival of DVDs in the late 1990s, which, as Barbara Klinger observes, inspired 'cinema's contemporary cultural omnipresence' (2006: 58). Chuck Tryon notices that DVDs with their inherent time-shifting, fragmentation and bonus materials (such as deleted scenes or alternate endings) turned 'films into objects that can be manipulated at will, not only by consumers but also producers [. . .]. In this sense, digital media, and DVDs in particular, work against the notion that media objects can ever be truly finished' (2009: 26). DVDs opened up the way for remakes to be perceived as yet another version of a story, to be treated in continuation and on equal terms. By allowing 'viewers to recognize that texts were ready to be ripped apart and reassembled in playful new ways' (Tryon 2009: 151), DVD culture fostered a remix sensibility that informs not only the fan activities of many modern-day YouTubers but is also a founding block of the contemporary film industry.

The second event was the launch of Web 2.0 in the late 1990s, which has connected once-isolated film consumers and given them a forum in which to voice their opinions, exchange knowledge and share expertise. Web 2.0 offered movie geeks of the VHS era and the later DVD generation a perfect outlet, providing them with a meeting place and companionship. Unlike in the past, today's viewers are no longer seen as a homogeneous and passive group (see Klinger 2006: 139–40; Tryon 2009: 32–37, 79–82; Gray 2010: 144–47; Jenkins 1992). Their interactive participation and 'the ability of networked movie audiences to shape the reception of a movie' (Tryon 2009: 2) need to be acknowledged, together with Henry Jenkins' important distinction between the old consumers as isolated, silent and invisible individuals and the new consumers who are more socially connected, noisy and visible (2006: 19). In fact, all these recent developments have led Richard Grusin to propose that, 'by looking at the relation between cinema and new media, we can see that we already find ourselves in a digital cinema of interactions', with 'an interactive spectator in a domestic or other social space rather than an immobilized spectator in the darkened dream-space' (2006: 73, 75).

Hollywood remakes of British films had only been sporadic and spread across decades in the years before the digital revolution. Some notable and frequently discussed examples include Alfred Hitchcock's auto-remake *The Man Who Knew Too Much* (1934, 1956), and Brian De Palma's and Francis Ford Coppola's musings on Michelangelo Antonioni's *Blow-Up*: *Blow Out* (1981) and *The Conversation* (1974), respectively.[4] An unprecedented increase in Hollywood remaking activities started in the mid-1990s and continued into the new millennium, with a focus on British films from the 1960s and 1970s. The list comprises an impressive number of titles,[5] making it as significant an occurrence as the other two more commonly discussed cross-cultural examples of Hollywood remakes of French and Asian films (see Crawford 2016: 115).[6]

Their unusual proliferation from the mid-1990s onwards can partly be explained as the outcome of the above-mentioned technological developments, which had a major impact on promoting a more reflexive form of film appreciation. DVD culture inspired people to revisit classic films and created interest in their new makeovers. A growing awareness of film history, film collectability, unlimited access to online film archives and the popularity of websites such as the Internet Movie Database (which figures in the top 50 most visited websites in the world) have all created an opportunity for interactive viewing. The audience is now able to find, compare and discuss different versions of the same story at the click of a mouse. Whether seen negatively as an echo chamber, feedback loop and 'the cult of the amateur' (see Keen 2007), or positively in terms of collective intelligence and 'We-Think' (Leadbeater 2008), the rise of the figure of the film geek means that viewers are now often better equipped to write about films than are professional critics, as numerous interpretations on IMDb prove daily. Film geek activity is equally essential in designating remakes their unique status since, as Constantine Verevis aptly points out, remaking is not just an inherent quality of the texts themselves, but 'the secondary result of broader discursive activity' (2006a: 106). This is made easier when both the British originals and their Hollywood remakes are in the English language, allowing for the two versions to interact with each other and facilitating the process of recall and cross-referencing. Also, as the original and its remake frequently have identical titles, a sense of seriality and continuity becomes even more firmly established. When one googles one title, the other is bound to pop up.

The arrival of the first VHS videos and then DVDs in the late 1990s encouraged film collecting and helped revive forgotten cult and classic films from the past. Tryon notices:

> Because of their collectability and their association with discourses of connoisseurship, DVDs contribute to what might be described as a new brand of cinephilia, one that is more willing to embrace obscure and virtually unknown films, as audiences seek to position themselves as insiders with a unique knowledge of film culture. At the same time, DVD audiences can revisit and embrace cult films or other movies that have typically been marginalized within standard reception cultures. (2009: 21)

In many cases, it was the release of the Hollywood remake that prompted the DVD release of the British original, confirming Verevis' claim that contemporary remakes enjoy a more 'symbiotic relationship with their originals, with publicity and reviews often drawing attention to earlier versions' (2006a: 17), as the two co-exist 'in the contemporary media marketplace' (138). The only notable exception is *Bedazzled*, whose troubled relationship with its 2000 remake represents the early phase of DVD culture. In 1999, Paramount expressed its interest in remaking *The Italian Job* with George Clooney and Ben Affleck in the leading roles and at the same time re-released the original film in UK cinemas, to the joy of British fans. Paramount issued the DVD of the original in 2002 in the UK and then in 2003 in the US, to coincide with the theatrical premiere of the remake. The studio's strategy of releasing the DVD of the original *Italian Job* to coincide with the pre-release marketing buzz surrounding its remake points to the distributor's efforts to promote both titles, raising interest in the earlier film and benefiting from its classic status. When in 1999 the BFI released a restored print of *Get Carter* for cinema exhibition, Warner Bros was already in the process of remaking the film with Stallone. When the remake was screened in American cinemas in 2000, the studio additionally released a remastered version of the original for the first time on DVD. Without ignoring mercantile reasons behind Warner Bros' decision to remake a well-respected title, one must also acknowledge that the remake further helped solidify the original's global popularity, leading to other additional revenue streams.

Bedazzled shows the process of slowly grasping how the contemporary marketplace operates in the digital era. Initially, the studio performed an uneasy balancing act between wanting to evoke the memory of the original and suppressing it as possible competition. According to Thomas Leitch, '[a]lthough remakes by definition base an important part of their appeal on the demonstrated ability of a pre-existing story to attract an audience, they are often competing with the very films they invoke, even if those films have been out of release for many years' (2002: 44). As a result, remakes can marginalise the original film, 'reducing it to the status of the unseen classic' (Leitch 2002: 40). He argues that '[t]he parasitism of the remake becomes clearest when re-releasing becomes a likely possibility, when the old film is available alongside the new for video rental, or when both films are in release in the same market at the same time' (40). As Joe Leydon speculates,

> [t]o be sure, it helps a bit that most ticketbuyers can't (or won't) make comparisons, since the original pic – starring and dreamed up by Dudley Moore and the late, great Peter Cook, with the latter penning the script – hasn't been easily accessible, even in well-stocked vidstores, for several years. (2000)

Looking at the IMDb user comments devoted to the update reveals that, despite the producers' efforts to the contrary, the memory of the original was alive and well. Many expressed hope that the remake would finally result in a DVD release of their favourite British film, which by then was fading away on old tapes due to repeated viewing. In the end, they had to wait five years after the remake's premiere for a limited DVD release of the original *Bedazzled* in the UK, handled by Hollywood Classics Ltd on behalf of Twentieth Century Fox. The release provoked joyful reactions such as this one:

> It's been unavailable for years, with crappy old commercial VHS copies with the soundtrack hanging off changing hands for silly money (I taped mine off the TV like everyone else.) But now it's out on DVD! As of this week (end of July '05). I haven't bought one yet but I'm sure I will. I hope there are some nice extras. (adamblake77 2005)

The bonus materials are quite modest, however, and omit to mention the remake. A further two years later, the original finally became available on disc in the US, but the studio did not even acknowledge the fact that its DVD premiere coincided with the film's fortieth anniversary. The remake was now clearly promoted as a vantage point from which to access the original, with Harold Ramis as the director, co-writer and co-producer of the remake sanctioning the original through his status as a comedy genius. It took Fox another eight years to finally release a 'double take: original and remake' box set in 2008, openly endorsing the relationship between the two films and, as a result, allowing them to enjoy a longer shelf life and the so-called long tail together.

By contrast, the DVD release of *Alfie* interestingly occurred in 2001, three years before the remake hit the screens in 2004. It is safe to assume that Paramount did this to start working on raising awareness of the original, in preparation for the remake's release. When the film premiered in 2004, shortly afterwards a DVD of the remake was released, containing extensive bonus materials that provided the viewer with many elaborate comparisons between original and source, including location, characters, cinematography, set design, genre and many others. Similarly, Paramount released *Sleuth* on DVD in 2002 in both the UK and the US, followed in 2004 by Jude Law's announcement in an interview for *Film Review* (October 2004) that he was planning to remake the film with Caine and himself in the main roles. The remake premiered in 2007 and was distributed on DVD by Paramount from 2008 onwards, showing the overall strategy of reviving originals well in advance of their remakes.

The Wicker Man's distribution history is so complex that there are book-length studies devoted to it (see Brown 2000). Warner Bros was first involved with the film in 1974 when, as Justin Smith notes, they 'marketed the film's horror elements with a lurid advertising campaign and sent it out around selected drive-ins. The studio claimed their tax losses, the film bummed and was soon forgotten' (2010: 95). Its popularity only stirred upon its second theatrical US release in 1977, thanks to several individuals unaffiliated to the studio who restored the film's extended version from Roger Corman's retrieved print. Warner Bros then returned onto the scene in 2003, once *The Wicker Man* had acquired cult classic status, to distribute The Director's Cut on DVD which, according to Smith, is 'noticeably better than many earlier available prints, transferred as we are told from the original "analogue telecine master"' (2010: 97). He further observes that – although the film had been broadcast on British television a few times since the early 1980s, creating its UK fanbase, and was available on VHS

> it has only been with the advent of DVD that *The Wicker Man* has been available in a full, 'restored' version following the reinstatement of lost or excised footage. The belated issuing of 'directors' cuts', to use the

marketing parlance, has been of considerable interest to cult fans, and this format also allows documentaries, interviews and comparative versions to be endlessly debated and discussed. (90)

The DVD consists of rich bonus materials, including two versions of the film, the 84-minute cut and the extended 102-minute one, as well as a fascinating discussion moderated by Mark Kermode, during which Christopher Lee reveals that he was approached to appear in a remake opposite Nicolas Cage. Lee's comment suggests that the reason behind Warner's sudden interest in the restoration of the original and rebranding it as a definitive must-see classic was to prepare the ground for their upcoming remake of the film. Warner released the remake a few years later, in 2006.[7]

Digital culture created the perfect conditions for the studios to revisit old classics, while at the same time promoting their remakes through ready-made associations, using the DVD format to establish links between the two versions to appeal to numerous audiences. By creating a sense of continuity across two works, both DVDs become promotional materials for both films, simultaneously opening them up to new readings and encouraging self-reflexive and interactive viewing. This discovery created new marketing strategies designed to appeal to the film buff, the collector and the cultist, by providing them with different versions to compare and analyse and include in their personal archive. The studios' involvement with these remakes relied on the existence of a pre-existing fan-base to whom they could additionally offer their favourite original films in new formats. Restored, repackaged and re-marketed, none of these originals have suffered from their associations with their remakes and often gained popularity on a much larger scale. By finding titles that have a cult or classic status and a built-in audience, Hollywood not only ensures continued financial profit, but also plays an active part in the originals' preservation and longevity. Looking at the significance of remakes in assisting the revival of iconic British films confirms Barbara Klinger's words about Hollywood's central role in the preservation and revival of bygone texts, with the studios functioning as museums and 'custodians of the past' (2006: 92). Although all the remakes of British classics were undoubtedly profit-driven, and Hollywood is by no means a philanthropic institution, the effects of such actions often offer 'meaningful and influential confrontations with its archive for viewers' (Klinger 2006: 93).

CULTURAL RETURN AND CRITICAL REAPPRAISAL

But there are also other equally powerful factors involved in giving these films a second life and second chance, aside from the digital revolution. In the 1990s, everything British became fashionable and 'cool' once again, in line with the country's own rebranding of itself as 'Cool Britannia'. The revival of pride in all things British manifested itself in several ways. The Union Jack featured in many unusual places, ranging from the skirts of the Spice Girls, David Bowie's *Earthling*-era frockcoat designed by Alexander McQueen, and posters for the 1997 release of *Austin Powers: International Man of Mystery* (Roach), to the bedsheets of Liam Gallagher and Patsy Kensit on the cover of *Vanity Fair* (1977) in a John and Yoko-esque homage, which proclaimed 'London Swings! Again!'

The 1990s saw a rise in the popularity of British film stateside, following the triumph of a few high-profile commercial hits. These included *Four Weddings and a Funeral* (Newell, 1994), *Trainspotting* (Boyle, 1996), *The Full Monty* (Cattaneo, 1997), *Lock, Stock and Two Smoking Barrels* (Ritchie, 1998) and the above-mentioned *Notting Hill*, often produced and/or distributed by the able hand of Hollywood, just as in the 1960s. Moreover, the success of British music – in particular Oasis, the Spice Girls and Blur – across the Atlantic reminded one of the first 'British invasion' in the 1960s, when for a brief time in history British bands dominated American music charts. Cool Britannia was imbued with nostalgia for the 1960s, borrowing heavily from its iconography. This nostalgia can be seen, for example, in the many replacements of the 1960s icons by their 1990s equivalents: Oasis was recognised as the new Beatles, Blur recalled The Kinks, *Trainspotting* was compared by many American reviewers to *A Hard Day's Night* (Street 2002: 11) and the wafer-thin top model Kate Moss was standing in for Twiggy. The newly found pride in British music, cinema and fashion – together with the popularity of the Labour government under Tony Blair – recalled the good old times under Harold Wilson and their optimism.

One of the films which literally 'revived' Swinging 60s was *Austin Powers: International Man of Mystery*. The film is about a 1960s British spy who, after hibernating for three decades, wakes up in contemporary London and shocks his co-workers with his open sexism, leading to numerous funny gags. While Powers' behaviour was clearly out of place and out of date in the late 1990s, it nonetheless revealed that part of the reason behind the nostalgia for the 1960s was the result of the rise of third-wave feminism and the desire to return to the times when male and female roles were more clearly defined. With Cool Britannia came a new Lad subculture propagated by men's magazines focused on promoting hyper-masculinity in opposition to the more sexually ambivalent New Man of the 1980s. *Loaded*, *FHM* and *Maxim* glorified male 'rogues' by featuring screen icons such as Gary Oldman or Oliver Reed. Caine's ruthless London gangster from *Get Carter* became the symbol of the movement, with the Lads embracing his 'classic blokey icon unquestionably' (Catterall and Wells 2002: 109), including his open sexism. Caine's anti-hero seemed to speak to a new generation of young men who found solace in his cool machismo.

Thus, the timing of the remakes of Caine's films in the new millennium could not have occurred at a better moment in time, as they followed a growing interest in his works by the Lads as well as a young generation of filmmaker geeks. In 1993, Tarantino claimed that *Get Carter* was his favourite British film (Chibnall 2003: 100). Then, in 1998, a thirty-year-old Guy Ritchie paid tribute to both *Get Carter* and *The Italian Job* in his debut *Lock, Stock and Two Smoking Barrels*. Nick James claims that, in the wake of the revival of *Get Carter* and the American success of *Lock, Stock and Two Smoking Barrels*, 'a new kind of character and class system has been created, mostly for export' to the US; this was seen in many British gangster flicks that followed at the turn of the millennium and featured 'a violent and vicious caricature of young working-class criminality' (2001: 303), as in *Rancid Aluminium* (Thomas, 2000), *Circus* (Walker, 2000), *Gangster No. 1* (McGuigan, 2000), *Love, Honour and Obey* (Burdis and Anciano, 2000) and others. However, the most impressive cinematic appropriation of *Get Carter* and the 1960s Zeitgeist to date came not from Britain, but from America, when in 1999 Steven Soderbergh created an extended homage/remake/sequel to Mike Hodges' classic in *The Limey*, which will be discussed in the closing chapter.

All of the above examples confirm Verevis' words:

> Critics and reviewers discuss remakes in relation to their originals, but only in those cases where the earlier films continue to *circulate* through the efforts of cultural taste-keepers (aesthetes, educators) and the agency of archives and distributors. Although television (broadcast, cable) and information storage technologies (VHS, DVD) have contributed to the number of films memorialised in *personal archives*, it is nonetheless the case that only a small fraction of world cinema output is seen, let alone remembered, beyond its initial appearance. More than this, in addition to 'the visible face of the canon' – publications, archives, home-video libraries – there is also 'a largely invisible cultural structure that underpins it: *a tissue of quotations, linkages, assumptions and ultimately memories*'. (2006a: 152–53)

One could add other reasons behind each individual remake, such as the release of the new BMW Mini Coopers in the case of the 2003 remake of *The Italian Job* (see Verevis 2017: 161–62, or Steenberg 2012b). However, one thing remains clear: the remakes' accumulation from the late 1990s onwards was the outcome of larger forces at work, rather than digital technology alone. An entire cultural environment existed for *Alfie*, *The Italian Job*, *The Wicker Man*, *Bedazzled*, *Sleuth* and *Get Carter* to be remade, including the rising interest in cult movies promoted by Alex Cox's long-running BBC TV series, *Moviedrome*. Its first episode in 1988 was dedicated to *The Wicker Man*, while another episode later in the series covered *Get Carter* in 1990.

The decade closed with the 1999 publication of the BFI's 'Best 100 British Films' list,[8] created after interviewing 1,000 people from the world of film, who had been asked to select the greatest British films of the twentieth century. After decades of negligence, some 1960s and 1970s films now featured prominently in the ranking. *Get Carter* was at number 16, *Alfie* at number 33, *The Italian Job* at 36 and *The Wicker Man* squeezed in at number 96. The list reflected a revival of interest in 1960s British cinema and a newly found appreciation for the neglected films of the past. The sudden growth in the number of Hollywood remakes of British films occurred exactly at a time when British film experienced critical validation and when the remake, after years of bad rep, was re-assessed by academia. These new research avenues found their perfect embodiment in the phenomenon of Hollywood remakes of iconic British films.

CROSS-CULTURAL REMAKES

Writing about Hollywood and creativity, Janet Wasko accounts that around 50 per cent of Hollywood films are adaptations and, more importantly, that films based on previous works tend to generate significant profit (2003: 16). As she comments, 'there are economic factors that contribute to this ongoing reliance on recycled ideas, already-proven stories and movie remakes and sequels' (16). Because the British originals are now engraved in popular memory and because many have cult classic status, remaking them was not so much motivated by the exploitation of unknown titles previously successful abroad. Rather, the motivation sprang from the economic imperative to ride the wave of nostalgia for the 1960s, which characterised the end of the millennium, and to benefit from the rise of interest in British cinema stateside.

However, while using a source material with a built-in audience has its benefits, it also has its pitfalls. In the case of remaking iconic British films, often regarded as national treasures, the stakes are quite high, and results have been variable in terms of critical reception and box office receipts. This chapter opened with Deeley expressing doubts about the commercial and creative success of the remakes that retooled iconic pictures of the past (2008: 271). The truth, as always, is somewhere in the middle. In economic terms, some of the remakes were financial liabilities, others spectacular successes. *The Limey*, with a budget of $10 million, made little over $3 million worldwide. *Get Carter* was never even released in the UK following poor reviews stateside, where it bombed. It came out the same year as *Bedazzled*, whose total lifetime grosses, however, almost doubled its budget. *The Italian Job* is the greatest box-office hit of all the remakes so far, almost tripling its budget. *Alfie* flopped, *The Wicker Man* was a critical and financial disaster (although by 2018 the film had almost broken even), and *Sleuth* has disappointingly made less than $5 million worldwide to date.[9]

Linda Hutcheon evaluates adaptations based on different measures when she proposes that '[p]erhaps one way to think about unsuccessful adaptations is not in terms of fidelity to a prior text, but in terms of a lack of the creativity and skill to make the text one's own and thus autonomous' (2006: 20). Since what lies at the heart of the pleasure of adaptation is the interplay between repetition and variation, the remake is required to perform two tasks: it tries to stand on its own two feet while also recalling the memory of the earlier work. As Catherine Grant argues,

> the most important act that films and their surrounding discourses need to perform in order to communicate unequivocally their status as adaptations is to (make their audiences) *recall* the adapted work, or the cultural memory of it. There is no such thing in discourse as a 'secret' adaptation. (2002: 57)

Remakes, just like any other adaptation, equally involve the following: 'an acknowledged transposition of a recognizable other work or works', 'a creative *and* an interpretive act of appropriation/salvaging' and an 'extended intertextual engagement with the adapted work' (Hutcheon 2006: 8). Their complex operations and intricate relation to the earlier works include all of the characteristics mentioned above. They also produce a similar kind of pleasure which Hutcheon identifies as repetition with variation, recognition, remembrance and change (2006: 4). As a result, the remake often welcomes comparison rather than hiding its roots. It acknowledges its predecessor, not only on a textual level, but also in industry-sanctioned paratextual materials, which is what all the Hollywood remakes of iconic British films do to some extent, using a variety of tools.

The most common adaptation strategy involved in Hollywood remakes applies here as well – except for *Sleuth*, which Michael Allen refers to as 'Americanising' the source texts to 'appeal to an American audience [. . .], giving it American cultural values and references' (2003: 85). However, the difference lies in the fact that these remakes also function within the shared transnational identity described in the previous sections. As a result, they attempt to appeal to both British and American viewers at the same time. They do so by including several types of cross-cultural references that are more than just an inside joke for those in the know, thus re-applying the same strategy to crossover used in the original films, but now in reverse.

Two successful British films in the 1990s featured American women visiting the UK and settling down with English men (*Four Weddings and a Funeral* and *Notting Hill*). Similarly, the remakes in the new millennium keep the tradition of referencing an Anglo-American special relationship, by either pairing them romantically or introducing a Brit into a multiracial, multigendered and multicultural American melting pot. To that effect, they feature known British actors in supporting and even main roles. Elizabeth Hurley appears in *Bedazzled* alongside Brendan Fraser and steals the focus away from his romantic entanglements with Frances O'Connor. Law as the new millennial Alfie relocates to New York and, thanks to his English charm, seduces numerous American locals, played by such stars as Marisa Tomei, Susan Sarandon and the British-American then-newcomer Sienna Miller. Jason Statham continues on from Caine's criminal masculinity; in his role as sidekick to Mark Wahlberg's noble hero in *The Italian Job*, he brings to the table charisma, bravado and charm with his Limey Lad identity. Stamp travels over winding California roads, confusing the locals with his Cockney rhyming slang and making an undeniable impression on his nemesis, Peter Fonda, in *The Limey*. Caine, in a typical case of celebrity casting, appears opposite Sylvester Stallone in the remake of *Get Carter* and retains his London accent, despite the film's location in Seattle.

But the presence of Brits in America seems to serve another purpose, too. When relocating the original British stories to the new American setting, the remakes not only perform a cross-cultural journey across the Atlantic, but also often make it a subject of the films themselves. They feature British characters who are migrants, travellers or outsiders, crossing borders or journeying across two continents, further experiencing and embodying relocation and assimilation issues inherent to the process of adaptation itself. To that effect, in *Alfie* and *The Limey*, the protagonists' Englishness sets them apart, and their foreignness either charms or threatens the natives, depending on the genre. In rare cases, their journey also embodies more than just the remake's spatial border crossing. The journey constitutes also a temporal one, such as when the titular Limey played by Stamp comes out of prison in 1999 to find himself in a new world that he cannot fully understand, as he remains stuck in the 1960s.

Aside from making the habit of employing British actors in crucial or supporting roles, the remakes also contain other, more commonly found, types of self-reflexive cross-cultural gestures. Such gestures may include certain object fetishes (the Mini in *The Italian Job*, Peter Cook's sunglasses worn by Hurley in *Bedazzled*) and the repetition of cult one-liners ('You're a big man, but you're in bad shape. With me it's a full-time job', repeated almost verbatim by Stallone as a new Jack Carter, or 'What's it all about?' asked in an identical manner by Law at the end of the remake of *Alfie*). Often, the remakes reference not just the original film, but also other British titles of the era, through more extended associations. For example, *The Wicker Man* remake rather heavy-handedly references visual tropes from *Don't Look Now* (Roeg, 1973), released as a double bill with the original *Wicker Man*, and *The Limey* samples Ken Loach's kitchen sink drama *Poor Cow* (1967), not only as a sign of cineliteracy, but also as a clever narrative device linking the main character to the 1960s.

The music and lyrics featured in the original British films and their Hollywood remakes also serve as another example of the film creators' efforts to appeal to audiences on both sides of the Atlantic. *Alfie* is a good case in point. The song to promote the 1966 version, titled 'Alfie', was written by Burt Bacharach and Hal David and performed by Cilla Black in the UK, since Paramount believed the film needed a British vocalist.[10] It is Cher, however, whose vocals are featured in the closing credits of the film. Both versions were released to compete against each other in the US, Canadian and Australian pop charts. In 1967, another cover was released, this time by Dionne Warwick, who with her performance of the song during the Thirty-Ninth Academy Awards ceremony sealed her success as the best interpreter of 'Alfie' in the US and, from then onwards, worldwide. The complicated cross-cultural trajectory of the song's many variants resulted in an international hit that has since then been interpreted by numerous artists – including Whitney Houston, Vanessa Williams, Barbra Streisand and Stevie Wonder – all adding to the film's classic status and its mystique. The soundtrack for the original *Alfie* was composed by the legendary American jazz saxophonist Sonny Rollins. As for the remake, it was commissioned from two heavy-weight British composers, Mick Jagger and David A. Stewart. Jagger and Stewart teamed up to recreate some of its original 1960s vibe, filtering it through their characteristic 1960s rock guitar and 1980s electronic music lenses, respectively. The new version closes with the theme song 'Old Habits Die Hard', performed by Jagger himself, which won the 2005 Golden Globe for Best Original song, but has failed to spawn any new covers as of yet. Then, there is the famous opening track to the original *Get Carter* by Roy Budd, a talented British jazz pianist and composer, whose haunting score was so engrained in the original film's atmosphere that it was then re-arranged in the remake by the then little-known American composer Tyler Bates. His sampling of Budd's original soundtrack brought him some attention, leading to the creation of more scores for horror remakes and eventually landing him high-profile jobs for *John Wick* (Stahelski, 2014, 2017, 2019) and *Guardians of the Galaxy* (Gunn, 2014, 2017). Finally, the famous folk music and lyrics adorning the original *Wicker Man*, which are now considered to represent quintessentially British pagan culture, were in fact created by the American musician Paul Giovanni. Angelo Badalamenti then stepped in as composer for the remake, to reshape the story with his signature eerie sound.

Looking at the different ways in which the originals and remakes interact with each other supports Lucy Mazdon's claim that '[t]he act of remaking the films and the various ways in which they are received should be seen as related components of a wider process of cross-cultural interaction and exchange' (2000: 1–2). Such a bilateral relationship is visible in the ways in which Hollywood remakes and their British originals talk to each other in many playful ways. The conversation also happens on another level. By introducing changes, remakes become 'a comment on societal and cultural transformations, providing us with countless clues to the medium, the culture, and ourselves' (Brashinsky 1998: 163). Jonathan Gray argues that, '[s]ince intertextuality works by placing the text at hand into a conversation with previously viewed texts, not only will earlier-viewed texts be able to talk to a current text – the current text will also be able to talk back to earlier texts' (2010: 57). By talking back to the originals, remakes possess the capacity to illuminate the anxieties at the centre of the original narratives (and vice versa), some of which were not obvious at the time. For example, writing about 1970s British cinema and class, Sue Harper and Justin Smith claim that '[t]he aristocracy no longer occupied the dominant narrative and symbolic space that it was formerly accorded. And authority figures were frequently mocked and undermined' (2012: 228). However, comparing power dynamics in the original *Sleuth* and *The Wicker Man* alongside their remakes helps one to notice that class issues remained a predominant force in both of these 1970s films. A further claim that, while in the 1970s 'many films exploited relaxations in censorship to present the female body for the sexual pleasure of men, most also expressed anxiety about sexually empowered women' (Harper and Smith 2012: 229) also needs investigating. Paradoxically, some remakes, such as *The Wicker Man*, now reveal more tension about female sexuality than their predecessors did thirty years earlier.

The case-studies are grouped less around genres than they are around common themes, although the generic variants are acknowledged as important factors in, for example, shaping the construction of male heroism or determining the film's endings. This focus on themes helps to scrutinise certain common denominators, in particular class and gender. It reveals how cinema can function as 'an especially illuminating social indicator of the realities of a historical era' (Kellner 2010: 4). Finding ways of updating class relations and gender conflicts – whether in comedies, dramas or horror films – poses many challenges for the Hollywood remakes in the new millennium. Each chapter focuses on two pairs of films, starting with the examination of the British originals, one from the 1960s and one from the 1970s, to trace the dynamically changing cultural landscape of the time. Each film is then accompanied by its remake, revealing the old versus new power dynamics brought about by several adaptation strategies. These strategies include gender-switching, the transformation of class into gender-based conflicts and the casting of specific actors whose iconographic status either recalls the original and pursues similar concerns or becomes a point of departure for something new. The following chapters attempt to determine how and if the remakes manage to 'adapt' to address contemporary concerns that resonate with a new audience.

Accordingly, Chapter 2, 'From British Working-Class Gangsters to Hollywood Heroes: *The Italian Job* and *Get Carter*', investigates the most common approach to updating working-class British masculinity to a new Hollywood setting. It focuses on Caine's gangster characters, which are then revisited by Wahlberg and Stallone in the two Hollywood makeovers, respectively. It examines the consequences of the casting decisions that reshape the remakes, as they become star vehicles for their Hollywood leading men and as the genre is tweaked to accommodate the requirements of Hollywood male stardom. Such films tend to endorse heteronormative relations and delegate any subversive elements present in the originals to the background.

Chapter 3, 'Gender, Stars and Class Wars: *Alfie* and *Sleuth*', examines what happens when Caine's 1960s and 1970s working-class lover is remade with a new British actor, Law, in the lead. It shows that such remakes tend to follow their predecessors more closely, rejecting formulaic resolutions or upbeat endings. Starting with *Alfie* as a more politically correct remake to appeal to the sensibilities of the contemporary viewer and closing with *Sleuth*, where Law clashes face-to-face with Caine, the chapter shows a complex entanglement of class, gender and star relations. The remake of *Sleuth* in many ways becomes a sequel to *Alfie*, and Caine becomes a surrogate father to Law.

Next, Chapter 4, 'From Devilish Masters to Evil Dames: *Bedazzled* and *The Wicker Man*', offers a chance to explore the transformation of upper-class charismatic male masters into she-devils and witches in their Hollywood makeovers. Interestingly, this gender reversal adaptation strategy applies equally to comedy and horror film genres back in 2000 and 2006, before gender-swapping became a popular Hollywood trend. From class power games that characterise the relationships in the original films, we move on to power games that result from male and female desires. Although women seem to take centre stage in these remakes, the chapter argues that their dominant position is problematic, since they are presented as either a visual accessory, as in the case of the remake of *Bedazzled*, or a heavily-drawn caricature, as in the case of *The Wicker Man* update.

Chapter 5, 'Remaking, Cultural Exchange and Personal Legacy: *The Limey*', analyses Soderbergh's unacknowledged remake/sequel to *Get Carter*, which offers a reminiscent look back at the 1960s' iconic films, stars and music. The film features Stamp and Fonda, whose presence reinforces its links to the 1960s counterculture. Whereas *Get Carter* was deeply rooted in the post-swinging pessimism of Northern England, *The Limey* takes place in a bright and sunny modern California. Soderbergh's film is a profoundly self-reflexive work that comments on the British and American counterculture movements and on cultural exchange. It sees remaking as a meeting place between the past and the present, which forever changes and continually impacts the reading of each work. The discussion of *The Limey* serves as a fitting conclusion to a book whose task it is to investigate other similar encounters between two film industries and cultures that are close yet distant, similar yet different.

NOTES

1. Preminger directed *Bunny Lake is Missing* (1965), which seems to be a loose remake of Hitchcock's *The Lady Vanishes* (1939) and *Into Thin Air* (1955). *The Lady Vanishes* was then later remade as *Flightplan* (Schwentke, 2005) – a Jodie Foster star vehicle (see Rasmus 2013). Ritt directed *The Spy Who Came In from the Cold* (1965), featuring Richard Burton. Lumet directed *The Hill* (1965), starring Sean Connery. Wyler's *The Collector* (1965) was a UK/US co-production with Terence Stamp in the lead role. Donen directed *Bedazzled*, which is discussed at length in Chapter 4. Mankiewicz directed *Sleuth*, which is covered in Chapter 3. Kubrick's *Lolita* (1963) started a whole series of US/UK co-productions which culminated with his posthumously released project *Eyes Wide Shut* (1999). Peckinpah directed *Straw Dogs* (1971), starring Dustin Hoffman, which was then remade in 2011.
2. I use 'British' in inverted commas for reasons other than Mark Glancy in his book *When Hollywood Loved Britain: The Hollywood 'British' Films 1939–1945* (1999). While he refers to films that were made in Hollywood during the Second World War and specifically targeted British audiences, I discuss films that were made in Britain with the assistance of Hollywood finance.
3. According to *The Time Out*'s ranking of British films from 2018, the 1960s were yet again the most highly evaluated decade, while 1968 and 1970 were the most popular years (https://www.timeout.com/london/film/100-best-british-films).
4. Other more prominent examples include *The Lodger* (Hitchcock, 1927; Brahm, 1944), *Whisky Galore!* (Mackendrick, 1949; Mackinnon, 2016), *Lord of the Flies* (Brook, 1963; Hook, 1990) and *Escape!* (Dean, 1930) as *Escape* (Mankiewicz, 1948).
5. The Cohen brothers' remake *The Ladykillers* (2004) also presents a good example of a Hollywood remake of an iconic British film, *The Ladykillers* (Mackendrick, 1955), but falls outside the scope of the present book, given that the original was not made in the 1960s. *Death at a Funeral* (Oz, 2007; LaBute, 2010) constitutes a recent example of a Hollywood remake of a British film, which occurred within three years from the release of the original, making it a separate case-study on par with *The Girl with the Dragon Tattoo* (Oplev, 2009; Fincher, 2011).
6. Starting in chronological order with the release date of the British films, these are: *Village of the Damned* (Rilla, 1960; Carpenter, 1995), *School for Scoundrels* (Hamer, 1960; Phillips, 2006), *Alfie* (Gilbert, 1966; Shyer, 2004), *Bedazzled* (Donen, 1967; Ramis, 2000), *The Italian Job* (Collinson, 1969; Gray, 2003), *And Soon the Darkness* (Fuest, 1970; Efron, 2010), *Get Carter* (Hodges, 1971; Kay, 2000), also remade as *The Limey* (Soderbergh, 1999), *Straw Dogs* (Peckinpah, 1971; Lurie, 2011), *Sleuth* (Mankiewicz, 1972; Branagh, 2007), *The Wicker Man* (Hardy, 1973; LaBute, 2006), *The Day of the Jackal* (Zinnemann, 1973), remade as *Jackal* (Caton-Jones, 1997), and *The Omen* (Donner, 1976; Moore, 2006). Two other British titles that are often mentioned as possible candidates for remaking are *Don't Look Now* (Roeg, 1973) and *Billy Liar* (Schlesinger, 1963), incidentally both starring Julie Christie.
7. Here, it is important to note the contribution of Alex Cox's long-running BBC TV series *Moviedrome*, which is dedicated to cult movies. The first episode aired on 8 May 1988 and was dedicated to *The Wicker Man*. The episode on *Get Carter* was broadcast on 20 May 1990.

8. As far as other rankings are concerned, *Sleuth* appears in the BFI's 'Michael Caine: 10 essential films' list, compiled in March 2018, which singles it out alongside *Alfie*, *The Italian Job* and *Get Carter* as one of the seminal works of Sir Michal Caine to date (https://www2.bfi.org.uk/news-opinion/news-bfi/lists/michael-caine-10-essential-films). As far as *Bedazzled* is concerned, it is mentioned by the BFI in a brief overview of the best ten films set during the Swinging 60s, published in March 2018 on their website. 'The 60s-set Faustian comedy *Bedazzled* proved the most popular choice when we asked you what we'd missed from the list', declares the BFI, showing that the film is still dearer to the hearts of the public than the establishment (https://www.bfi.org.uk/news-opinion/news-bfi/lists/10-great-films-set-swinging-60s). This seems further supported by a comment from Eleanor Bron, who, during a 2012 BFI retrospective to celebrate Peter Cook's career, observed that the film had been 'undercherished' in Britain. In September 2018, *TimeOut* published 'The 100 best British films' list which includes *The Wicker Man* (twenty-eighth place) and *Get Carter* (thirty-second place) (https://www.timeout.com/london/film/100-best-british-films).
9. Figures according to Box Office Mojo.
10. The choice of Black is interesting in itself. She was promoted as a working-class talent originating from Liverpool and discovered by the Beatles' manager Brian Epstein.

CHAPTER 2

From British Working-Class Gangsters to Hollywood Heroes: *The Italian Job* and *Get Carter*

With the increasing global popularity of British romantic comedies since the 1990s, it is sometimes easy to forget that British cinema has produced some of the most striking examples in the crime genre. Two of them, *The Italian Job* (Collinson, 1969) and *Get Carter* (Hodges, 1971), are discussed together in this chapter. They stand out in the British crime genre, albeit for different reasons. Steve Chibnall observes that, in both, 'the social realist aspect of the crime genre remained in creative tension with its melodramatic and comedic elements' (2009: 376). While the comedic elements that the producer and the director added to *The Italian Job* may have obscured the film's social comment, in the case of *Get Carter*, the combination of realism and classical American film genres punctuated by moments of dark humour creates a richly layered text reflecting on the time and place of its production.

Both belong to the gangster genre, yet each is located at the opposite end of its spectrum. *The Italian Job* is a comedy caper, whereas *Get Carter* belongs to the world of the neo-noir thriller. Chibnall's distinction between 'gangster light' and 'gangster heavy' (2009: 377), even though referring to the cycle of British films at the turn of the new millennium, applies equally to these two classics. Since both star Michael Caine, they also show the development of his gangster persona, in sequence exhibiting a hardening of his screen masculinity from a softer London manhood in the earlier film to a more sinister Northern masculinity associated with the British New Wave in the later one. In *The Italian Job*, he plays the leader of a gang that tries to steal gold from the Italian Mafia; in *Get Carter*, he is a violent racketeer who returns to his hometown to avenge his brother's death.[1] The chapter starts by investigating the transformation of Caine's working-class gangster from the cheerful swinging 1960s landscape to the pessimism and delusion of the early 1970s. Both films are then compared to their Hollywood remakes, as the stories are transformed to fit in with the image of their respective stars, Mark Wahlberg and Sylvester Stallone, often with mixed results and containing some contradictions.

THE ITALIAN JOB (COLLINSON, 1969)/(GRAY, 2003)

As this section will show, in *The Italian Job* original, the changes that the director introduced to the screenplay reveal how genre tweaking determined the overall presentation of gender. These changes reduced the role of the female characters and the film's overall political message, in order to focus instead on Caine's screen charisma and the performative nature of his masculinity and class. The remake's priority, then, was to create a more gender-balanced approach to replace the inherent misogyny of its 1960s progenitor, by increasing the role of its female star (Charlize Theron). In line with the 2000s' rising popularity of heist films that culminated in successful robberies, the film's genre was also tweaked to open up the possibility for a happy conclusion to all of its narrative threads, combining and in the process confusing the gang's members pursuit of financial rewards with romantic fulfilment and personal growth. However, the remake inadvertently replicates some of the original's film's 'gender trouble', even if it tries to delegate it to the background. In the process, the new version becomes just as laden with contradictions and ambiguities as its British counterpart.

Troy Kennedy Martin wrote the script for *The Italian Job* specifically for Caine, building on the actor's previous roles of the Cockney womaniser Alfie, the matter-of-fact spy Harry Palmer from *The Ipcress File* (Furie, 1965) and the cat burglar Harry Dean from the romantic comedy caper *Gambit* (Neame, 1966). The film was meant to ride on the popularity of Swinging London with its Carnaby Street fashion, Mini Coopers, youth culture and pop music. It also followed in the footsteps of two earlier Ealing comedy capers, *Lavender Hill Mob* (Crichton, 1951) and *The Ladykillers* (Mackendrick, 1955), whose winning formula about a bunch of losers led by Alec Guinness had previously appealed to American viewers. More than that, it was also to be Kennedy Martin's chance to prove himself to Hollywood bosses and hopefully move from writing for national television to working for Hollywood majors. In some sense, then, the plot about a group of Brits hoping to get rich by stealing gold from the Italian Mafia self-reflexively represents the dreams of many young British filmmakers in the 1960s, including the writer himself, of looting Hollywood and returning home with bags full of money, as he reminisces on the DVD commentary track. The lines spoken by Charlie Croker at the beginning of the film also address these sentiments. When his heist plan is rejected by the big crime boss Mr Bridger (Noël Coward), Charlie muses: 'I could always take it to the Americans. They are the people who recognise young talent. Give it a chance, they are'. And this is exactly what happened when Kennedy Martin's screenplay was picked up by Paramount and the project greenlighted with Caine in the starring role.

Upon its release, the film had a somewhat lukewarm reception in Britain and completely flopped in the US, even though it supposedly contained all the necessary ingredients to guarantee cross-Atlantic appeal. The ingredients included a soundtrack composed by Quincy Jones, a pretty American actress and an Americanised promotion campaign, whose poster mixed the iconography of the violent heist genre, such as a machine gun, with attributes of Britishness, such as a cup of tea. The truth, as producer Michael Deeley elaborated years later, was that *The Italian Job* was very un-American, and a few token gestures were not enough to convince the public and the reviewers otherwise:

> I have come to the conclusion that the reason the film did not click in the USA is because it had nothing to do with America – nothing at all. It is a playful look at differences between the British and their European neighbours. It would have worked equally well had we shot in Paris instead of Turin because it was the same old 'us against them', love/hate relationship that flourishes to this day between mainland Europe and Britain. Looked at this way, it makes perfect sense that *The Italian Job* received a Golden Globe nomination in the category of Best English-Language Foreign Film'. (2008: 76)

His opinion has been confirmed more recently by the film's repeated association with Brexit, with Anne McElvoy of *The Guardian* (2016) and Fintan O'Toole of *The Irish Times* (2018), among many others, referring to its cliff-hanger ending as a metaphor for the current political crisis, which still dominates British politics at the time of writing (2021). McElvoy professes: 'We are living in the real-life remake of *The Italian Job*', with the line 'You're only supposed to blow the bloody doors off' acquiring a new meaning (2016).

Thus, although in the original *Italian Job* various concessions were made to increase its chances of success in America, the film did not initially manage to cross over well. Its reception in Britain was not very warm either; it took several decades for the film to gain its present status. Rediscovered in the 1990s due to the prevalent nostalgia for the Swinging 60s, it was quickly adopted into the 1990s Cool Britannia Zeitgeist and endorsed by Lad culture when, as Kennedy Martin told *The Sunday Times*, it was 'alright to be a lad again' (quoted in Field 2001: 110). Since then, in November 2004, *Total Film* voted *The Italian Job* the twenty-seventh greatest British picture of all time. In a survey carried out in 2017 by Vue Entertainment, one of the leading cinema operators in the UK, it was voted the best British picture by 2,000 fans, beating

Zulu (Endfield, 1964), *Trainspotting* (Boyle, 1996), *The Full Monty* (Cattaneo, 1997) and *Love Actually* (Curtis, 2003) ('We Polled the Public on the Best Ever British Films – Can You Guess the Winner?' 2007). Deeley observes:

> In the forty years since its making, *The Italian Job* has become the cinematic equivalent of England's legendary 1966 World Cup victory, an evergreen topper of polls in lads' mags, the all time fantasy flagship of *Austin Powers*-style Britpop pride. If its reputation was first built on the back of multiple bleary-eyed TV viewings on Boxing Day afternoon, *The Italian Job* has become a cherished part of British culture, embedding itself quite firmly in the psyche and the vocabulary. (2008: 46)

The film's firmly established status made it a perfect contender for remaking in the 2000s. This was aided by the fact that the new millennium opened with a surge in heist films, especially following on from the success of Steven Soderbergh's star-studded *Ocean's Eleven* (2001) remake of Lewis Milestone's 1960 picture, which confirmed that 'The heist film, or "big caper" as it is sometimes called, is back on the marquee' (Lee 2014: 1). Writing about the early 2000s, Daryl Lee noticed: 'Crime pays very well these days; recidivism even better. It is not a bad time to be thinking about the heist as a genre' (2014: 2). Thus, when *The Italian Job* remake came out in 2003, it joined other releases of heist films that year, such as Frank Oz's *The Score*, Barry Levinson's *Bandits* and David Mamet's *Heist*, all reinventing and reinvigorating the genre.

Before discussing the remake, a few words about the plot of the original film are necessary to explain what makes the film so highly quotable to this day. It opens with Croker's release from Her Majesty's prison. The first close-up of the actor shows him scanning his surroundings before then briefly acknowledging the camera with a smile. This insolent gesture of breaking cinematic conventions will from now on define his character's lack of respect for rules. Charlie is next picked up by his American girlfriend Lorna (Meggie Blye) in a posh stolen car and taken to a hotel where she offers him a coming-out present: a girl of his choice from a line-up of beauties. Unable to choose, Croker beds them all. He then receives a posthumous message from his Italian thief friend, detailing a perfect heist opportunity in Turin. Freshly released from incarceration, he now decides to break back into prison to ask Mr Bridger to support his plan. He hides in the prison toilet and accosts Bridger in a cubicle just as the man is about to relieve himself. In the process, he crosses not only the boundaries of good taste but also of class, as symbolised by Bridger's criminal aristocratic status exemplified by newspaper cut-outs of royalty covering the walls of his cell. In response, Bridger sends a few heavies to Croker's Portobello flat to teach him some manners. However, upon finally learning about the details of Croker's plan, he then agrees to help him in the name of boosting the British economy and to supply him with everything he needs. Croker's team now consists of a few eccentrics, the most memorable being the computer expert Professor Peach (Benny Hill) with a weakness for corpulent ladies. Upon arrival in Italy, they are threatened by the Italian mafia who seem to have already been alerted to their plan. Undeterred, the English break into a traffic control centre, cause a massive traffic jam in Turin, dress up as English football fans, apprehend the gold bullion from its convoy amidst the confusion, place it in three Mini Coopers and escape into the crowded streets of Turin in a spectacular car chase with the Italian police. The gold is then loaded onto a coach. Upon exiting the city, the whole crew starts celebrating their victory when the bus suddenly swerves off a winding Alpine road, to be left half suspended over a cliff. If the gang tries to reach for the gold, the bus will topple over. If they jump from the bus, they will lose the gold. The film finishes with a literal cliff-hanger, as Charlie announces to his gang: 'Hang on a minute, lads, I've got a great idea, err . . .'.[2]

In terms of tone, the film was changed substantially from page to screen in director Peter Collinson's hands. Whereas the original screenplay contained a mixture of comedic and serious elements, Collinson eliminated any shades of grey and turned the story into a cheeky camp spectacle. Kennedy Martin's first draft featured a strong political theme, with Croker portrayed as an anarchist disregarding all social order. It was a darker action-packed thriller with social commentary (Field 2001: 26), a satire on Britain's uneasy relationship with Europe at the time when Britain was applying to join the European Economic Community (Cook 2007: 50). Steve Chibnall explains:

> In fact, Kennedy Martin had conceived a very different film: a more realistic underworld story with undertones of social and political criticism, more in sympathy with the contemporary rage on the streets of Paris than the patriotic chanting of the terraces at Wembley [. . .]. Collinson would play up the satire of English chauvinism already evident in the screenplay, and add a dose of camp excess that was not entirely to the author's taste. As the sexual proclivities of characters like Croker and Professor Peach were exaggerated for humorous effect, Kennedy Martin's critical drama became Collinson's comic book. (Chibnall 2005: 147)

Kennedy Martin addresses the difference between the script and the film in the following words:

> What I was doing was saying right well that was the first half of the thing and we laughed at them and we thought these cheerful cockney chappies, like the people who did the Great Train Robbery, all artful dodgers, but now this is reality, the reality is that there's blood on the pavements and then it went on to the second half [. . .] they found great difficulty

in taking that on board and they did their absolute best to choreograph the fight and stylise the violence. (quoted in Cook 2007: 49)

Aside from downplaying violence, the inclusion of cameo performances by beloved TV actors such as Benny Hill and Irene Handl was meant, as Deeley explains, to inject more humour, colour and richness into the script (2008: 54–55). However, with Hill on board, it acquired a new quality, becoming over-the-top, if not cartoonish, as the screenwriter recalls on a DVD commentary. It is understandable how Vincent Canby of *The New York Times* could describe the film as 'technically sophisticated and emotionally retarded' (1969). Looking at the original screenplay and the final cut, although the genre on the surface remains the same, the tone of the piece was drastically altered. It was deprived of harder edges, realism, romance and political or social allusions, in favour of over-the-top acting, cartoonish characters, as well as a chauvinistic and camp atmosphere.

The script for the remake was commissioned from the writing duo Donna and Wayne Powers. They repeated the title, the names of key characters and narrative units such as the hatching of a heist, collecting a team with unique skills and tools, the rivalry between competing criminals, the traffic jam and the car chase using Minis. The remake departs from the original film, however, in some crucial ways, including tone, realism and elements of romance, becoming surprisingly closer to Kennedy Martin's original concept. Lee notes that looking at the etymology of the words 'heist' and 'caper' reveals that the former is 'a dramatic form' whereas the latter 'tends towards the comic' (2014: 12). Although the distinction between the two terms tends to be 'mildly elusive' and not set in stone, 'heist' usually evokes 'the serious, dramatic, violent and perhaps professional dimensions of criminals carrying out ill-fated robberies' – this applies more to *The Italian Job* remake, while 'caper' suggests 'the colourful and amateurish side of such crimes' (2014: 12), which seems to characterise the original. Thus, whereas the original could be screened to a hall full of cheering British kids at a school Christmas party (G rating), the remake has a PG13 (parents strongly cautioned) rating. It appears to be more of a heist film than a caper, as it contains less humour, invents the death of Mr Bridger and includes a strong revenge and family theme, making it much darker in tone.

While the British version consisted of the preparation and execution of one big job in Italy, the remake features two robberies, thus initially remaking the original film's botched job and then providing us with a much more satisfying conclusion in the second robbery. The first one takes place in Venice, to justify the repetition of the title. Its success is thwarted by Steve (Edward Norton), who not only steals all the gold from the gang but, more importantly, kills Bridger. This then provides the gang with the motivation for the second heist in Los Angeles to avenge Bridger's death, which is foreshadowed in the film's taglines 'Not for the pay but payback' and 'Get in. Get out. Get even'. Furthermore, seeing Donald Sutherland, cast as Bridger, carry out his last fatal job in Venice in winter creates an additional sense of foreboding for anyone familiar with *Don't Look Now* (Roeg, 1973).[3] Introducing the motif of revenge romanticises the original Cockney rogues and makes them more likeable as heroes, since they now appear to be on the side of justice and honour. Finally, instead of the cliff-hanger that frustrated so many viewers at the end of the original story, this version offers the audience a classic Hollywood resolution, with the hero getting both the woman and the money, in line with the trend for happy endings prevalent in many American heist films at the time. As will be seen below, the remake of *The Italian Job* thus represents what Andrew Higson calls the 'rhetoric of democracy and populism [which] is built into the formal organization of the American film' whose narrative structure focuses on individual achievement and 'the formation of the heterosexual couple', with the figure of the star holding together 'these various formal strategies, narrative, visual and identificatory' (Higson 2002: 57–58).

One of the fundamental problems with which the remake had to deal was the dated presentation of women. In retrospect, Collinson's film appears to be very much a product of its times, appealing to male viewers' fantasies of women's constant availability and featuring promiscuity as a token of the Swinging 60s permissiveness. Despite the producer insisting that casting Caine should not send out the wrong message about *The Italian Job* as the second instalment of *Alfie* (Gilbert, 1966), the reverse seems to have been the case. The call-girls he beds after leaving prison and the wife of his deceased Italian friend all seem happy to pleasure him, bringing clear associations with his former role of a Cockney lothario, always on the lookout for another 'bird' and never wasting the opportunity of a new conquest. Vincent Canby finds that the film's humour thus consists of references to 'Caine's sexual promiscuity, shown obliquely in his physical exhaustion after various off-screen encounters' (1969).

Croker's attitude to women, therefore, remains a product of its time and place. The presentation of Croker matched Caine's public image of the time, since his supposed real-life promiscuity was regularly reported on in gossip columns. As Christopher Bray observes, the actor equally accentuated his sexual prowess and liberal attitude to matters of sex, merging life with fiction. Interviewed about his time in Hollywood while promoting *Gambit*, Caine said:

> Most stars here go to bed early because they're afraid of looking horrible in the morning. I look horrible all the time, so I have the advantage. In any event, I sleep between takes during the day. So I can stay up late with impunity, whoever she is [. . .] They seem convinced that we English are just a bunch of Limey fags and I'm determined to change the image.
> (quoted in Bray 2006: 93)

Even *The Encyclopedia of British Film: Fourth Edition* (McFarlane and Slide, 2013) mentions that '[o]ff-screen, his freewheeling sex life – he and Terence Stamp shared a King's Road flat and were committed to "pulling the birds" – merely reinforced his laconic film persona, apparently irresistible to women of all ages'.[4]

This is further accentuated by a change in the portrayal of Croker and Lorna's liaison. While it was much more developed in the original screenplay, in the film the girlfriend, played by Maggie Blye, 'a pretty young American actress' who was 'introduced to the mix specifically in the hope of adding some appeal to the US audience' (Deeley 2008: 56), was turned into a dolly bird whose screen time was reduced to her attractive appearance. Even as a secondary character, she remains irrelevant to the plot. In the opening scene, she picks up Croker from the prison in a stolen car and retorts with amusing remarks, implying that she might be able to hold her ground. Next, when she arranges for Charlie to receive his welcome-back gift, she surprises with her liberal approach, especially as in Kennedy Martin's original screenplay she seriously contemplates marriage – a motif which did not make it to the final cut. However, later, when she discovers Charlie's betrayal, she becomes hysterical and lashes out at him while he is holding an enormous teddy, reducing the argument to a cartoonish farce. Lorna is then considered a liability once in Turin and dispatched to Geneva to, as Chibnall notices, await the arrival of the conquering heroes (Chibnall 2005: 149). Blye's overall contribution to the film, therefore, seems so insignificant that Matthew Field, the author of *The Making of The Italian Job* (2001), does not even mention her in his section devoted to the discussion of casting. On the DVD commentary, Kennedy Martin recalls that there was a lot of male chauvinistic feeling present on the set, which, he believes, imparted itself on the picture. These sentiments were then picked up and reflected in the film's American promotion campaign; the poster featured the tattooed back of a woman in a bikini sitting on the ground at a mobster's feet (resembling Caine) in an extremely subservient position, sealing the image of women's position in the film.

It is for these reasons that the first major difference between the original and its Hollywood remake concerns the function of the central female character. She is no longer the dolly bird from the 1969 picture, but a professional safecracker and vault expert whose skills are essential for the successful completion of the second heist. Stella (Charlize Theron) joins the gang to avenge her father's death and, despite their initial prejudice, wins them over, thanks to her dedication to the cause, professionalism and maniac driving skills.

Stella's importance is emphasised by the fact that she both opens and closes the film. The remake starts with the close-up of a beautiful diamond necklace, then cuts to a bedroom showing a young blond woman, Stella, in bed. She is woken up by a phone ringing, then picks it up to hear that she is about to receive a gift. If one were to miss her greeting – 'Daddy' – the rest of the scene could easily be misinterpreted as a typical phone conversation between two lovers, a young woman and her older partner. This gives their relationship an incestuous undercurrent, as well as a chance for the viewers to see Stella in her negligee. On a narrative level, Stella will later become an important element of the second heist the success of which relies on her skills and talent. However, on a visual level she, just like her progenitor, is still at the outset established as eye-candy, showing the remake's intention to both have its cake and eat it. Stella is a progressive young woman, yet she remains visually objectified, like the women in the British original.

The next time Stella receives mention is when Bridger shows Charlie (Mark Wahlberg) her photograph after the first successful heist in Venice, to which Charlie responds: 'Stella's a beautiful girl'. Bridger then expresses his regret at spending half of his life away from her in prison and urges Charlie not to repeat his mistake. This parting advice given to Charlie by his surrogate father figure occurs just before Bridger is murdered by Steve, laying the foundation for Charlie's subsequent actions. For Stella to become available, the script calls for her father to die and then be avenged, so that he can be substituted by his alter ego, Croker, not only as the master thief but also as the object of her affection. What follows next is not only a revenge-motivated heist to retrieve the gold, but also a love story about Charlie and Stella burying old ghosts so as to be able to enter into a heteronormative relationship.

Figure 2.1 *The Italian Job* (1969): 'Now, what would you like?' 'Everything'.

Stella's growing sexual availability to Croker is manifested in the way in which her clothes change from the moment when Croker enters her life. At first, she is presented as a single woman in impeccable dark clothes; her appearance when she first joins the gang resembles Hitchcock's immaculately dressed icy blondes. When Charlie unexpectedly visits her in her hotel room to accidentally reveal her in her bra, her behaviour reveals embarrassment and sexual unavailability, in stark contrast to the original where women were open to view and sexually available. However, the scene yet again discloses a contradiction, demonstrating that the remake tries not to sexually objectify Stella on a narrative level: it shows that Charlie respects her privacy; yet it connotes her to-be-looked-at-ness by allowing the viewer to peep. Later, during the preparations for the heist, she practices her driving skills in her red Mini, wearing a matching red top, to indicate her awakening desire and availability to the hero. When the gold is safely retrieved towards the end, prompted by Charlie, she breaks her golden rule and looks at the contents of the safe she has just cracked open. She is now ready for her relationship with Croker.

When comparing the presentation of Charlie Croker in both versions, it becomes obvious that one crucial element that characterised the original character is now missing from the remake. In Collinson's film, the presentation of Croker was very much determined by its star's class and working-class masculinity, established by Caine's earlier starring roles in *Alfie* and *The Ipcress File*. In terms of class, the film seems to contain one crucial paradox, however. On the one hand, Caine's Charlie appears to epitomise a young working-class meritocrat who opposes the old order. Chibnall notices that, '[i]n posing a challenge to the reactionary *ancien régime* represented by Bridger, Charlie Croker was to embody the spirit of anarchy that was so much a part of youth rebellion in 1968' (2005: 147). On the other hand, however, Croker desperately tries to ingratiate himself with Bridger, going to great lengths to earn his approval so as to gain entry into the world of the criminal aristocracy. The irony of this attempt lies in the fact that, in reality, both Caine and Coward came from humble backgrounds, which adds to the impression of class being an act and furthermore comments on the rigidity of the British class system (Bray 2006: 120). In this respect, the two scenes in which Croker feigns aristocracy are quite revealing. When he picks up his car, he puts on a posh accent, adopts a stiff way of holding his shoulders (perfected previously in *Gambit*) and all too easily passes for an aristocrat.[5] In another scene, he arrives at a hotel in a freshly tailor-made suit and introduces himself as 'Lord Croker'. Both scenes support Bray's claim that class, just like gender, is a performance whose success depends in great measure on the right costume and accent. They also remind one of Caine's first major role in *Zulu*, where he plays a high-rank British army officer.

Thus, rather than just aping or mocking the gentry, the film creates the impression that Croker would quite happily step into their shoes, given half

Figure 2.2 *The Italian Job* (2003): 'This is a love story, actually'.

the chance. This becomes even more evident when analysing the way in which he treats his team by continually barking orders at them and assuming a dominant position. 'It's a very difficult job and the only way to get through it is we all work together as a team. And that means you do everything I say', is one of the most memorable lines in the film. The team is now reduced to responding only 'Yes/No, Charlie', as they become completely overshadowed by Caine's starring role. This impression of Croker's central position aided by Caine's screen charisma is so strong that it obscures the fact that he is always acting on behalf of Mr Bridger. Hence, a role that was supposed to challenge the status quo never quite delivers on its promise. In the end, Charlie is no more than an opportunist without any political or social agenda, best summarised by his disarmingly honest response to Lorna's question when she presents him with a few beautiful women to choose from: 'Now, what would you like?' To which he answers, 'Everything'.

If there is any class allegory, it soon becomes subsumed by the film's overriding focus on gender representation. In Collinson's hands, it is Caine's performance of masculinity, rather than class, that becomes imprinted on the viewer's memory. As Lindsay Steenberg argues, 'Caine's embodiment of a working-class London masculinity is self-consciously highlighted in *The Italian Job*; Charlie Croker draws our attention to the fact that criminal masculinity is a seductive performance at the heart of the genre' (2012a: 88).

As Robert Shail correctly points out, writing about this and other roles that Caine reprised in the 1960s and early 1970s, 'in conventional terms of gender politics, Caine's persona remains rooted in a fairly traditional discourse of masculinity' (2004: 73). In contrast to the Northern masculinity of the British New Wave, we are now offered 'a southern masculinity rooted in the cultural landscape of working-class London', replacing the 'tough, aggressive, sometimes violent, maleness of Finney and Harris' with 'a more playful, humorous, although equally self-confident, identity' (Shail 2004: 68).

In hindsight, it is difficult to believe that, during the pre-production phase, the British producer Deeley was briefly faced with an unexpected problem related to casting. Even though the role had been modelled on Caine's earlier working-class screen persona and created specifically for the actor, Paramount was now speculating about casting Robert Redford instead (Deeley 2008: 53–54), a move which in hindsight seems quite absurd. It seems especially absurd considering that *The Italian Job* is quintessentially a tale about a few eccentric English underdogs who team up to fool their Italian adversaries, with Englishness being flaunted all over the screen – from the presence of the English football insignia to the above-mentioned beloved Mini Coopers painted in red, blue and white to represent the Union Jack. In the end, Caine, who was then quickly becoming the icon of the Swinging 60s, took the lead, and with his presence turned the film into one of the most iconic pictures of all time.

In the remake, on the other hand, the issue of class becomes irrelevant, and Croker's behaviour is transformed to fit in with the convention of romance. In fact, the whole heist plot can be read as a test that the lead character must undergo to win and bed the woman at the end of the film, making Stella not only an important addition to the male gang but also the driving force behind the action. As a result of his love interest, the American Charlie Croker drastically differs from his British prototype. The director, F. Gary Gray, observes on the DVD commentary: 'This movie is like a love story actually'. This statement reveals that the love angle is the greatest departure from the original as, by introducing this romantic subplot, Croker is changed from a womaniser into a caring partner, first in crime and then in life. The film shows that '[w]hat motivates the thieves appears to be straightforward: cash for a better life, the means to get out of financial trouble or stagnancy. But as critics and audience members alike know, while the leader's motives may start there, they are inescapably more complicated' (Lee 2014: 9). Love and revenge then become personal drives for the hero, just like in the case of Danny Ocean's motivation for the robbery in Soderbergh's film, showing the affinities not only between the remake and its British source but also other genre films of the time. Stella is just as much an object of desire as the gold, something to be studied and eventually possessed. Her presence directly affects the portrayal of the lead character, whose respect and romantic feelings for the daughter of his friend and mentor mean that, in the Hollywood version, Charlie must remain a perfect gentleman at the expense of further character development. It is hard to disagree with Stephen Holden, who argues that

> Charlie is Mr. Wahlberg's latest attempt to present himself as a contemporary James Cagney-like hybrid of action hero and leading man, and once again this pug-faced actor falls short. The blank, opaque quality that served him in 'Boogie Nights' and can make him a sinister villain works against him here. He simply lacks the charisma of a credible ringleader and displays little passion, even when riled. (2003)

Stella Papamichael also notices Wahlberg's 'cosmic anti-presence' and observes that it is Charlize Theron who 'is left to drive the movie, taking the wheel with quiet confidence and steering it home' (2003). This is deserved praise for Theron's acting while failing to notice her overall function in the film.

However, despite these criticisms, casting Wahlberg as the new Charlie Croker seems to have paid dividends, turning the remake into the most commercially successful Hollywood remake of iconic British films to date. As a leading man, he offers a version of Hollywood masculinity that is surprisingly unthreatening, despite his physical abundance, since he uses his brains, rather than his muscles, to solve problems. Caine's Charlie does not come up with the heist plan himself but quite simply follows it exactly as specified by his deceased Italian colleague. By contrast, Wahlberg's Charlie is the creative spirit of the heist, working it through with the help of his equally ingenious teammates, emphasising the equality of the team where each member is not just a cog in the machine but a crucial ingredient for achieving a common goal, with the team's racial, gender and national diversity essential to its success.[6] His democratic leadership stands in stark contrast to the class divisions that informed the relationships in the original, which in one scene features a huge desk in a modern office block with gang members seated around to listen attentively to Croker's plan. In the remake, this more class-based corporate gangster culture with its officious, bureaucratic and hierarchical structure becomes replaced with scenes of camaraderie, such as playing a game of basketball. Wahlberg's Charlie does not lead his eccentric team through non-negotiable orders, since they all are on equal footing. The crew is much more democratic, and responsibilities are more evenly distributed. Even with his commanding physique, Wahlberg comes across as a rather ordinary bloke. In comparison to his quirky gang members (a computer nerd who claims to be the real Napster, or an explosives expert with a love of shoes and first editions), each with their individual backstory introduced via flashbacks, he is a rather surprising choice for the mastermind of the intricate heist. The backstory of Wahlberg's Croker is so insubstantial that the viewer may intuitively fill in the gaps with the actor's biography. His working-class upbringing, troubled past as a young criminal and later reformation are often discussed. The actor's strong family ties, loyalty to his kin, pride in gaining his degree at a mature age and an extremely regimented daily routine seem to show that he is both ordinary and extraordinary, therefore making him an ideal Hollywood star according to John Ellis's theory (see Ellis 1992).

Despite his star status, it appears that Wahlberg/Croker needs the other members of the gang, not only to perform the perfect heist, but also to hold the film together and give it variety and humour. He does not outshine the other members of the gang, nor upstage his supporting cast in any way. Even though the new Charlie is a much nobler version of Caine's character, this does not mean that the remake shies away from jokes based on womanising and objectifying women, which characterised the first version. For the romance to happen, these elements must be delegated to the background characters, leaving Wahlberg unsoiled.

In the original *Italian Job*, the function of women in the film as sexual objects determined the way in which they were presented, as either accessories or objects of male desire. It also affected the presentation of the main hero as well as other gang members. For example, Collinson transformed the character of Professor Peach, who in the original screenplay was a quiet train spotter, into a man with a penchant for obese women. In the remake, Benny Hill's character becomes Lyle aka 'Napster' (Seth Green), who is also awkward and obsessed with women; it is made clear that he is not allowed to have any intimate contact with Stella in the scene where he accidentally hurts her by trying to pin a US badge/camera onto her top.

The remake does feature, however, Caine's closest 'cultural replacement'. Thus, although the actor is missing from the film, the type of screen virility he embodies is not. When asked in 2001 whether he would consider appearing in the remake, Caine said he would enjoy the challenge (Field 2001: 132). When he was eventually approached, the actor was committed to another project at the time; hence, the role went to Sutherland instead. Even though Caine briefly appears in a small cameo in the scene where the villain (Edward Norton) watches the 1969 *Italian Job* on his newly acquired Plasma TV, his presence is nonetheless evoked by another British actor – Jason Statham, the then-emerging icon of Lad culture – who serves as a tribute to Caine's original Cockney rogue. Caine may be absent from the screen but the type of masculinity he embodied is revived by another Limey lad's presence.

Casting Statham is not a coincidence, for several reasons. First of all, at the time, he was strongly associated with Guy Ritchie's low-budget debut caper *Lock, Stock and Two Smoking Barrels* (1998), and then with Ritchie's second feature *Snatch* (2000), another violent caper but this time with an international Hollywood cast added to the mix. Shail argues that Statham's role in *Lock, Stock and Two Smoking Barrels* immediately established his screen image as that of tough London working-class masculinity, bringing to mind such 1960s actors as Caine, Terence Stamp and Sean Connery. Unlike his predecessors, however, he finds Statham's Englishness, working-class identity and mock Cockney to be mere comedic tools (2019), which became especially evident in the actor's later Hollywood work. Statham's would-be gangsters in the two British capers by Ritchie could not have arrived at a better moment. As Ali Catterall and Simon Wells remind us, 'British gangsters, so beloved of the New Lads, had been transformed into shotgun-toting clothes horses: likeable, mythological pop culture icons, the stuff of celluloid, photo shoots, magazine columns and best-selling autobiographies' (2002: 270). They further add: 'The belated commercial success of a number of British cult films from the 1960s and 1970s has been closely allied with this backwards-looking retro craze' (275). Ritchie's timely exploitation of gangster chic – where clothes matter as much as class identity and accent – creates a stylish and attractive package less rooted in reality than in the film iconography of the 1960s and 1970s, with *The Italian Job* and *Get Carter* as two preferred sources of inspiration. Thus, it seems that now the true successor to Caine's Croker is Jason Statham, who at the turn of the millennium became a new British movie icon of London's cinematic underworld and Lad culture. A comment by an IMDb user confirms that 'Jason Statham (who would have made an excellent Charlie in a more faithful remake or sequel) is great as the driver and ladies' man, Handsome Rob' (LennyRenquist 2003). Significantly, Statham's Handsome Rob is the most sceptical gang member regarding Stella's competence and involvement in the heist, and it is possible to read this reluctance as yet another continuation from his roles in Ritchie's male-centred films,[7] as well as the original *Italian Job*, which deprived women of agency.

Moreover, Statham's presence in *The Italian Job* is not only a token British ingredient to appeal to British audiences, but also a reference to the simultaneously occurring waves of heist films on both sides of the Atlantic, with the proviso that on American soil the stories tended to end in victory, while in Britain the outcomes were often disastrous or at least uncertain. Lee believes that Ritchie's 'exhilarating depictions of lad culture' in both films 'rejuvenated the genre and marked the heist lexicon' (2014: 95). Brian McFarlane goes as far as claiming that *Lock, Stock and Two Smoking Barrels* was responsible for the renaissance of gangster genre cycle in the late 1990s in the UK (2009: 369). As a result, more gangster films were released in the UK between April 1997 and April 2000 than in the two preceding decades (Chibnall 2009: 376), becoming the most important cycle in British cinema since the British New Wave (Chibnall 2009: 384).

In line with 1950s British comedy capers, the British *Italian Job* shows that the heist does not always have to go according to plan. Its famous cliff-hanger was the proverbial final nail in the coffin, sealing the film's fate stateside upon its first release. The idea of a sequel was quickly abandoned, to the chagrin of all those involved in the production, to this day leaving fans to speculate endlessly about the methods with which the gold might have been safely retrieved from the bus.[8] Surprisingly or not, the ending continues to divide the viewers, as seen by some unfavourable comments from those IMDb users who have grown accustomed to successful thefts in Hollywood heist films in the 2000s, to which the remake belongs. Thus, instead of the cliff-hanger that frustrated so many viewers, the remake offers a classic Hollywood resolution, as the two narrative plotlines arrive at a single destination. The film closes with a romantic image of Charlie and Stella embracing in a gondola in Venice, where the film opened. It also reveals that the successful completion of 'the Italian job' entails getting the gold as well as the woman. Charlie's voice-over informs us that he decided to follow Bridger's advice and settle down with the woman he loves. As Lindsay Steenberg notes:

> It is telling that the 2003 US remake did not include a closing mystery, ending instead with a celebratory montage of each member of Croker's team enjoying the consumer goods that they had earlier fantasized about – Handsome Rob (Jason Statham) enjoying his Aston Martin car, Lyle (Seth Green) enjoying speakers so loud that they literally blow women's clothes off, and Croker (Mark Wahlberg) enjoying the hard-won love and respect of glamorous safe-cracker, Stella Bridger (Charlize Theron). (2012b)

The ending conclusively proves that Stella is an object to be won, like a car or a sound system. Except for Left Ear (Moss Def), who spends his money on a house in Andalusia packed with a collection of shoes and first editions, all the other members of the gang use their fortune to impress and seduce the opposite sex.

To date, this update has received the highest score of 7 out of 10 from IMDb users, when compared to the other Hollywood remakes of British films included in this study. Even some ardent British fans of the original give it a high score and admit to enjoying it, despite their initial prejudice. This is possibly because the remake affords numerous pleasures based on the knowledge of the original. For example, Charlie announces to the gang that they should stage their robbery in LA, just 'like the Italian job', referring not only to the first heist in Venice, but also to the original film. Another instance is Left Ear's response to Napster's convoluted computer jargon – 'We're in Italy. Speak English' – recalling the original's xenophobia and jingoism. With the original's classic status now firmly cemented, it comes as little surprise that the creators of the remake attempted to make numerous concessions to appease its British fans by including other British references. Such references include the new model of the Mini Cooper embedded in the story – confirming Verevis' suggestion that a possible motivation behind the revival of the classic was also the relaunch of the Mini Cooper (2017: 159–60) – and the cross-cultural cast. Following the success of the remake, *The Brazilian Job* sequel was occasionally mentioned in the industry press. However, history uncannily repeated itself, and the idea never materialised, despite the film's handsome box-office receipts.

Finally, in terms of gender, it is worthwhile highlighting one last thread that runs through a few disgruntled IMDb user comments and blames the remake's high rating on young female viewers. Indeed, the user rating report for the film shows that many young women under 18 give it the highest score, showing how its increased gender balance translated into a more gender-balanced audience appreciation. However, it could also indicate that, despite having a strong female character at the centre of the story, the film heavily relies on fairy-tale elements – a single female orphan waiting for her prince charming who, with her dead father's blessing, undergoes a successful test to win her heart. Seen in this light, the remake, through its gender and genre transformation, becomes a closet Cinderella story whose hidden contradictions continue to match those of the original.

GET CARTER (HODGES, 1971)/(KAY, 2000)

Hodges' *Get Carter* was, in fact, remade three times. The first remake was in 1972, as the blaxploitation movie *Hit Man* (directed by George Armitage and starring Bernie Casey, Pam Grier and Lisa Moore), which MGM produced to recuperate their losses after the original's unsuccessful financial performance. Then, it was remade as *The Limey* in 1999 by Steven Soderbergh, the discussion of which concludes this book. Finally, in 2000, it was updated by Stephen Kay. Since the film had already experienced its own revival in Britain by the end of the millennium, it is not surprising that Kay would comment: 'We're going to get crushed in London. It's tantamount to a British film-maker remaking *Mean Streets*' (quoted in Chibnall 2003: 110). He was fully aware that, by then, *Get Carter* had become 'a cult classic, recognized as an innovative and morally complex crime thriller that has influenced the development of both British film noir and American noir' (Spicer 2010: 112). This section will look at the original's complex generic heritage and the film's social implications, before moving on to the discussion of its 2000 remake, whose function, so it seems, primarily was to serve as a Sylvester Stallone star vehicle.

According to Robert Murphy, the idea for *Get Carter* first came in 1969 when

> Klinger was approached by Nat Cohen [. . .] to help make a couple of films for MGM, who were in the process of closing down their Borehamwood studios but didn't want to be seen to be deserting

Britain completely. Klinger had already decided to exploit the recent upsurge of interest in the English underworld aroused by the trial of the Richardson and Kray gangs to make a hard-hitting, realistic British gangster film and he had bought the film rights to an as yet unpublished crime novel, Ted Lewis' *Jack's Return Home*. (1999: 128)

The novel was based on a real-life event, the so-called 'one-armed bandit murder', which had taken place in the northeast of England. But pinpointing the film's exact origins is by no means easy. As will be seen below, in the process of adaptation, other notable influences came into play – from American film genres, British New Wave and European art cinema to British literary tradition. What makes *Get Carter* unique, therefore, is its close resemblance to its American counterparts at the time, while simultaneously remaining deeply embedded in its British context.

After the prosperity of the Swinging 60s, full of hope for a better future, the 1970s in Britain to many felt like a cold shower (see Newland 2013: 10–17). Britain had to wake up from its swinging dream and face a harsher reality. There was a growing realisation that, behind the 1960s' swinging veneer, there may have been corruption, violence and criminality involved. The infamous Kray brothers were now behind bars, and other British productions of the time offered further reality checks, including the cult gangster film *Performance* (Cammell and Roeg, 1969) and *Villain* (Tuchner, 1971), starring Richard Burton as the incarnation of the Krays in one. *Get Carter* was equally topical, tapping into the then media coverage of a more realistic vision of London's criminal underground.

The film's plotline begins as Jack Carter travels from London to his hometown, which he deserted many years earlier for a more liberating life in the capital, to track down his brother's murderer. His unexpected appearance in Newcastle soon opens up old wounds, brings back memories of unresolved past feuds and distorts the order of previously smoothly run criminal activities between the London gang lords and their Newcastle allies. As a reluctant return traveller, Carter unforgivingly refers to his hometown as a 'crap house'. Still, he continues to undertake his journey, urged on by a sense of familial duty and possibly feelings of guilt, since it is implied that he is the real father of his brother's daughter, Doreen (Petra Markham). In the pre-credit scene in his boss's London penthouse, Carter is shown staring blankly into space. He is literally entombed by the darkness of the frame, making the audience realise that his journey can only ever be one-way, since such an opening immediately marks him as a neo-noir protagonist. As he plunges into the depths of Newcastle's criminal world, his gentlemanly manners and elegant London exterior give way to outbursts of unchecked and often unjustified violence. His manic laughter at the film's closing as he fulfils his revenge throws us out of the world of western and gangster iconography and into a world inhabited by mad avengers of the Jacobean revenge tragedy (Murphy 1999: 136). Carter must die in order to comply with the requirements of that dramatic tradition, with Hodges having to 'fight hard for his preferred ending against his financiers at MGM, who would have liked the protagonist to survive for a possible sequel' (Chibnall 2003: 23).

Although panned at the time of release for its high level of brutality, misogyny and lack of characters with any redeeming features, *Get Carter* has experienced a veritable renaissance since it was rediscovered by Lad culture in the 1990s and adopted as the mouthpiece of masculinity in crisis. As Patrick Tobin observes, 'Caine's performance as Carter set the mould for generations of London hard men in film – violent men who possess a sick and twisted sense of honour about themselves even when they are abusing women and murdering their enemies' (2012: 102). The film's renewed popularity, together with the revival of interest in Caine's other iconic parts from the 1960s and 1970s, reveals nostalgia for a time when films featured 'unacceptable pre-feminist representations of women' (Murphy 1999: 135) and when the roles of women and men were more clearly defined and divided. Carter seemed to speak to a generation of young men who similarly liked lager and violence and who treated the opposite sex instrumentally. Troubled by the film's endorsement by New Lads, Hodges wondered if the attention his film received in the 1990s may reflect

> a certain confusion or sadness that modern men have. They don't always know who they're supposed to be, or what their roles are, do they? A character like Carter makes them nostalgic for a time that they didn't necessarily know but that they've heard about from their fathers. Carter gets things done his way, no messing about. That can be comforting to a lot of men. (quoted in Gilbey 2004)

Moreover, its revival and transformation from cult to classic exemplify the changes in the film canon, signifying, as Chibnall notes, that '[t]he conception of nationhood and national character that the British cinema canon has always reflected seems to have swelled to encompass the sordid and sensational as well as the saintly and sober' (2003: 121). Perhaps he is right that it was easier for the film to finally become accepted by the establishment because it is not just an average gangster flick, but a work that derives from both American and European cinemas, as well as 'respectable traditions of British drama: the role of tragedy in the theatre, and social realism in the cinema' (2003: 113). However unaccepting we may be of Carter's violent behaviour, we know exactly where it is coming from, in terms of both literary and cinematic traditions, as well as a particular historical moment.

Acknowledging the film's level of brutality should not overshadow its important social implications, as the violence that springs from the genre also derives from a specific social context and location. The movie had to wait until the 1990s not only to be discovered by a disenfranchised male youth, but also to be recognised as a work of social commentary. Its bleak vision reflects the morals and mores of the late 1960s and provides a visual record of the post-industrial Newcastle cityscape that has since changed beyond recognition. If, as Hodges claims, '[t]he 1960s for many of us was a hopeful and exciting decade when radical ideological dreams seemed realisable[, t]hose dreams, however, soon faded, overtaken like many human endeavours by greed and corruption' (2009: ix). *Get Carter* painfully discloses this.

To start with, generically, the film seems to be rooted in the American gangster and western tradition. The credit sequence on the train shows Carter reading Raymond Chandler's *Farewell, My Lovely* (1940), in a tribute not only to Chandler's book, but also its first screen adaptation, Edward Dmytryk's *Murder, My Sweet* (1944), a noir classic shot in Los Angeles. Later, the Hollywood remake of *Murder, My Sweet* (1975), starring Robert Mitchum, would go on to pay homage to the pre-credit London sequence of Hodges' *Get Carter* by replicating it almost shot for shot in its opening scene (Fuller 2000: 36). This tribute shows the mutual creative impact between Hollywood and British cinemas and *Get Carter*'s influence on the development of not only British but also American film noir.

Indeed, Hodges admits to having been greatly influenced by American films which he calls 'the best films in that genre, without a doubt' ('Mike Hodges Discusses *Get Carter* with NFT audience' 1999: 124). In 2009, he explained in a forward to *Neo-Noir* that *Get Carter* was made out of 'anger and revenge against social injustice wrapped up as a thriller' (2009: ix), similar to 1940s American noir. The American poster seems to have picked up on this generic association by presenting Carter as a lone ranger, recalling other neo-noir protagonists of the period, such as Callahan in the *Dirty Harry* (Siegel, 1971) marketing campaign. *Get Carter* also follows in the footsteps of the first 'true neo-noir' (Spicer 2010: 215) – *Point Blank* (1967), about a lone vigilante roaming the streets of Los Angeles. Incidentally, *Point Blank* was directed by a British filmmaker, John Boorman, which points to yet another continuity. In a fashion similar to Boorman's classic, Hodges' film displays self-conscious reflexivity and creative appropriation of various generic traditions, 'reflecting different national and transnational influences', while remaining 'carefully located in national and regional contexts' (Bould et al. 2009: 6).

Moreover, as Tobin observes, '*Get Carter* may well be Britain's most complete and brutal response to the mythical culture of film Westerns' (2012: 101), with Carter walking around a lawless Newcastle holding a rifle against a vast desolate landscape. Chibnall describes these generic affinities in the following way:

> In this 'north-eastern', the familiar iconography of the western genre is knowingly adapted to give Newcastle a frontier quality: gangsters cruising the town in Jags stand in for gunslingers on horseback, drinks are knocked back in a long saloon bar, a shotgun rests on top of a wardrobe, there is a conspicuous presence of good-time girls and a conspicuous absence of lawmen. When a tough, taciturn loner rides into town, we know there is going to be business for the undertaker, just as we do in the 'spaghetti' westerns of Sergio Leone. (2003: 6–7)

However, as Tobin notes, '[t]he main difference, of course, is that there is no endless frontier or Technicolor sunset for him to ride off into – just a cold beach in Newcastle, caught between coal slag and an unfriendly ocean, while listless grey skies hang above' (2012: 102). Perhaps more surprisingly, Hodges' playful appropriation of the western also offers moments of comic relief, such as the high-angle shot of Caine's naked thighs forming a frame-within-a-frame, as he stands at the top of the stairs with his legs wide apart, pointing his rifle at the London hoodlums in a classic cowboy pose.

Beyond these parallels, the film is also equally indebted to the tradition of 1960s British New Wave, through its focus on depicting the life of the working class in Northern England. It is significant that for his cinematographer Hodges insisted on Wolfgang Suschitzky, who had developed an acute eye for location through working on documentaries. Designed by Antonioni's former collaborator, Asheton Gorton, *Get Carter* was shot on location but, as Laurie N. Ede notices, in contrast to *Blow-Up*'s (Antonioni, 1966) reconstructed mise-en-scène

> *Get Carter* made straight presentation of some stark modern settings, such as the Brutalist Trinity Centre multi-storey car park in Newcastle and Blackhall Colliery near Hartlepool. Such godless places performed an essentially sociological function for a key film of the post-New Wave era, hinting at the environmental influences on ugly human behaviour. (2012: 52)

Andrew Spicer observes how 'Hodges' documentarist's eye and Wolfgang Suschitzky's long-lens camerawork contrast the city's pre-war terraced housing with its new tower-block developments and multi-story car parks' becoming a comment on 'a rapid modernization that embraced two of the major growth industries of 1960s Great Britain, gambling and pornography, which turned Newcastle into the Las Vegas of the northeast of England' (2010: 112).

Another reference to the British New Wave comes from a somewhat ironic casting choice. Hodges wanted Cyril Kinnear, the pornography baron stereotypically depicted in the novel as an obese baddie, to be played by John

Osborne as a seedy intellectual. As Murphy writes, the director persuaded the producer 'to cast John Osborne, the Angry Young Man whose play *Look Back in Anger* had rudely shattered the conservative consensus in 1956. He was tall, thin and bearded' (1999: 130). Responsible in no small degree for the revolutionary changes in contemporary British theatre and cinema by bringing the subject of class injustice to the fore, here he is at the criminal epicentre of a Northern town, whose poverty he exploits for his shady business dealings.

Although Caine's London accent should have been a source of confusion, considering he plays a Geordie and the film draws from the British New Wave's authenticity traditions, it nevertheless serves to register the gulf between London and Newcastle. It also seems to provide continuity between *The Italian Job* and *Get Carter*, allowing us to trace the development of Caine's gangster persona. The former film's optimism is now matched by the latter's omnipresent darkness. The lightness and humour of the earlier role are replaced by sombre and sinister tones, as we observe Caine change gear from a gangster light mode to a gangster heavy one, simultaneously displaying important generic differences within these two categories of crime film. The accent could additionally be explained by Caine's admonition that 'Carter is the dead-end product of my own environment, my childhood. I know him well. He is the ghost of Michael Caine' (quoted in Chibnall 2003: 27). It is, therefore, not only a marker of location, but also a signifier of class identity which by then had already become an integral part of Caine's star image, as he frequently mentioned his humble roots. As Shail explains, the actor is unique in 'never having made any attempt to disguise his origins as the son of a porter at Billingsgate fish market, a working-class Londoner who had come up the hard way. In fact, he has created a screen persona which deliberately plays upon the qualities associated with his background' (2004: 69). Paradoxically, then, Caine's London accent may have even further contributed to the impression of realism with critics praising his 'nuanced, realistic acting' (Murphy 1999: 133). Just as in the case of *Alfie*, whose posters exclaimed that 'Michael Caine is Alfie', conflating the actor with the role, the posters all over the country now proclaimed that 'Caine is Carter'.

With the role of Carter being so closely bound with Caine's star persona, it is no wonder that the director of the remake would feel some trepidations when embarking on the project. His apprehension was soon confirmed by critics who, despite the lack of a press screening, soon jumped on the film. *The Washington Post* called it 'uninspired', *The New York Times* 'pointless', *SFGate* 'conventional' and *Variety* 'useless' (McCarthy 2000), to quote the mildest of the criticisms. Consequently, the film was never even released in the UK, and the British public had to wait two years until Warner Home Video released it on DVD.

On the DVD commentary, it appears that Kay's only solace came from Caine's involvement in the project, who told him on the set that Sly made a great Carter. Caine plays Brumpy, the villain he kills in the original, evoking the memory of the earlier film by 'celebrity intertextuality' (Verevis 2006a: 20). This is a strategy common in remakes where actors associated with previous works make cameo appearances, which can function either as homage to the earlier work, or as endorsement of the new version, or both. It seems that, in this case, Caine's cameo sanctions the new version, with the actor naming Stallone as his worthy namesake. It is significant that some of the first words that Stallone utters in the film are 'My name is Jack Carter', as if to establish the character's new celluloid identity. Hodges was baffled by the actor's endorsement of the Stallone remake ('*Get Carter* Director Deems Remake out of Shape' 2002); he found his appearance disappointing since Carter was, in his opinion, the actor's definitive role. Indeed, Caine's decision to appear alongside Stallone appears more complicated and less clear-cut in retrospect. Following the remake's bad reception, he dismissively referred to his participation as a joke. Even though the remake is located in Seattle, Caine speaks in his usual London accent, which provoked Elvis Mitchell of *The New York Times* to suggest that 'Mr. Caine appears here in a role that will increase regard for the original. Maybe that was his intention' (2000).

Still, despite unfavourable reviews, the remake with its new hero warrants investigation, provoking one to ask whether its purpose was really to remake Hodges' crime classic or rather become a springboard for something else. In fact, upon scrutiny, it appears that, in this case, the function of the remake extends beyond the updating of the old story for modern times. Instead, it became an opportunity to reboot Stallone's declining screen image.

Significantly, the term 'reboot' came into prominence together with 'the increasing industrial importance and cultural popularity of movies and television programmes based on comic book characters' (Herbert and Verevis 2020: 7). Although Stallone has avoided playing comic book characters like Superman, the role he rejected in 1979, he is equally placed 'in a paradoxical temporal situation, where narrative events occur over time and yet the character remains unchanged' (Herbert and Verevis 2020: 1). This applies especially to Stallone's two most iconic creations, Rocky Balboa and John Rambo, and by extension also to Stallone as an actor, who, like a comic book character, is remarkably one of a few Hollywood actors whose celluloid manifestations never die. In his long-spanning career, he is killed only once in *F.I.S.T.* (Jewison, 1978).

Moreover, Stallone's iconic roles emerged on screen at the same time as many comic book characters figured 'centrally within movie and television franchises of the 1980s and 1990s' (Herbert and Verevis 2020: 8). In parallel to the millennial vogue for rebooting such movie franchises, Sly as a cultural figure equally needed rebooting. By the end of the millennium, he had become branded as the muscle man of the action genre whose body, as Paul McDonald writes, 'had made millions at the box office but was critically dismissed' (2014: 150). Thus, even though the reboot is most often analysed in the context of film franchises and series,[9] I wish to propose a further approach to the term, with the new version becoming an opportunity to reboot the career of a star in need of a new direction.

Previously, before he took the part of Jack Carter, in an effort to achieve critical validation, Stallone gained 40 pounds to transform his hard body into that of a disabled, overweight and impotent sheriff, Freddy Heflin, in *Cop Land* (Mangold, 1997), where he appeared opposite such heavy-weight actors as Robert de Niro and Harvey Keitel. According to McDonald, the weight gain not only 'carried narrative meaning, with Heflin's spiritual and physical inability to act symptomatically displaced onto the flaccidity of his body', but also departed from the 'ideological legacy of Rambo' whose hard body had by then become 'a sign of Reaganite jingoism' (2014: 163). Finally, this reflected Stallone's own desire for 'actorly legitimisation, distancing him from the mass popular market while also "embodying" his commitment to actorly craft' (McDonald 2014: 165). Despite his efforts, the film garnered lukewarm reviews, and Stallone's physical transformation did not translate into critical rehabilitation or audience approval. The legacy of his two iconic roles, Rocky and Rambo, remained dominant in the background (McDonald 2014: 165–67).

Cop Land was then followed by *Get Carter*, this time with Stallone as a lead. Its function, it seems, was to reboot Stallone, with Todd McCarthy of *Variety* seeing the remake of *Get Carter* as the 'latest Sylvester Stallone "comeback" picture' (2000). As Proctor writes,

> the term reboot, in its original context, is 'used to describe the process of restarting a computer or electronic device [in order] to recover from an error' ('Reboot Definition' 2010) [. . .] Shutting down the computer [. . .] and rebooting it, resets the hardware and, hopefully, restores the unit to optimum functionality. As with a computer's internal memory, rebooting the system does not signify total loss of data. (Proctor 2012: 5)

In *Get Carter*, Sly is similarly restored to optimum functionality after his disabled, bloated body and general incapacity throughout most of *Cop Land* proved unsuccessful in gaining him actorly legitimisation or audience appreciation. *Get Carter* resumes the tradition of Sly's hard iconic body, thus not losing the data, but rebuilding and resetting its function for the 2000s. The remake thus marks his return to the action genre through its continued emphasis on his muscular body and physical prowess. At the same time, it attempts to become a starting point for something new, with Sly's muscles no longer in the service of the nation or state, as in his *Rambo* and *Rocky* series – especially *Rocky IV* (Stallone, 1985) – but rather helping his own family.

Leonardo Quaresima believes that the remake 'assumes that its viewer is an intertextual viewer [who finds pleasure] in juxtaposing and comparing' (2002: 80). The 2000 *Get Carter* offers the viewer many such points of comparison, not only because of the celebrity casting, but also because of the repetition of iconic lines. 'You're a big man, but you're out of shape. With me it's a full-time job' is one of the most famous one-liners from the original, spoken by Caine's Carter. Repeated verbatim by his Hollywood counterpart, it seems to acquire a double meaning: it becomes Sly's proclamation that he has finally accepted his fate and his professional calling as an action-movie star whose body serves as the main attraction.

The film appears to be a relatively faithful remake in terms of plot and key ideas, and it is easy to see how the original's American roots could have appealed to Hollywood producers because of its generic familiarity. However, as a star vehicle for Stallone made at the turn of the millennium, the remake departs from its source in a few crucial ways. When Caine accepted the part back in 1971, Hodges was surprised that he was willing to risk his reputation by playing 'such a shit'. When it comes to contemporary Hollywood stars, Divine believes that, '[w]ith the exception of Harvey Keitel, a Hollywood star today would not dare play Carter as an amoral angel of vengeance' (2000: 18–19), and Stallone was no exception.

Hodges' protagonist is a morally corrupt anti-hero who will stop at nothing in his pursuit of revenge. He says so little that his occasional outbursts of violence become even more terrifying. His obsession with hygiene and health (he cleans cutlery on the train to Newcastle, pops pills and applies nose drops) implies that, under the confident and elegant veneer, there is possibly a vulnerable mind and a body that may eventually crack. Another troubling aspect of his behaviour is his misogyny, a trait that started with *Alfie*, resurfaced in *The Italian Job*, then found its most violent expression in *Get Carter*. Yet again, women are drawn to Carter, even though he treats them instrumentally as a source of sexual pleasure, a means to get his way or a source of information. Over the course of this film, Carter sleeps with three women – his boss's wife, Anna (Britt Ekland), his Newcastle landlady, Edna (Rosemarie Dunham), and the local gangster moll, Glenda (Geraldine Moffat). All three women are then endangered or even die due to his actions. Anna most likely suffers serious physical harm due to her infidelity. Edna's brief affair opens her home to a visit by professional gangsters. Glenda's death is indirectly caused by Carter, since he forces her into the boot of a car which then sinks. Carter does not flinch at the sight of this unnecessary and accidental death, because to him, as Chibnall correctly observes, women are either whores or saints. This binary opposition becomes evident when he compares Doreen to

Figure 2.3 *Get Carter* (1971): 'Slags like your Sandra can get away with it, can't they? The Doreens of this world can't, can they?'

Brumpy's own teenage daughter before he kills him: 'Slags like your Sandra can get away with it, can't they? The Doreens of this world can't, can they?'[10] His staging of Margaret's death when he forces her to strip, drugs her, gags her and dumps her limp body into Kinnear's lake is as chilly and shocking today as it was in 1971. Murphy's comparison between the women's fate in Lewis' novel and Hodges' film shows most poignantly that such changes were introduced not because of any plot development, but rather because of a morbid fascination with Carter as a psychopathic killer.

Kay's Carter, on the other hand, possesses a moral compass. As Christian Divine comments in *Creative Screenwriting*:

> The new script by David McKenna (revised by Stephen Kay) shows how Hollywood 2000 deals with moral ambiguity. In the first five pages, Jack Carter, now a Vegas mob flunkie, defends a woman's honor; helps lift an old lady's bag; plays ball with a child; and gives a big tip to a cabbie. There is no doubt this confused man is a good guy. (2000: 18)

Even though these scenes failed to be included in the final cut, with Stallone in the lead, the viewer is left with no doubt regarding the new Carter's moral integrity. Thus, he is no longer a misogynist with psychopathic traits, but

BRITISH WORKING-CLASS GANGSTERS TO HOLLYWOOD HEROES 57

Figure 2.4 *Get Carter* (2000): Stallone's Carter clumsily comforts his niece.

rather a nice guy who somehow got mixed up with the wrong crowd. It should, therefore, not be surprising that, once back home in Seattle, Carter's first goal is to comfort his brother's widow and clumsily counsel his niece. As one satisfied IMDb user comments, '[t]he remake is a brave attempt. All the nasty stuff has been removed. The right morality, the right politics and the right family values have been poured in' (tober 2011).

Unlike in Hodges' film, which showcases Carter's virility and sexual prowess, in Kay's version, Jack does not engage in any sexual antics. Whereas Caine's Carter is directly involved in the porn business and does not mind watching such films until Doreen appears on the screen, Stallone's Carter works as hired muscle in Las Vegas and is in no way related to the digital porn industry opening up in Seattle. He watches a porn DVD only as part of his investigation; when he then sees the exploitation of his niece and other young girls, he finds it very disturbing. The remake clearly shows that Carter is in no way responsible for her downfall.

To further showcase his noble qualities and moral integrity, Carter's body count in the remake is also much lower, despite delivering many punches. In the end, he only kills the young Eddie (Johnny Strong), who spiked Doreen's (Rachael Leigh Cook) drink to rape her, and Brumpy, who tried to cover this up. He shoots him in the back, recalling Carter's death at the hands of a nameless assassin at the end of Hodges' film. Geraldine (who is a blend of Margaret's and Glenda's roles, played by Rhona Mitra) is killed off-screen by Cyrus Paice (Mickey Rourke), whom Carter beats to a pulp but does not kill. He also decides to give the big boss Kinnear (Alan Cumming) a second chance. The return of equilibrium at the film's closing re-establishes the importance of family values, with Carter able to leave the city because he has purged it of its criminal filth and helped to reunite his family.

Caine's Carter was focused on revenge due to an old-fashioned moral code rather than his genuine concern for the well-being of his relatives. Stallone's Carter's family-oriented narrative springs from the significant changes that the 1980s hard body hero underwent in the 1990s. Drawing a comparison between Rambo and Reagan, Susan Jeffords notices that their astounding achievements in the 1980s left little room for improvement, since '[t]hese characters had made themselves so spectacular that they began to verge on comic representations of themselves' (1994: 176). She explains how, in the first years of Bush's administration, the alternative was not to exceed their predecessors, as this would be unrealistic, but to show that 'the qualities of spectacle and violence are no longer sufficient for determining character, and that action takes more than ability – it takes heart' (176). As a result, by 1991, the hard body hero from the 1980s, epitomised by Rambo and Rocky, had already started to feel guilty when delivering a punch. Likewise, and significantly, Terminator 2 dies at the end to protect the family, showing the complete change of motivation for masculine heroism by the 1990s (Jeffords 1994: 141–43). This transformation is observable in the example of Stallone's Carter. He combines the lethal quality of his earlier roles with a softer and more caring side to American manhood, which is 'capable of change' thanks to families providing 'both the motivation for and the resolution of changing masculine heroism' (Jeffords 1993: 197).

Another difference between the original and its remake concerns the development and purpose of the motif of the journey. Hodges' film is built around this theme, with Carter's travel from London to Newcastle slowly acquiring a symbolic dimension. Thus, while on a literal level *Get Carter* is the story of one man's odyssey into the depraved underworld of Newcastle in search of justice, it also becomes, as Pamela Church Gibson and Andrew Hill argue, 'pivotal in understanding the transition from the 1960s to the 70s' (2009: 333). The movement from the South to the North bears profound significance, representing a threshold between two geographically distinct locations, as well as the chasm between the old and the new. The appearance of Jack Carter back in his old town shows the stark contrast between the glamour of London and the poverty of the post-industrial North. In the pre-credit scene shot in a luxury London penthouse of Carter's boss, the gang members watch a cheap porn film produced for them in the North. The first comment that registers the gulf between the two cultures and locations is uttered by one of the gangsters who jokingly points out: 'Bollock naked with his socks still on?' 'Yeah, they do it like that up North', replies another.[11] Later, Carter's first words when he arrives back in his hometown demonstrate his new status as a sophisticated

Southerner in a rough and uncivilised Northern environment. In a scene in a public bar, he orders a pint of bitter instead of his favourite London scotch. He snaps his fingers at a bartender and demands: 'In a thin glass'. The scene also explains why his brother's death caused by an overdose of whiskey seems suspicious. Newcastle's local alcohol is the less sophisticated and much cheaper brown ale.

Hodges further juxtaposes the superficial sophistication and confidence of Londoners with the Geordies' lack of style, through contrasting Carter's fashionable Soho look suit with the 'tatty sack suits and grubby tweeds' and 'polyester trousers and nylon shirts' (Laverty 2011) of the locals. In Newcastle, even places of entertainment are shown as imbued with a melancholy spirit and a far cry from their Swinging 60s London equivalents. As Sue Harper and Justin Smith comment:

> The film's geographical space juxtaposes decaying infrastructure and entrepreneurial modernity, suggesting that this is a community trapped between the old world and the new. And it is important to recognise the almost perfunctory manner in which realist constructions of geographical spaces are internalised in the lives of their protagonists. (2012: 176)

The film implies that the Swinging 60s not only sealed the growing divide between the North and the South, but also brought no benefits to the working class of Northern England. The only few permitted luxuries associated with the Swinging London scene are collaborating with the criminal underworld in the capital. However, although this northern elite seems to be in a never-ending party mood, Hodges soon turns this into the morning after. In one of the final moments of the film, we see the guests outside the front of Kinnear's mansion. As the police raid the luxurious residence, the visitors are brought out into the cold light of day. Their blank faces covered with thick layers of make-up register little emotion, nor any awareness that their Swinging 60s are now over.

As Murphy argues, films like *Get Carter* show 'a post-swinging Britain where permissiveness has curdled into pornography and violence' (1999: 128). The film unveils the deformation of 1960s ideals by using the example of the Northern setting. Rather than benefiting from the sexual revolution, the 'salt of the earth' Northerners lose their innocence and integrity as sexual liberation is monetised by a southern-owned pornographic business. Women's lib and the pill have resulted in only illusory freedoms, with most of the women in the film now victimised, including Doreen, whom her father's girlfriend introduces to the local porn business at the age of sixteen. Thus, the honest community and family ties that Northern England always stood for appear to have fallen by the wayside, with absent mothers, fathers unable to establish authority and teenagers losing their innocence for thrills and small change. The 1960s values have been turned into short-term profits, as counterculture is commercialised and criminalised through the affluent London exploiting Newcastle as a possible new satellite town.

When Carter discovers that his niece/daughter has become involved in the local porn business, he realises that his actions have indirectly implicated her in the system that took her innocence away and murdered his brother. His corruption has crossed borders that he thought were impenetrable, and it is his past mistakes that now haunt the present. With his daughter's downfall, we see the next generation suffer the repercussions of the previous generation's decision to live outside established rules. Thus, the idea of one gangster's journey from London back home to Newcastle presented the director with a chance to reflect on the then passing era that seemed to offer so much possibility yet ended up in so much disappointment.

On the level of the plot, the idea of a journey from one geographically and culturally distinct location to another is also seemingly preserved in the remake. Upon hearing the news of his brother's death, Carter travels from Las Vegas to Seattle by train to find out what happened. However, Stallone's impenetrable face hidden behind sunglasses makes it hard to tell whether the trip brings back any memories or traumas from the past. Caine's Carter had a very good reason to leave his hometown for London: it seemed to be a move forward, a rebellion, a gesture discarding the old ways for newly found liberation and an escape from past mistakes, such as fathering his brother's daughter. The 2000 Carter's decision to desert his original hometown remains unclear, unless we take the comment of one of the Seattle gangsters about his Las Vegas tan as indicative of a possible cause. After all, the film visually exploits Seattle as the rainiest place in the US, from the moment when the hero arrives in town until the symbolic spell of dry weather at the film's closing as he leaves, determined to change his life. The film tries to convince us that, unlike in its British prototype, Jack's trip from Las Vegas to Seattle does not represent his moral descent but, on the contrary, becomes his journey towards redemption. Chibnall correctly points out that '[f]or this Carter, the return home to Seattle is not the end of the road but a rediscovery of the righteous path' (2003: 109).

In the remake, the Seattle to which Carter returns is now a city with one of the highest levels of literacy in the country, liberal views and respect for green issues. Furthermore, unlike 1970s Newcastle, it is a place of prosperity and advanced technology. The only thing that it has in common with Newcastle is its claim to being its country's northernmost coastal city. In the original, Jack's movement from London to Newcastle, two geographically but also culturally specific locations, indicated not only a spatial but also temporal journey from the Swinging 60s optimism to 1970s pessimism. The 2000 *Get Carter* now shows digital media as a dangerous new source of corruption and criminal activity, with the big boss Kinnear, now a Harvard graduate computer geek millionaire, setting up a digital porn business with the help of Cyrus Paice. Here lies excellent potential to juxtapose the fall of the utopian ideals of the 1960s counterculture with the fall from grace of the digital revolution, easily observed from today's vantage point, given the growing awareness of digital disruption and the violation of personal data on social media. However, Kay instead seems more focused on rebooting Stallone's star persona, whose mythical figure overshadows all of the film's other social implications.

Thus, if there is a journey in the remake, then it seems that the most likely candidate for transformation is Stallone's own acting career since, as noticed earlier, the film clearly builds on pre-established elements of his screen persona. Stallone's role in *Cop Land* as a mumbling sheriff with a disabled body and mental malaise differed from his more typical roles. It is only towards the end of this film that he takes action into his own hands and purges his hometown from corruption, bravely exposing his fellow cops and thus breaking the bonds with his pseudo-family. The function of *Get Carter*, it seems, was then to restore Stallone to full functionality once more, which the remake emphasises by having the actor's able hard body very much on display. The film's frantic camera work pauses only during scenes of reconciliation with his family and in the rare moments of the protagonist's contemplation, allowing the viewers to dwell on his vein-bulging muscles.

Unlike Caine's Jack Carter, who is killed at the end, Stallone proves yet again to be invincible. Reminiscing about the ending of the original, Caine says: 'I would have loved him to have walked away but we used to kill people in pictures those days. They were no sequels [laughs]. Maybe it's better that there's just *Carter* instead of *Carter* 1, 2, 3 and 4' (DVD commentary). But, in some sense, the new version provided Caine with the opportunity to appear in *Carter* 2, even if he had to die on screen once again to make room for his replacement. Stallone's Carter can never die because, unlike Caine's anti-hero, he is a confused good guy who has returned to the righteous path. The film finishes not only with a clear indication of Carter opening a new chapter in his life, but also the possibility of a next instalment. This never materialised, since the film bombed.

Get Carter was followed by a streak of similar and similarly critically dismissed action films, such as *D-Tox* (Gillespie, 2002) or *Avenging Angelo* (Burke, 2002) going direct to DVD. As Adam Lippe writes, '[y]ou would think that after *Cop Land*, Sylvester Stallone would have understood his new niche and retired his action hero poses to move on to different and more challenging projects' (2009). This shows the impossible task that Stallone faced at the beginning of the 2000s, when he could not please his audience and critics either way. *Cop Land* would not provide Stallone with the actorly recognition he desired, but it led to his return to the action genre. Thus, even if *Get Carter* may be a failed remake, in a sense, it is a successful body reboot. With Stallone now back in shape, it was only a matter of time until the actor realised that, instead of stepping into someone else's shoes, perhaps it was time to revisit his own iconic roles. The sequel to the *Rocky* franchise, *Rocky Balboa* (Stallone, 2006), was welcomed even by the sceptics. Stephen Holden of *The New York Times* confessed: 'When I first learned of this film, presumably the final episode in the "Rocky" franchise, the idea of the 60-year-old Rocky going at it one last time sounded risible. Reports of audiences snickering derisively at trailers for the movie seemed to confirm my expectations. Surprisingly "Rocky Balboa," is no embarrassment' (2006).

CONCLUSION

Caine's working-class gangsters seethe with cool charisma. The actor explained the iconic appeal of his roles from the period in the following words:

> If you look at English males in our films, they're either homosexual, bisexual, cold, repressed, fucked up, no good with women, bad lovers, kinky or insane . . . The Englishman in films has always been weird with women. Here you have an actor who in *Alfie* went out and screwed them all, in *The Italian Job* he stole the gold and screwed them all, and in *Get Carter* he killed all the bad guys and screwed all the girls. So there you have three icons . . . which is me'. (quoted in Field 2001: 110)

Yet, at the same time, these films trouble with their outdated representation of women, displays of violence and overt endorsement of patriarchy. For Gibson and Hill, for example, in *Get Carter*, '[t]he troubling portrayal of women in the film can be taken as a further comment on the anxieties of the period and its concerns about the excesses of permissive sexuality' (2009: 334). Harper and Smith agree that the film represents a tendency in the crime films of the decade, whose narratives 'endorse patriarchy and punish sexual deviance violently' (2012: 142).

To reflect the changes in women's position in society, both remakes distance themselves from the inherent misogyny of their forbears, by turning women into a positive catalyst of change. In *The Italian Job*, Charlie's criminal and materialistic intent is subsumed by his desire to help Bridge's daughter come to terms with her father's death; in *Get Carter*, the teenage Doreen helps her estranged uncle return to the righteous path. This does not entail, however, that the images they portray are without problems, as Stella is a sexual object reserved for the conquering hero, and Doreen's rape is avenged so that she can be restored to her virginal state. The presentation of other secondary female characters that briefly come and go remind us, however, of Caine's Carter's division of women into two categories, saints and whores, which still holds.

The two Hollywood remakes discussed in this chapter thus adopt a seemingly similar adaptation strategy: they update the troubling aspects of the stories for the new millennium by removing any uncomfortable elements to the background, in the service of their leading Hollywood stars. Neither remake chooses to centre around class issues, as the focus is placed on the representation of gender instead. The emphasis on class distinction is replaced by a different binary opposition of good guys versus bad guys. With this problem resolved, life can return to normal, in contrast to the British films where chaos and uncertainty prevailed.

Led by Wahlberg, the British underdogs are transformed into an American success story focused on individual abilities and personal fulfilment, which all of the gang members achieve in the end. Their commercial motivations are subsumed by their revenge imperative and romantic involvement. Although including numerous nods to the original film, the remake manages to offer a new spin on the story, enabling audiences to judge it on its own terms and avoiding unfavourable comparisons to the original – a fate that seems to have consumed the 2000 *Get Carter*.

As a result, unlike *The Italian Job*, the remake of *Get Carter* was a critical and financial disaster. In *The Italian Job*, Wahlberg's Croker is surrounded by his diverse team to inject humour and variety into the film. *Get Carter*, however, rests entirely on Stallone's broad shoulders, who, despite his impressive physique, struggles with this weight. The film, therefore, fails to satisfy on numerous levels. It fails both those who grew up with Stallone's no-nonsense tough-guy masculinity of the 1980s and those who wanted the return of the original ruthless Carter despite contemporary sensibilities. As one IMDb user comments,

> Stallone hasn't had it easy. As soon as the eighties ended he was pretty much an obsolete joke, the occasional decent film (Cliffhanger, Copland) hasn't changed that one bit. Here he is in a remake of the British Caine classic [. . .] trying to be both a cool mofo and an involving character at the same time; neither is a success. (DaveNoodles 2006)

Contrary to Kay's expectations, Caine's presence did not seem to help either. Unlike the cleverly interwoven British references in *The Italian Job* remake, Caine's occasional appearances pepper the film and, like Hamlet's ghost, keep reminding the viewer of its British progenitor. It is important to note that the remake came out just at the same time as the original was back in vogue, with Caine's gangsters serving as a model of fashionable criminal on-screen masculinity that, according to the Lads, needed no reformation or rehabilitation. Stallone's hard body with the heart did not appeal to anyone. However, it turned out to be a stepping-stone towards the realisation that rebooting his screen image for the new millennium could be achieved through returning to and rebooting his own franchise.

NOTES

1. A link between the two films can be observed in the poster design for the British release of *Get Carter*, which depicts Caine in an exuberant floral jacket entirely out of place for the dark crime thriller, yet closer to the image of Caine's lighter gangster persona in *The Italian Job*. The American poster for *The Italian Job*, however, mistakenly portrays Caine's gangster in a dark suit, a black hat and leather gloves, which does not match the tone of this cheerful comedy caper.
2. The final scene is so iconic that it inspired sculptor Richard Wilson to place a full-size identical bus on top of the De La Warr Pavilion in East Sussex in order to promote the London Summer Olympic Games in 2012.
3. In 1999, just as the original film was being re-released in British cinemas, rumours about the possible casting for the remake circulated, mentioning Caine as a possible contender for the part of Mr Bridger and Rowan Atkinson as Professor Peach (Dilley 1999).
4. Even today, in the documentary *My Generation* (Batty, 2017), the actor nostalgically remembers the 1960s when women were called 'birds' and cannot stop himself from making sexual innuendoes at Maude Garrette while promoting his latest caper film *Going in Style* (Braff, 2017), coincidentally also a remake.
5. Charlie explains his long absence by saying that he was in India shooting tigers with a machine gun, in a sarcastic reference to the former British empire and its attitude towards the colonies.
6. Mark Gallagher notes how the remake 'grants agency to men of different races, with instrumental roles for Mos Def [. . .] and Franky G, the latter of whom achieves an iconographic weight disproportionate to his small role in the film', receiving 'a number of lingering camera shots, emphasizing his heavily muscled arms and also granting him an empathetic presence, perhaps evidencing African American director F. Gary Gray's investment in men of color' (2013b: 271). While he is right in identifying this new racial dynamic and agency, he is wrong in claiming that the original gang consisted solely of white men. In fact, his argument would have been even more poignant, had he investigated the original film's 'racial profiling', visible in the final moments of the film. It is the mistake of the only black member of the gang, the driver of the coach, Big William (Harry Baird), that causes it to swerve and land on the edge of the cliff, resulting in the failure of the entire operation.
7. The lack of women in Ritchie's two films could be interpreted as either misogyny (see Monk 1999), or the expression of male solidarity and brotherhood (see Chibnall 2009).
8. The Royal Society of Chemistry organised a competition meant to solve that problem, and the winner was announced in 2009 (https://www.theguardian.com/film/2009/jan/23/italian-job-ending-solved).
9. However, some essays contained in the edited collection *Film Reboots* (Herbert and Verevis 2020) extend this discussion to include stand-alone titles.
10. Even though Hodges interprets this as Carter's violent reaction to the inequality at the heart of the British class system (Chibnall 2003: 82), Carter cannot be considered a modern-day Robin Hood. If it had not been for his personal injustice, there would be no hint that he would otherwise oppose his bosses and other profiteers of their business. Moreover, if we are to believe in his rage at society's corruption, this still does not necessitate the level of violence inflicted on female characters who are mostly victims of the system.
11. The line was dubbed for the US viewer as 'Bare ass naked with his socks still on'.

CHAPTER 3

Gender, Stars and Class Wars: *Alfie* and *Sleuth*

In Lewis Gilbert's *Alfie* (1966), which catapulted Michael Caine to international stardom, his working-class character beds numerous women from all walks of life. In Joseph Mankiewicz's *Sleuth* (1973), which then confirmed Caine's status as one of Britain's most significant cinema actors, his working-class hero seduces the wife of a wealthy aristocrat. This chapter will show how both films engage even more overtly with the theme of class identity and its importance in personal and sexual relations than either *The Italian Job* (Collinson, 1969) or *Get Carter* (Hodges, 1971). Alfie suggests that his girlfriend gives their son away for adoption, because only a rich woman could 'dress him handsome' and teach him how to 'talk proper'. Milo in *Sleuth*, however, already knows how to dress and talk to win the heart of a classy woman, since his father worked hard to pay for his education in a second-rate public school. However, as his aristocratic opponent played by Sir Laurence Olivier makes him acutely aware, pretending to be something is not the same as being it, since 'qualities that breeding brings can't be acquired' – an attribute echoed by the film's casting, which adds an extra layer of irony to the film's conflict.

In 2004 and 2007, respectively, *Alfie* (Shyer) and *Sleuth* (Branagh) were remade with a surprising twist, as both featured the same actor – Jude Law. The result was a fascinating transformation of both films. Not only did elements of class and gender come up for re-appraisal, but a more complex interconnection between all four films was established through Caine and Law's on- and off-screen relationship. This extended across the films into new elements of seriality, in a way similar to the current trend in 'legacyquels' where 'beloved aging stars reprise classic roles and pass the torch to younger successors' (Singer 2015), with Caine now appearing opposite Law in the remake of *Sleuth*.

Linda Hutcheon writes that sequels are about 'never wanting a story to end', whereas remakes are about 'wanting to retell the same story over and over in different ways' (2006: 9). But, as the case of *Alfie* and *Sleuth* will show, the difference between sequels and remakes is often blurry. Both are preoccupied with repetition, yet also spring from the desire to continue and add on to the previous story. *Alfie* and *Sleuth* are primarily remakes, as their titles and repetition of basic narrative units suggest, while also containing elements of sequelisation. They seem to feature the same characters and continue the story of a previous film. They take up 'the action where it left off; the characters' history in the earlier film is mentioned, understood or otherwise significant in the later one' (Jess-Cooke 2009: 3). Both remakes are now intrinsically bound together through the presence of the same actor(s), inviting the viewer to actively engage in the process of comparison, not only between originals and their remakes, but also across all the four interconnected films.

ALFIE (GILBERT, 1966)/(SHYER, 2004)

'Hello. They never make these cars big enough, do they? Well, you all settled in? Right, we can begin. My name is . . . Alfie. I suppose you think you're gonna see the bleeding titles now. Well you're not. So you can all relax' – Gilbert's famous opening makes no qualms about the film's frivolous subject-matter and its rule-breaking hero right from the first scene. After having intercourse with a married woman, Siddie (Millicent Martin), in the back of his car parked on the Embankment, Caine's Alfie Elkins emerges from the vehicle and introduces himself, speaking directly to the camera and charming the audience. As testament to a bygone era characterised by the tumultuous changes taking place in the country, this British classic seemed like a perfect contender for remaking in the new millennium, since many of its troubling aspects needed updating to fit in with the contemporary Zeitgeist. These troubling aspects include Alfie's misogyny and the outdated portrayal of women who required transformation into their third-wave feminism equivalents, not to mention the film's kitchen-sink heritage that had to be adjusted to contemporary Hollywood generic conventions. Before looking at these transformations in more detail, however, I will first try to place the original within a larger cultural and historical context to understand what led to the creation of one of Caine's most iconic heroes, which Law then decided to revisit almost forty years later.

As Alexander Walker points out, '*Alfie* was a London cockney boy's dream of a Casanova-like existence which might have been lived out in reality – and in some cases was so – by the self-same cockney boys from South London who had become film stars and fashion photographers' ([1974] 2005: 303). He aptly remarks that 'Alfie's eye for a "bird" is as sharp and pitiless' as David Bailey's camera lens (307). In terms of the plot, the film is precisely that: a few seemingly unrelated snapshots featuring brief appearances by women that come and go as they catch Alfie's eye. According to John Hill, '[i]n formalist terms, i.e. in terms of narrative function, one woman is as good as another and the film could quite easily be re-edited without causing any particular violence to its thematic continuity' (1995: 164). Gilda, Siddie, Lily, Annie, Ruby, Dora, a manageress of a dry cleaner's, a chiropodist with a ginger moustache, a hospital nurse and countless other nameless conquests become episodes joined together by the protagonist's direct address to the audience. It is only thanks to the birth of his son Malcolm that we get the sense of the passage of time and despite (or rather thanks to) it realise that Alfie is just as stuck in his ways halfway through the story as he was at the beginning. Even his relationship with his son is at one point literally presented as a collage of photographs that capture a few fleeting happy moments.

One event that drastically changes the mood of the film from comedy to heavy drama misleads the audience into thinking that Alfie might reform his ways. When he impregnates the married Lily (Vivien Merchant), who later arrives at his bedsit to undergo an illegal abortion, he leaves her alone in agony. As he professes, '[m]y understanding of women goes only as far as the pleasure. When it comes to the pain I'm like any other bloke – I don't want to know'. Despite the gravitas of the abortion scene, the story surprisingly returns to where it first started – the Embankment at night, where Alfie now bumps into Siddie and awkwardly tries to patch things up. His final monologue addressed to the camera when he implores 'So what's the answer? That's what I keep asking myself. What's it all about?'[1] does not suggest any real reformation. This theme is further underlined by the presence of the same stranded dog that featured in the opening scenes.

Gilbert does not provide his protagonist with any backstory to justify his selfish acts. All we are given is his repeated invocation that one is alone in this life and can never rely on anybody else. Ian Nathan points out that Caine's Alfie 'was shagging away under the ever-present threat of nuclear fall-out' (2004), which, though no excuse, provides his live-for-the-moment lifestyle choices with some context.[2] The film reflects well the ambiguity of the times when moral codes were in the process of transformation, forcing one to adapt to the new circumstances. Alfie exemplifies one way of exploring and exploiting the new mores through making up his own code of conduct based on personal freedom. While open to criticism, Caine's Alfie, as Will Self claims, 'was such an iconic figure because he signposted the dark side of the Sixties; after all the swinging came the backstreet abortions, the abandoned children and the shattered psyches of runaway girls' (2004).

The iconicity of the film derives from the fact that it captured a moment of social revolution with ethics and laws changing, creating new gaps to be filled.

According to Claire Hines, after the end of World War II, the economic boom was initially slower in Britain than it was in America, '[w]ith rationing continuing and austerity measures in place into the 1950s, for a time Britain was struggling with economic recovery. However, by the early 1960s consumer culture had spread on both sides of the Atlantic' (2018: 84). Numerous films reflected the social, cultural and political conditions of the 1960s, often featuring 'hedonistic and sexually liberated characters' (Chapman 2000: 115). But perhaps the most perfect cinematic incarnation of the new circumstances was Sean Connery's Bond, who, by the time *Alfie* hit the screens, had become a fantasy figure for men on both sides of the Atlantic. Connery's Bond embodied 'the lifestyle that can be contextualised within the ascendance of male consumerism in 1960s Britain and America' (Hines 2018: 84), representing classlessness and modernity. *Dr. No* (Young, 1962), *From Russia with Love* (Young, 1963), *Goldfinger* (Hamilton, 1964) and *Thunderball* (Young, 1965) depict Bond's exquisite taste for fine wines and food, tailor-made suits, expensive accessories and automobiles, with beautiful women added to the mix. When asked to explain the franchise's success to *Playboy* magazine in November 1965, Connery said that 'Bond came on the scene after the War, at a time when people were fed up with rationing and drab times and utility clothes and a predominantly gray color in life' (quoted in Hines 2018: 84). His hero projected a type of masculinity that was closely bound to the idea of consumerism, with Bond becoming 'a walking and talking advertisement for a range of brand-name products' (84).

Understandably, Alfie's consumerism is of a different kind and on a level different from that of 007, because he does not belong to the universe of spy fantasy, but rather the Swinging 60s combined with kitchen-sink drama. Yet, his careful attention to appearance and male grooming mark him as a new type of working-class hero, much closer to Bond in many ways than the characters occupying the universe of the earlier British New Wave. Examining Alfie's appearance, Walker notes that he is 'a recognizable pretender to middle-class status in his flannels and navy blazer with its Services badge on the breast pocket' ([1974] 2005: 306). Alfie enjoys his elegant shirts, suits, accessories and a Rolls-Royce which he drives as a chauffeur for the establishment. For him, a nice car, even if it is not his own, is a status symbol that allows him to get his foot through the door of high society's places, such as when he invites Lily to an exclusive tea shop out of town. Apart from being a status symbol, the car also stands for Alfie's mobility, as he can easily move around the city and drop in on his girlfriends whenever he pleases. His arrival is immediately announced, not just visually, but also auditorily, as it is often accompanied by a snazzy jazz soundtrack that enlivens the otherwise drab-looking indoor and outdoor locations.

Thus, even if Alfie is not travelling around the world with a licence to kill, he nevertheless, just like Connery's Bond, exemplifies 'the changing concept of masculinity shaped in part by consumerism, and the commodification of sexuality' (Hines 2018: 144). For instance, Robert Murphy notices that Alfie's

> characteristics – an almost psychopathic vulgarity which links women, clothes and cars as commodities to be flaunted to prove to the world that he has achieved success without privileges of birth or education – could be tentatively identified with the working-class actors, photographers and pop stars who were supposed to inhabit Swinging London. ([1992] 2008: 143–44)

Alfie's behaviour resembles that of Bond's, who was equally promoted as the ultimate sexual nomad, 'a highly mobile and assertive man sworn to bachelorhood', who rejected 'the values and permanence of monogamy, fatherhood, and family life', to seek instead 'casual sexual encounters with women while exercising emotional and sexual control' (Hoxna 2011: 194). Sarah Street compares the James Bond series to the British New Wave, going as far as to suggest that the differences between them are merely stylistic because, '[i]n terms of ideology, the Bond films were not escapist aberrations', but rather revealed what the social realist films were equally preoccupied with – namely the 'masculine nightmare of being trapped in the provinces of wife and family' (1997: 87). This explains why Alfie remains a hardened bachelor and, despite his growing attachment to Malcolm, refuses to settle down with Gilda, choosing instead to be a weekend father, unhindered by any commitments.

Another aspect of Caine's working-class masculinity that stands out is his choice of occupation for the leisure industries. Traditionally, working-class masculinity was associated with physical labour, as evidenced in the opening sequence of *Saturday Night and Sunday Morning* (Reisz, 1960). Its protagonist, Arthur Seaton (Albert Finney), gets his hands dirty performing a repetitive menial task at a bicycle factory in Nottingham. This indicates that, as Nicola Rehling puts it, 'physical strength has been a determining characteristic of modern, capitalist, Western masculinities, especially working-class masculinity', with the focus placed on 'production and activity' and 'a stoical transcendence of pain and bodily needs' (2009: 92). Rather than being trapped in a factory or down a mine, however, Alfie's work allows him to lead a lifestyle constantly on the move, whether driving the elite to luxurious locations or taking photographs of visitors to London at tourist traps, which is how he meets the wealthy American widow Ruby. Thus, Alfie's, and by extension Caine's, confident representation of masculinity is to a large extent contrasted with the maleness of the Northern 'angry young men'.[3] Robert Shail compares the two in the following words:

> In place of a masculinity forged in the harsh industrial landscapes of the north of England, Caine offers us a southern masculinity rooted in

the cultural landscape of working-class London. The tough, aggressive, sometimes violent, maleness of Finney and Harris is replaced by a more playful, humorous, although equally self-confident, identity. (2004: 68)

From the vantage point of the decade after the film's release, Walker observed: 'Had *Alfie* come out in the 1970s, when Women's Lib was digging its spurs into male flanks, it would have been dubbed a crude propaganda tract for chauvinist male pigs' ([1974] 2005: 307). The film provokes this sentiment even more so from a contemporary perspective. The role is still regarded as Caine's defining performance and one that is powerfully imprinted on viewers' memory in Britain and across the Atlantic. The film's supposed sequel, *Alfie Darling* (Hughes, 1975), dismally lacked its predecessor's social relevance and its star's magnetism. It proves that, when deprived of their cultural context, Alfie's sexual exploits do not lend themselves well to serial treatment, becoming a soft-porn sex comedy curiosity instead.

Almost forty years passed before another attempt at reviving the old classic would take place. The new version offered a second chance at figuring out 'What's it all about?' – a question that bothers the original Alfie at the end of the film. Unlike most remakes discussed in this book, this one retains the nationality of its protagonist and, as is to be expected, provides many continuities with the original film. It draws from and sometimes even augments some of the aspects of Caine's Alfie's masculinity, while reshaping it through the lens of Law's sexual and gender ambiguous charm for the new millennium. While understandably a risky undertaking, it must have helped that Caine seems to have personally endorsed the project and that, over the years before the remake hit the screens, he had repeatedly voiced his admiration for the younger colleague. During his Oscar speech in 2000, for example, he said: 'Jude [is] gonna be a big star no matter what happens'.[4] He then later openly promoted Law as the perfect choice for the new Alfie in an interview with *The Telegraph*: 'I think it's great that Jude is playing Alfie. He is a friend and I'm a great admirer of his. I think he's a wonderful actor and it will be very interesting because Alfie was a male chauvinist pig in the 1960s, and the story is being re-written by an American woman. I'll be intrigued to see it' (Davies 2004).

Stuart Henderson remarks that 'sequels ostensibly inherit DNA from their predecessors, along with the family name, a relationship which [. . .] occasionally finds itself reflected in narrative terms, as in the numerous "Son of" films'. He finds that many sequels dramatise 'some form of genetic, psychological or economic inheritance from one protagonist to the next' (2014: 145). In the case of the remake of *Alfie*, the idea could be substantiated by the fact that Caine's character fathers a cute blond boy in the original film.[5] And although Law was born in 1974, rather than in 1966, when the original was released, in terms of the time frame and generation gap between the protagonists and the two films, the notion of a father-and-son relationship is still quite workable. Moreover, over the course of the remake, Law's Alfie refers to his father once, when he shares some advice that he was given: 'Son, whenever you meet a beautiful woman . . . just remember, somewhere there's a bloke who's sick of shagging her'. This statement could have just as well been uttered by Caine's Alfie. Some viewers have also commented on a physical resemblance between the two actors: 'For one thing, Jude Law is as close a match physically to a young Michael Caine as you could hope to find among the current crop of Hollywood actors' (livewire-6 2004). They even called him 'the next generation Caine' (matties25 2004). James Mottram of *Film Review* observes: 'Let's get one thing straight, however – no one but Law could replace Caine in this role. He has the requisite roguish looks and the right amount of cocky swagger and cheeky charm to play the role' (2004: 102).

As mentioned above, Alfie's British nationality creates a sense of continuity with the original work. It is also a good marketing strategy that draws from the popularity of the cycle of Anglo-American rom-coms. As Law points out, '[s]etting the film in New York made him a bit of a fish out of water, a bit of an alien. He's rootless, familyless . . . that modern sensibility that when you go somewhere new, you start again: You can project what you pretend is you' (quoted in Levy 2004). Moving the British character across the Atlantic and surrounding him with a plethora of attractive American women opened up numerous opportunities for cross-cultural romance. The remake follows on from successful romantic comedies whose humour relies on the pairing of an American woman with a British man. Such pairings were initiated by Hugh Grant's appearance as Charles, an attractive, dithering loser in *Four Weddings and a Funeral* (Newell, 1994), who wins the heart of a sophisticated and confident American (Andie MacDowell). Grant's English charm – characterised by 'commitment-phobia, self-effacing awkwardness, and verbal incontinence' (Rehling 2009: 41) – was then further exploited in *Nine Months* (Columbus, 1995), *Notting Hill* (Michell, 1999), *Mickey Blue Eyes* (Makin, 1999), *Two Weeks Notice* (Lawrence, 2002), *Music and Lyrics* (Lawrence, 2007), *Did You Hear About The Morgans* (Lawrence, 2009) and *The Rewrite* (Lawrence, 2014).[6] This analogy was not lost on some viewers who remarked the following:

> Clearly the writers/producers of this remake felt that the behaviour of the original Alfie – a cold-hearted sexual conqueror with, by today's standards, an appallingly chauvinistic attitude to women – would not be credible today [. . .] So instead they give Alfie a soft-focus, almost Hugh Grant-style makeover, place him in New York (where his English manners inevitably come over as slightly quaint) and ask us to simply bask in his good looks and charm. (philip-63 2004)

Accordingly, despite his ability to convincingly portray Americans in supporting roles in *The Talented Mr Ripley* (Minghella, 1999), *Road to Perdition* (Mendes, 2002) and *Cold Mountain* (Minghella, 2003), *Alfie* would provide Law with his first Hollywood leading role, but on the condition that he remained as British as possible. His Englishness is announced from the first moment in the opening credits, thanks to his accent and words such as 'smashing', 'blimey', the infamous 1960s 'birds', the way he jokingly refers to his penis as 'Big Ben'[7] or explains his reason behind moving to New York by saying 'Location, location, location' in reference to a popular British show on Channel 4 (2000–).

But where the Anglo-American romantic cycle typically finishes with boy getting girl, the remake does not. The presence of the British actor forms closer links with the original film and, as a result, destabilises Hollywood conventions. Thus, unlike the remakes in Chapter 2, which devise new upbeat endings or heterosexual pairings for their American heroes, *Alfie* offers up more challenging material in terms of genre and gender representation. The film appears to be a romantic comedy at first, but gradually proves to have less humour, to then end on a serious note, depriving the viewer of a typical Hollywood resolution. Over the course of the film, Alfie dates many American women, but none of them manages to tame him. In the end, even if he does learn from his mistakes, he is not rewarded by a successful relationship, which makes the conclusion more British than American. This ending produces an interesting hybrid that could upset viewers familiar with director Charles Shyer's previous Hollywood works with its upbeat endings in *Father of the Bride* (1991), *Father of the Bride II* (1995) and especially the Anglo-American romantic comedy *The Parent Trap* (Meyers, 1998).[8]

Other than the successful transatlantic rom-coms, the inspiration for the cross-cultural romance could also have derived from Gilbert's film, in which Alfie is only prepared to give up his free-wheeling bachelor's lifestyle for the American Ruby (Shelly Winters). Ruby is not only in 'beautiful condition', but also more sexually adventurous and emancipated in contrast to the more 'mumsy' British women he dates. Her sexually predatory behaviour is an exception that could be explained by her nationality. In Bill Naughton's play and novel, Ruby is British, and the contrast instead is placed on wealth and social mobility, which initially makes Alfie uneasy and affects his sexual performance. The film avoids the question of nationality on the level of dialogue, but the casting of Winters as Ruby introduces this notion and functions as a smart marketing strategy to ensure the film's cross-Atlantic appeal. Winters had by then been a two-time Academy Award winner, first in 1960 and then in 1965. She was also well known for 'her stormy marriages, her romances with famous stars, her forays into politics and feminist causes' ('Shelley Winters, Two-Time Academy Award Winner, Dies at 85' 2006). Winters' Ruby brings with her the confidence of foreign capital and a large sexual appetite, making

Figure 3.1 *Alfie* (1966): 'Going up in the world, aren't I?'

her almost like a stand-in for Hollywood's activities in 1960s London, hungry to move on from one project to the next and at the peak of its productivity.

Because the lead character is again British, many of the features of Caine's Alfie resurface. Some are even given more emphasis, especially seen in Law's Alfie's interest in fashion, style and appearance, admiration of his own body and the awareness of his physical attractiveness. However, the remade Alfie's narcissism is now a notch above Caine's: it reflects the changes taking place in mainstream society, with its supposed gradual acceptance and integration of gay culture and decreasing fear of divergence from pre-existing concepts of heterosexual masculinity. Law's Alfie seems to capture on screen the essence of a type of masculinity that Mark Simpson calls metrosexuality:

> The typical metrosexual is a young man with money to spend, living in or within easy reach of a metropolis – because that's where all the best shops, clubs, gyms and hairdressers are. He might be officially gay, straight or bisexual, but this is utterly immaterial because he has clearly taken himself as his own love object and pleasure as his sexual preference [...] For some time now, old-fashioned (re)productive, repressed, unmoisturized heterosexuality has been given the pink slip by consumer capitalism. The stoic, self-denying, modest straight male

didn't shop enough (his role was to earn money for his wife to spend), and so he had to be replaced by a new kind of man, one less certain of his identity and much more interested in his image [. . .]. (2002)

Alfie calls himself a fashion whore, proudly displaying to the viewer his collection of top-designer men's wear, asserting that, '[i]f you ooze masculinity, like some of us do, you have no reason to fear pink'.

The difference between the two actors' representation of masculinity is best observed in their treatment of direct address to the audience. Caine's does not so much reveal his true nature, as this is no secret, but rather seduces the audience, winning their sympathy with his charming nod at the camera and easy camaraderie. He does not share his feelings with the women he dates but can divulge his philosophy on life with the viewer, assumed to be male (while the female members of the audience are eavesdropping). Viewers equally appreciate that owning a couple of nice suits, a car, 'a few bob' in your pocket and a constant flow of available 'birds' is what defines a swinging bachelor's lifestyle. By contrast, Law's Alfie's seduction of the camera is ambiguous, oscillating between men and women in the audience. For example, his remark that 'even though the PC boyfriend sat next to you with his arm slung around your shoulder will deny it . . . And he will deny it. For us boys, it's all about F. B. B. Face. Boobs. Bum' is addressed directly to women. However, another comment could only ever be spoken to men: 'Now, lads, learn from my mistake. Never get involved with a single mum'. With the new *Alfie* now clearly functioning as a date movie, the direct address tries to accommodate both female and male viewers, swapping allegiances and confusing its recipients as to who and when is granted a privileged one-to-one with the character and his tips on seduction. The confessional tone is no longer as effective for one more reason – by the time of the release of the remake, its novelty factor had worn off, as it had already been successfully used in such earlier titles as *Ferris Bueller's Day Off* (Hughes, 1986) or *Full Fidelity* (Frears, 2000).

It seems that this ambiguous gender flirtation with the camera could be further explained by yet another continuity. This time it is with Law's earlier role as an amoral American playboy seducer in *The Talented Mr Ripley*, whose 'teasing powers of manipulation [. . .] make him ardently courted by every man or woman he knows' (Maslin 1999), with either sex unable to resist his easy charm. Ariel Levy from *New York Magazine* semi-jokingly confirms the power of Law's sexually ambivalent appeal with the following anecdote:

A friend of mine has a joke. He raises his eyebrows, shrugs his shoulders, and says, 'Jude Law . . . ?' Which means that he is a straight guy, but given the chance? With Jude Law . . . ? Because obviously, Jude Law is beautiful in a way that transcends regular handsomeness, even movie-star handsomeness: Jude Law is art, walking. Who could resist? (2004)

Law's beauty was also exploited in Steven Spielberg's *A. I. Artificial Intelligence* (2001), where he plays the character of a camp, gracefully moving sex-mecha lover, Gigolo Joe, constructed to satisfy all kinds of female customers. Thus, it appears that, with Law as the new Alfie, the director, who co-wrote the screenplay with Elaine Pope, tried to capitalise on the actor's ambiguous sexual appeal.[9]

At the end of Naughton's novel, after Alfie is rejected by Ruby, he notices a lonely young man in the street and speculates whether he is 'queer' and is there to

> look around for one of these bent old boys who was rich, and who would take him in, give him a home, buy him his gear over in Jermyn Street or somewhere, shirts made to measure and all that caper, and make a fuss of him, perhaps set him up as his chauffeur, and see he was never short of a tenner, and at the same time relieve him of his responsibilities. ([1966] 2012)

He finds that gay men function within similar social mechanisms of commodification as women, with their transactional value as lovers without the consequence of family or pregnancy being of crucial importance. This notion did not find its way into Gilbert's film. That film's purpose was to build on Caine's previous role as the sexy heterosexual Cockney spy Harry Palmer in *The Ipcress File* (Furie, 1965), whose success with the opposite sex is indicated right in the opening credit sequence by the presence of two empty wine glasses on a table and Palmer's discovery of a woman's bracelet in his bedsheets.[10] It is tempting to assume that Pope and Shyer had familiarised themselves with the film in addition to the original *Alfie*, as the remake seems to recycle the introduction to Caine's Cockney spy, even though it is filtered through Law's sexually ambivalent charm. In *The Ipcress File*, we notice Palmer asleep in bed, before then watching his morning routine as he wakes up, gets out of bed, reads the morning paper and grinds his own coffee beans, an activity that identifies him as a sophisticated London bachelor. *Alfie* also starts in the protagonist's flat (rather than an empty street, as featured in Gilbert's film). We see a close-up of Law's bare arm and foot sticking out from under his red bedsheets as the camera caressingly tilts and zooms, putting his body very much on display. This time, instead of peeping, however, we receive an open invitation into his bedroom. There, we watch him prepare to leave for work (a deleted scene shows Law having a shower) and learn about fashion, accessories and how to apply cologne: 'Now, in the cologne department, most men overdo it. Americans practically spray it on with a crop-duster. My rule: Nothing above the neck, though I do like a little splash on Big Ben'. This possible borrowing from *The Ipcress File* suggests that Law's reappraisal of Caine's iconic Alfie is not just motivated by the need to update the old classic for the new millennium, but also constitutes an attempt at establishing him as his generation's 'Michael Caine'. This is then further supported by his affiliation with the remake of *Sleuth* discussed below.

In the original, aside from Alfie's sexual exploits, to further reinforce the image of Alfie's heteronormative masculinity and his role as the only Alpha male in town, the film contrasts him with other men, such as his only friend, Nat – played by Murray Melvin, known for his breakthrough role as a gay man in the British New Wave film *A Taste of Honey* (Richardson, 1961), or the incapacitated Harry (Alfie Bass), trapped in a hospital wheelchair.[11] Whereas in the novel and play Alfie is upstaged by Lofty (Frank in the film), a heavily-built lorry driver who replaces him as Ruby's lover, in the film it is an anonymous pretty boy with a guitar. This reduces the impact of Alfie's humiliation and, through marginalising Frank's function in the film, deprives Alfie of any convincing competition. Pope explained on the DVD commentary that they struggled to find anyone even vaguely as attractive as Law for the scene described above. In the end, they settled for enigma, a reaction shot that leaves the viewer to imagine what kind of man could upstage the beautiful actor as Liz's next sexual partner. This does not mean, however, that the remake follows the original in refusing to present any viable alternative or competition to the protagonist's charisma. In the original, Gilda agrees to marry the decent but boring and unattractive Humphrey (Graham Stark). Her counterpart in the remake, Julie (Marisa Tomei), settles for Adam, who, played by Stephen Gaghan, makes a brief yet strong appearance and upstages Law's Alfie with his soft-spoken yet confident masculinity. The presence of Alfie's friend, Marlon (Omar Epps), also serves as a counterpoint to Alfie's philandering, showing that being physically attractive does not have to translate into commitment phobia and responsibility-free lifestyle choices.

Alfie uses his nationality to justify his European, as he calls it, philosophy on life – in this European philosophy of life, consumerism is focused on sensual pleasures, such as good wine and beautiful women, rather than on the pursuit of financial rewards, which he identifies as American. He professes that he does not understand those Brits that move to the US in the hope of coming back home with buckets filled with money. Ironically, however, his attitude to sex simply represents a different type of consumerism: 'Dating is a kind of shopping for Alfie; a way to get himself the best and the most pretty things. Alfie has come here from London primarily because "the most beautiful women in the world reside in Manhattan"' (Levy 2004). For Alfie, women are commodities with 'an expiration date' who 'have a shorter shelf life'. Just as his clothes are carefully selected to represent top designer labels, such as Gucci, his women also need to be physically stunning and off the top shelf to sustain his sexual interest.[12]

In the original, women are also treated as disposable sex objects. As the film derives from the kitchen-sink realism tradition, however, they are a far cry from James Bond's Playboy bunnies; their casting was determined by a very particular set of physical attributes, even if 'the publicity discourse around Bond girls suggested that they were modern, liberated, independent women' (Chapman 2000: 95).[13] Compared to Bond's conquests, Alfie's vary in age and appearance and are more complex characters, with a more active role in the progression of the narrative. Rather than being presented as two-dimensional playthings to be discarded by the man, the film brings aspects of realism into play, positing an important question about the supposed gains of a permissive society and their impact on both sexes. Alfie's women tend to be predominantly filmed indoors, trapped scrubbing floors, preparing dinner or quite simply killing time, waiting for Alfie to arrive, as in the case of Annie and Gilda. Their presentation challenges the concept of female modernity and independence attached to, for example, Julie Christie's character in the British New Wave film *Billy Liar* (Schlesinger, 1963), whose first sixty seconds on screen immediately marked her as a new female icon of modernity.[14] In *Alfie*, however, except for the emancipated American Ruby, most women are modest and quite shy. Siddie and Lily are housewives trapped in mundane marital relations, and while the former engages with Alfie to enjoy some of the freedom and anonymity of a big city, the latter is a tired mother of three who struggles to cope while her husband is away recovering in a health clinic. None of these women are presented as stereotypical 1960s conquests, but rather as old-fashioned girls in a way similar to the novel, where most of Alfie's girls are past their prime and far from good-looking. To substantiate the idea that Caine's Alfie is both modern and irresistible to all, the film, therefore, requires other additional women who engage in casual sex with him just for the sake of it, such as the pretty hospital nurse (Shirley Anne Field), who is anything but attractive in the novel. However, this is not enough to convince the viewer that the promiscuous lifestyle in Swinging London is equally shared by all sexes or indeed commonplace. As Murphy observes, '[a] survey carried out in 1970 found that only 19 per cent of married couples under forty-five used the pill, and the idea that most single girls were sexually promiscuous had little foundation in fact' ([1992] 2008: 142). The film seems to confirm this notion. Unlike the Bond girls, the women in *Alfie* are far from enjoying the 1960s sexual revolution without the consequence of pregnancy or abortion. In this respect, *Alfie* recalls the British New Wave's preoccupation with male misogyny and its impact on women's lives. Yet, Murphy claims that Alfie's 'attitude to women is less misogyny than a failure to communicate on anything but the most basic level' ([1992] 2008: 144), as he 'plays according to the rules that assume women to be helpless, brainless and inherently inferior – "She, it, what does it matter, they're all birds"' ([1992] 2008: 145). Both Gilda and Lily become pregnant. The former decides to keep the baby and works long hours to support her child before marrying Humphrey, a man whom she respects

Figure 3.2 *Alfie* (2004): Ruby is now the cosmetics mogul Liz.

but does not love.[15] Lily pays most dearly for her momentary lapse by having to undergo the horrid abortion.[16]

As for the women in the remake, Pope rightly observes on the DVD commentary that they needed more updating than Alfie, who, in her opinion, appears to be a timeless and universal character, almost set in stone. On the face of it, the updated female characters appear to be much more progressive versions, with financial independence, self-confidence and beauty to match, but there are some aspects in their presentation that are troubling. For instance, in contrast to the original, all the women are now hypersexualised eye-candy to sustain Alfie's interest, and they also provide the viewer with titillation, as the women are often open to view, parading on screen in revealing outfits or without tops on. This function of female to-be-looked-at-ness in the film is sealed by a powerful *Gilda*-like image, with Susan Sarandon's Liz admiring her body in multiple mirrors in a Chanel boutique, with Alfie by her side looking on approvingly.

According to Pope, Dorie/Siddie (Jane Krakowski) needed the least updating as a bored and sexually frustrated trophy wife of a wealthy businessman. Julie/Gilda is now a single mum who sees some potential in Alfie and hopes that he will settle down with her and her son. When she discovers his infidelity, she breaks up with him on the spot and quickly moves on to date other men.

Lonette/Lily (Nia Long) is the girlfriend of Marlon, Alfie's best friend. After a drinking session, the two flirt and end up having unprotected sex. In the original, Lily's moral lapse occurred under massive strain, when she was at the point of mental and physical exhaustion, juggling too many responsibilities on her own. Lonette, however, seduces Alfie because she is upset with Marlon and curious to find out what makes him so irresistible to women. When he accompanies her to an abortion clinic, she does not inform him that she has decided to keep the baby in the hope that it could be Marlon's. Since both Marlon and Lonette are black, Alfie's one-night stand with Lonette is only revealed when the child is born interracial. According to Cynthia Fuchs:

> Presumably, this turn of events underscores Alfie's contemporary coolness, as he has sex with black, married, and childed women, his apparent lack of discrimination serves as sign of his social and maybe even his political progressiveness. At the same time, the danger of discovery lies in the potential baby's appearance, that is, in its embodiment of miscegenation. No surprise, the film is unable to work through this crisis coherently, but instead makes it into Alfie's personal predicament (as he literally worries about his losses), leaving out the historical, cultural background of Marlon's (possible) distress and sense of betrayal. (2004)

Finally, Ruby is turned into the cosmetics company mogul Liz, a modern female cougar who possesses none of Ruby's crassness. In the original, Alfie is impressed by the fact that she is financially independent and owns three hairdressers. His visit to her apartment turns into a showroom display when, instead of focusing on his date, he makes sure we notice a king-sized bath and a mirror on the ceiling in the bathroom. 'Going up in the world, aren't I?' he proudly informs the viewer, well-aware of the perks that would come with marrying the wealthy American widow, including the enjoyment of her luxury apartment with its amenities, such as central heating. Once rejected, he realises that he may have feelings for her, but it is uncertain whether he is smitten with her or rather the middle-class lifestyle she represents. In the remake, Liz encourages Alfie to start a new career and helps him come up with a business proposal, playing the role of lover and mentor in one. Played by Sarandon, she impresses Alfie with her understated elegance and sophistication, and is genuinely embarrassed when he discovers her affliction for young men.

However, one female stands out above all others in the new version. Annie, originally played by 1960s icon Jane Asher, known for her highly publicised relationship with Paul McCartney, becomes Nikki. This volatile bi-polar dope-smoking and pill-popping glamorous party girl, played by the British-American actress and trendsetter Sienna Miller, is Alfie's perfect match, mirroring his interests in fashion and satisfying his high beauty standards. They meet soon

Figure 3.3 *Alfie* (2004): Match made in heaven.

after Alfie's brush with mortality, which forces him to adopt a healthy lifestyle. However, Nikkie lures him back to old habits: all-night partying, reckless driving, smoking and drinking. Whereas in the original Caine's abusive behaviour pushed Annie away, in the remake Nikki's antics after she stops taking her medication drive Law's Alfie away.[17]

Thus, whereas in the original our sympathies lie with the abused women, the remake clearly redirects these feelings towards Alfie, who is now presented as a victim of his own actions. As Fuchs points out, the inclusion of Alfie's boss, Mr. Wing (Gedde Watanabe), who repeatedly mistreats his wife, makes 'Alfie look relatively sensitive (he only abandons his girls, but doesn't berate them)' (2004). All the women feel sorry for Alfie. Despite being betrayed, Julia is concerned about his well-being. When he apologises to Dorie for standing her up, she forgives him on the spot and wishes him good luck in the future. Other adaptation changes lessen the impact of Alfie's actions, such as his one-night stand with Lonette, who appears to initiate the seduction, or Nikki's mental volatility. Towards the end, Alfie has regrets and acknowledges his mistakes. The women, however, either bounce back or show incredible resilience. As Timothy Corrigan notes, 'even the young women whom Alfie beds and abandons take his departure in stride, not undone by hooking up for a night or two with this shallow pretty boy' (2012: 111). In contrast to the original, where the women are victims of Alfie's misogyny, their modernised counterparts are now either partly to blame or take everything in their stride, remarkably powering through with a smile on their face. This approach not only reduces the impact of Alfie's conduct, but also eclipses or simply brushes off its long-term consequences. Even Alfie's health scare, such as when he discovers a possibly cancerous lump on his penis, functions to increases the viewer's sympathy for the hero, via the invented character of an elderly man named Joe (Dick Latessa), who provides him with emotional comfort and some important life lessons about the benefits of monogamous relationships.

When asked if there was anything in the script that worried him in terms of making his character too reprehensible, Law answered:

> I was constantly trying to drag him into the mire. I'm always a bit scared of crystal-clean, candy-smile characters, but Charles [Shyer, director] pushed me to embellish that side of the performance rather than play it down. And I was like, 'No! Let's play it really fucked up!' In the end it came out as quite a nice balance between the two. ('The Total Film Interview – Jude Law' 2004)

However, although Law's Alfie continues and develops his predecessor's preoccupation with style, accessories and his overall narcissism, his misogyny and brutality are both toned down to lessen the impact of his selfish acts and to ensure that our sympathies remain with the hero. With Alfie now deprived of a darker side, the film struggles desperately to fit into a romantic comedy mode. Instead, it provides the audience with a modern morality tale whose message – looks are not everything and think before you unzip – is spelled out at the end of the film. The remake ends up being less dark than the original, and yet much darker than any British-American romantic comedy would allow. When Law's Alfie at the end of the film implores 'What's it all about?' the question no longer represents the voice of the lost generation of the 1960s who had every right to ask this, but rather that of the lost boy who is almost expected to make mistakes, even though he should know better.

SLEUTH (MANKIEWICZ, 1972)/(BRANAGH, 2007)

In Gilbert's *Alfie*, Caine's protagonist can only dream of marrying wealthy. In Joseph L. Mankiewicz's *Sleuth*, he is a working-class success story intent on marrying the wife of his aristocratic opponent. And yet, surprisingly, it is in *Sleuth* where his class belonging is most accentuated, revealing, as Shail puts it, that '[t]he promised classless society of the 1960s had patently failed to materialise for the vast majority of British people and there was a consequent hardening of politicised class positions in the new decade' (2004: 75). As this section will show, when adapting his play for the screen, Anthony Shaffer redirected its focus from sexual jealousy to class conflict, which becomes further accentuated by the casting of the story's antagonists. The remake of 2007 then puts the focus back on sexual tension, but with a surprising homosexual twist. Before addressing the changes introduced to the remake, however, I will first look at the original film and how it interweaves class and casting to become a powerful reminder that, despite the new working-class ascendancy in the 1960s, class conflict on- and off-screen remained a powerful force to be reckoned with in the decade that followed.

Shaffer, the author of Hitchcock's London-based *Frenzy* (1972) and *The Wicker Man* (Hardy, 1973), adapted *Sleuth* from his play of 1970, in which he subverted and parodied most of the rules of the detective genre popular in the 1930s. Unlike in Agatha Christie's works, in his play the murder does not occur at the beginning but in the middle of the action and, as it turns out, it is not a real murder as this occurs only towards the end. The play had a very successful run in Britain and on Broadway, where it earned a Tony Award in 1971. Its great popularity was the most likely reason why, within two years from its theatrical premier, it was adapted for the screen to great accolades. Roger Ebert called it 'a totally engrossing entertainment' that is both 'funny and scary by turns' (1972). Shaffer had two actors in mind when he was approached to adapt his play for the screen – Alan Bates for the role of Milo Tindle, and Anthony Quale for the part of Andrew Wyke, since the actor had by then successfully embodied the character on stage. The producers, however, insisted on Laurence Olivier, who was an obvious audience draw, and Michael Caine – who with the roles in *Alfie*, *The Italian Job* (Collinson, 1969) and *Get Carter* (Hodges, 1971) under his belt – was quickly becoming a new household name.

Although a great success on Broadway, the play was not without challenges when it came to adapting it to the big screen since, as R. Barton Palmer explains:

> In accordance with Broadway trends of the late sixties, Shaffer's play is a two-hander involving minimal action that unfolds on a single set. Its drama is largely conversational and mental, a battle of words between two intelligent, witty, and inventive characters from different social backgrounds, whose contrasting experiences and views must largely emerge from how they speak and what they say. (2001: 166)

Shaffer's task, therefore, was not to make the screenplay less wordy, since dialogue was its main attraction, but to accentuate the difference between the antagonists by introducing small yet significant changes.

Whereas initially Mankiewicz's film makes us suspect that Andrew's intrigue is motivated by hurt male pride and that the prize in the game is the woman, it soon transpires that a typical Hollywoodian 'boy loses girl, boy wins her back' is not its sole subject. This becomes apparent when we examine how Shaffer transformed the dialogue. For example, Andrew's 'You know even in these days I still set my own work among the gentry. And a great number of people enjoy it, in spite of the Welfare State' (Shaffer [1970] 2004: 14) becomes: 'Even today I still set my work amongst the gentry. Many *ordinary* people seem to enjoy them in spite of our *classless* society' (emphasis added). His request to call his guest 'Milo' meets with a simple 'Of course' (Shaffer [1970] 2004: 15) in the play; yet, in the film, Milo answers quite sarcastically: 'We are all on first name terms these days, Andrew'. Many other small additions stress the class difference between the two men. Thus, the most important alteration concerns putting class animosity at the centre of the conflict, whereas in the play the emphasis was equally, if not more, placed on sexual jealousy.

As a result, from the beginning of the film, the two protagonists are presented as each other's opposites, not only in terms of appearance, age and sexual competence, but primarily in terms of class. When Milo pulls up at Andrew's old country manor in his red convertible sports car with engraved initials, we immediately get the sense of two different worlds about to collide. While in the play Milo owns a travel agency, in the film it is an up-and-coming hairdressing salon, which reflects the newly found affluence of the working class and references

Figure 3.4 *Sleuth* (1972): 'We are from different worlds, you and me'.

the booming beauty industry in the 1960s (as exemplified by the career of Vidal Sassoon). Andrew proudly displays his aristocratic quirkiness – collecting and playing games, his favourite pastime activity aside from writing crime fiction, which suggests his emotional immaturity, intellectual snobbery and an increasing loss of touch with reality. His pattern of speech is very affected, convoluted and full of references to literary and historical figures, all supposed to make Milo uncomfortable. In contrast to the play, the film is packed with examples of Andrew correcting Milo's 'foul' English and of the two men mocking each other's accents. Prompted by Wyke, Milo makes an effort at self-correction, swapping 'birds' for 'ladies' and 'to nick for 'to steal', as he is repeatedly reminded of his shortcomings in the aristocrat's eyes. As the writer nostalgically reminiscences, the 1930s were the glorious times when every prime minister had a thriller by his bedside and every detective was titled. Of modern times he speaks ironically and with contempt, 'We're all liberals now'.

Given that 'the erosion of the landed gentry', which Andrew represents, was 'accelerated by the rise of the comparatively new urban middle class' that profited from the growth of the 'consumer society' (Cashmore 1989: 49), to which Milo belongs, one can see that Andrew's hatred is not simply the outcome of hurt male pride but also of class transgression. For him, their worlds can only peacefully coexist on the condition that they do not permeate or affect one another. Thus, even though Milo is, as Andrew ironically asserts, 'nicely-spoken, well-dressed in brand new country gentleman's clothing' and lives in an old Georgian house, being dressed the part is not the same as being the part. He is unable to reconcile with the fact that his opponent is the working-class son of an English farmer's daughter and an Italian immigrant watchmaker, who, as he sarcastically comments, managed to move 'from Genoa to Georgian in a single generation' – a line added to the screenplay. Thus, he designs a cruel game of humiliation to teach Milo a lesson. Knowing that, despite the young man's efforts, he will never be able to match his wealth, Andrew teases his guest with an offer of quick and easy profit. Duped into believing that the writer is well-meaning, Milo dresses up as a clown and performs a fake burglary. The whole affair ends up with the novelist aiming a gun at him and for the first time openly declaring why he hates his guest: 'You are a culling blue-eyed wop and not one of me' and 'a jumped-up pantry boy who doesn't know his place' (lines added to the screenplay). Later on, in the second act, Wyke explains to inspector Doppler (Milo dressed up and made-up) that he had to teach 'young master Tindle' a lesson to test his mettle since '[h]e came here aping the gentry hoping for acceptance [. . .] You don't join just like that [. . .] Qualities that breeding brings can't be acquired'.

For Tindle, however, Wyke's games are a childish and mindless activity that fills the empty lives of the upper classes. When he realises the novelist's cruel game, he addresses the class difference in the following words:

We are from different worlds, you and me, Andrew. In mine, there was no time for bright fancies and happy inventions, no stopping for tea. The only game we played was to survive, or go to war. If you didn't win, you just didn't finish. Loser, lose all. You probably don't understand that.

He adds: 'I don't play games of humiliation. I know too much about that'.

When these words are uttered by Caine, the conflict acquires an extra sense of irony: Caine's star persona overshadows any aspects of Milo's Italian heritage, as we begin to realise that we are watching an English working-class actor clash with Britain's most respected thespian. Mankiewicz insisted that Caine slips into his Cockney accent, even though the original character in the play was not a Cockney. As he explained, 'I tried to get him to use his accent like a violinist uses his violin. He puts on the accent of a proper gentleman and then drops it' when under pressure (quoted in Ciment 2008: 129). Thus, Mankiewicz's *Sleuth* addresses the issues of class wars in more ways than one. As we witness the protagonists' games and enjoy their battle of wits on screen, it becomes impossible to separate the characters from the actors' personas. *Sleuth* becomes a self-conscious display of its two leads' acting skills and acting styles, while also acquiring an even more personal dimension. Real-life class differences are bound to affect our perception of *Sleuth* when we realise that we are watching Baron Olivier clash with Caine, not a 'Sir' then, but the son of a charlady and a fish-market porter, whose own East-End roots well matched his screen persona, an aspect of Caine's craft that he had often explored. In fact, Caine's description of his early struggles in the acting profession uncannily echoes Milo's speech about the social injustice mentioned above:

> It was very difficult for me because I had the wrong voice and the wrong accent. I refused to change my accent because so many people had said to me, 'Who do you think you are?' I thought to myself, 'If I can become a success, it will be an inspiration to other boys. You don't have to have a posh accent to succeed'.
>
> It's very hard to explain class boundaries to an American. But the mistake they made in England was equating accent with intelligence – not to mention skill, determination, and ability. I flouted it all, didn't talk posh and kept the accent, and even went to America and became a success. I'm quite disliked by some people because of that [laughs], although not by others. I'm sort of a subversive within the English class system. I fouled it all up, which I so enjoy doing at times. (quoted in Porton 2004: 6)

Such statements not only equate actor with character, but also show a possible strong link between on-screen and off-screen rivalry.[18] Caine also frequently mentions a letter that he received from Olivier before the shoot of *Sleuth*:

> Larry wrote me a letter saying 'you may be wondering how to address me when we meet' because he was a Lord. I hadn't wondered for one moment how to address him when we meet. He very kindly said 'you must call me Larry the moment we meet and for the rest of our relationship', so that was . . . there was that class thing there [. . .] (quoted in Weintraub 2007)

As he further recalls:

> So there's this incredible snobbery that goes on and that did impart itself to the original movie in the script. Out of the script it did because everybody, the papers said Michael Caine working class Alfie, he's going to have to work with Lord Olivier. Boy is he gonna get showed a lesson, this little scum-bag [. . .] (quoted in Weintraub 2007)

The class conflict depicted in Mankiewicz's film and accentuated by the casting could never have worked as well in 2007. Caine explains: 'Now today, I am Sir Michael Caine but the idea that I would write to Jude and say: "You may be wondering how to address me . . ." He'd probably think: "Piss off"' (quoted in '*Sleuth*. Sir Michael Caine Interview' n. d.). This section looks at how Harold Pinter returned to the source and transformed the 'innocent' sexual banter originally present in Shaffer's play by giving it a distinct homosexual spin. I will also discuss the film's casting, which not only connects both versions of *Sleuth*, but also the *Alfie* remake. Finally, I will explore how the remake of *Sleuth* functions as a legacyquel, a neologism first coined by *ScreenCrush* film critic Matt Singer to describe a 'very specific kind of sequel [. . .] in which beloved aging stars reprise classic roles and pass the torch to younger successors' (2015). While it is more commonly used to discuss Hollywood movie franchises – such as *The Force Awakens* (Abrams, 2015), *Terminator: Genisys* (Taylor, 2015) and *Creed* (Coogler, 2015), revitalised 'through the notion of legacy' (Singer 2015) – the term could equally apply to the *Sleuth* remake, which further validates the notion of Law's function as the new Michael Caine.

Although remakes usually provoke negative comments in the press, this time the project was in the able hands of Oscar-nominees and winners, Noble-prize laureates and the titled. The idea was initiated by Law who, despite Pinter's life-threatening illness, visited the legendary playwright at regular intervals between 2003 and May 2005 to work on the screenplay. This clearly showed that *Alfie* was never intended to function as a stand-alone remake, but rather as part of a series. Securing the involvement of Pinter, Kenneth Branagh and Caine further raised interest in the project and created high expectations. The end result, however, was considered disappointing by many. *Sleuth* has been variously called 'an interesting failure' (Berardinelli 2007), 'a pissing contest' (Taylor 2007), a 'sterile, mindless, pointless and wearisome' film (Ross 2007) and even 'a Dead Film Walking' (Bradshaw 2007). Even if there may be a grain of truth to some of these harsh accusations, what the film does succeed in is updating for the new millennium the conflict presented in the earlier version, while continuing its predecessor's self-reflexive trajectory.

Like the remake of *Alfie*, *Sleuth*, although not a sequel in the strictest sense of the word, still creates a strong sense of continuity. Law steps into Caine's shoes for a second time, this time to play Milo Tindle. Caine is faced with the unique opportunity to not only play Olivier's part of Andrew Wyke, but also to explore what would have happened if Milo from the original film had somehow survived and then become a thriller author, channelling his traumatic experience into creative writing. Even the way in which Caine describes the character of Andrew in the remake recalls his earlier incarnation of Milo: 'And in my head back-story on this writer, Andrew Wyke in this, is that he is working class who has gone to university, changed and gotten rid of any thick accent of wherever he came from, but he's still tough enough'. He adds that he always envisaged him 'as having a tough working class background' (quoted in Weintraub 2007). As for Law, it is not without significance that in *Sleuth* he plays an out-of-favour and jobless actor, as he had to personally push to produce the film following *Alfie*'s critical and financial failure. To Law, the benefits of co-starring with Caine in *Sleuth* were quite apparent. Not only could he test if he would be able to hold his ground next to Caine, but he could also lay to rest the pretty-boy image that had characterised many of his earlier performances, including Alfie. According to Ebert, the film is 'so much about dialogue and performance that I, at least, found myself thinking more about the actors than the characters' (2007).

The screenplay was Pinter's first in over a decade. The playwright claimed not to be familiar with Mankiewicz's film and to have based his version solely on Shaffer's 1970 play. When promoting the film, Pinter, Branagh, Law and Caine repeatedly distanced themselves from the idea that the new version was a remake, choosing instead to promote it as a re-adaptation.[19] The film self-reflexively brings this up when Andrew teases Milo whether he understands what the term 'to adapt' means. As a re-adaptation, *Sleuth* derives from Shaffer's play rather than Mankiewicz's film, and Pinter's name as a distinguished British playwright and screenwriter serves as the anchor of the entire undertaking, giving it an aura of prestige, especially as it turned out to be his last piece of writing. However, the origins of the new film are more complex.

Despite Pinter's assurance that he re-adapted Shaffer's play, Andrew refers to Milo as 'a hairdresser' on four different occasions throughout the film, thus alluding directly to Mankiewicz's film version, since Milo owns a travel agency in the play. In addition, in Pinter's version, Law's Milo introduces himself as a jobless actor who makes ends meet by chauffeuring, creating further parallels between both *Sleuth* and *Alfie* versions. The recasting of Caine and the fact that Law had already by then played in the remake of *Alfie* must have also undoubtedly added to that perception. Branagh mentions in the DVD commentary that viewers responded enthusiastically to a line uttered by Law at one point in the film, when he asks Caine's Andrew 'What's it all about?' This line further attests to the existence of unavoidable associations between the originals and their remakes, and the viewer's active role 'in carving out alternative pathways through texts' (Gray 2010: 156) that might run contrary to the creators' expectations.

In fact, Pinter's screenplay seems to have a number of antecedents, creating a complex intertextual web of allusions, not only to Shaffer's play or Mankiewicz's film, but also to other works. Of particular importance, it seems, may be Pinter's first adapted screenplay, *The Servant* (1963), directed by Joseph Losey. The play likewise depicted power games between two men from dissimilar social backgrounds, whose roles eventually reverse as the servant comes to dominate his master. In *The Servant*, the house's increasing claustrophobic and menacing character accentuates the disintegrating mental state of its inhabitants whose relationship begins to verge on homoerotic sadomasochism. Pinter appears to have introduced the same idea of 'sexuality as an instrument of power' (Billington 1997: 152) and the symbolic function of mise-en-scène into *Sleuth*, whose protagonists go on to cross the borders of sexual and gender normativity as the action moves from the lounge to the master bedroom.

On top of the more obvious references and connections mentioned above, *Sleuth* also offers points of comparison with other films. Some viewers additionally spotted parallels with Sidney Lumet's *Deathtrap* (1982), which also stars Caine. In *Deathtrap*, he played a famous Broadway playwright, who comes up with an elaborate plan to kill his wife with the help of his younger lover (Christopher Reeve), himself a fledgling writer, who eventually tries to outsmart his mentor. Based on Ira Levin's play of 1978, the premise of a fake murder in the first half recalls Shaffer's idea, which was duly noted by numerous reviewers upon the film's release (see Maslin 1982; Ebert 1982). This reveals an intricate web of influences and continuities between the originals, their remakes and other supposedly unrelated titles, which all become connected retrospectively through the presence of the same actors and reoccurring motifs. This web offers 'the navigational viewer', described by Janet Murrey, numerous pleasures 'in following the connections between different parts of the story and in discovering multiple arrangements of the same material' (quoted in Jenkins 2006: 119).

Even though Branagh's film similarly opens with Tindle's arrival at Wyke's impressive mansion, the generic transition between the two versions soon becomes apparent. In Mankiewicz's film, the comedic atmosphere of the battle of wits in the first half is then juxtaposed with a more 'macabre game of cat and mouse' (Ebert 1972) in the second. Here, however, the mood is immediately imbued with tension, as from the opening sequence we are invited into the world of the thriller genre. Andrew's house is no longer filled with antique furniture, games and automata. Instead, it resembles a sterile and modern high-tech art gallery where every move activates remote sensors and is recorded on surveillance cameras. This time, rather than being a landowner, Wyke has acquired his fortune writing thrillers, earning him the nickname 'master of menace' and making us suspect that the game he has designed for his guest will be just as sinister as the titles of his books – *Rat in a Trap*, *Loser's Kiss*, *Dead Fish* or *Blind Man's Bluff*. His dark intentions are immediately hinted at by his choice of a smart black suit. His greeting handshake shot from a bird's-eye-view perspective shows Andrew to be an extension of the house, as his hand emerges from the lifeless building, giving the film a strong gothic undercurrent. Tindle is no longer an up-and-coming travel agency proprietor, but an aspiring unemployed actor, which gives more credibility to his later impersonation as Inspector Black, as well as self-reflexively indicating Law's awareness that *Sleuth* is his second chance to prove that he can successfully deliver Caine's iconic character on screen.

Although, on the surface, the reason for the conflict is again Maggie's betrayal with the younger lover and Andrew's morbid jealousy, there are too many sexual innuendoes in the men's exchanges from start to finish to treat them as merely male banter. This is especially because, over time, they appear to flirt with each other and eventually openly challenge each other's sexual orientation and gender identity. In Shaffer's play, their competitiveness was visible when they tried to question each other's sexual competence. For instance, Wyke calls himself 'an Olympic sexual athlete' who could 'copulate for England at any distance', which Milo ridicules, saying that taking part matters more than winning ([1970] 2004: 23). Shaffer's witty verbal play becomes much more menacing in Pinter's hands. In his ambiguity-ridden dialogue, it is hard to tell the difference between homophobic, homosocial and homosexual. Indeed, as Michael Billington points out, 'Pinter had always been fascinated by the thin dividing line between male bonding and homoerotic instincts', especially if the two men are 'drawn together by the desire for the same woman' (1997: 138). *Sleuth* serves as a good example of such ambiguities.

Figure 3.5 *Sleuth* (2007): Jude Law is Michael Caine.

Already the very first exchange between the two adversaries contains homoerotic innuendoes and sexual tension. Despite seeing two cars parked in front of his house, Andrew asks his guest if he came by train. When Milo tells him that he drove and points to his car, Andrew asks: 'The little one?' Milo then answers: 'Not the big one'. To this Andrew responds: 'No, the big one is mine. What do you think of it?' Milo replies: 'Very handsome'. Although cars are commonly referred to as female, Milo's response subverts this, setting the tone for the rest of the film, as gender roles will also become fluid and malleable. This is implied by an exchange that follows, in which Andrew's traditionalist view of a relationship involving an active male and a passive female is challenged, as he tries to emasculate Milo by his provocative homosexual word play:

> Andrew Wyke: I understand you're fucking my wife.
> Milo Tindle: That's right.
> [. . .]
> Andrew Wyke: I thought you might have denied it.
> Milo Tindle: Why would I deny it?
> Andrew Wyke: Well, she is my wife.
> Milo Tindle: Yes, but she's fucking me.
> Andrew Wyke: Oh, she's fucking you too, huh? Well, I'll be buggered. Ha ha. Sorry.
> Milo Tindle: Yes, it's mutual.

Andrew Wyke: You take turns?
Milo Tindle: We fuck each other. That's what people do.

Moreover, if we add Milo's clothes and accessories – such as cowboy leather boots, a thumb ring and highlighted hair – giving him an aura of, as Law explains on the DVD commentary, 'a rent boy', we might find another interesting role reversal. If we are to believe that Maggie designed the house herself, then she must be an independent and successful woman in her own right. Milo, therefore, may be cashing in on his pretty looks through his affair with the mature and wealthy woman, which is reminiscent of the Alfie-Ruby/Liz relationship.

Initially, it seems that the novelist is teasing, testing and challenging Milo's sexuality. At the end of the first act, it appears as if he has won this game of humiliation when the young man resorts to a surprising line of defence, claiming that he is not into women at all. Later, as the film progresses, however, it appears that Andrew starts to succumb to Milo's sexually ambivalent charm. As he explains to Inspector Black in Act Two, '[a]s a matter of fact, I liked him. I thought he was attractive. I thought we could've become good friends [. . .] I put myself in my wife's shoes. He was terribly sweet'. This recalls Pinter's *Collection*, where, according to Billington, a lot of the dramatic tension derives

Figure 3.6 *Sleuth* (2007): Caine's iconic tough-guy image mocked.

from the husband's obsession with and attraction to the wife's lover (1997: 139). After Milo removes his costume and make-up, the game continues but takes yet another surprising turn. Now it is Andrew whose own gender and sexual identity become questioned when he is forced at gunpoint to wear his wife's jewellery in what becomes an emasculating drag performance and a way of mocking Caine's iconic tough-guy screen image.

The most significant twist in the Branagh version is that, in the end, neither Milo nor Andrew want Maggie back. The woman is no longer the prize in their game or the object of their desire, even though her presence is much more tangible than in the original movie, as we assume her to be behind the wheel of a speeding car approaching the mansion towards the end of the film. Indeed, the two protagonists briefly fantasise about moving in together and making the female redundant. In Act Three, during a seduction scene in a red-lit guest bedroom, Andrew proposes that the jobless actor moves in: 'Forget her. Let her rot. Stay with me. You're my kind of person'. He promises expensive holidays and making acquaintances with powerful and famous people. A flattered Milo approaches Andrew, toys with the belt of the writer's dressing gown and then, in a gesture implying that he is about to perform fellatio says: 'I've always been attracted to rich and powerful men. Rich and powerful men make all the girls quiver. Like a jelly on a plate'.[20] One IMDb user commented on the scene with the following words:

> Michael Caine and Jude Law are inches away from a kiss here and that's a bizarre turn of events. True, Jude Law has a sexual presence that he carries as if he didn't know was there. Everything he says has a sexual connotation whether consciously or unconsciously. His Milo Tindle looks decidedly post coital. A bit undone, unwashed. (primodanielelori 2007)

Another one asserted:

> The homosexual element is a novelty but, I must say, not a surprise. Jude Law exudes sex. It's impossible to put him in a confined environment with just one other person and not be sensitive to the sexual possibilities. He provokes without half trying. He plants sexual ideas in your mind and you feel compelled to break rules and go for it. (littlemartinarocena 2007)

Milo says he might accept the offer on the condition that the writer is nice to him; to assert his dominance, he then demands that Andrew pour him whisky. This scene recalls a similar exchange in *The Servant*, which Walker describes as 'the aggressive ball-game, in which Barrett gives Tony his first order ("Well, go and pour me a glass of brandy"), and clinches his dominance' ([1974] 2005: 214).

The final scene takes place in the master bedroom, with both men lying on the bed. At this point in the film, it is difficult to predict what card each opponent has up their sleeve, as they both seem to have let their guard down. Andrew tries to stroke Milo's hair as the young man starts crying, apparently touched by the generous proposition. But what happens next comes as a great shock when, in response to physical contact, Milo suddenly bolts upright and from a gay seducer turns into a homophobic bully:

> Take your hand off me [. . .] Fuck off, you big puff. Jesus, I come here as an innocent bystander, as a totally respectable individual. A humble part-time hairdresser. And you try to corrupt me. You try to seduce me [. . .] You're a menace. Also, you're a cunt.

In the original film, Milo collects Marguerite's coat to claim his victory over Andrew and to ascertain his possession of the woman. Here, however, Milo announces that Maggie plans to return to Andrew. He then grabs her black leather coat, reminiscent of the wardrobe that Law wears as Gigolo Joe in *A. I.*, puts it on and, acting very camp, kisses Andrew goodbye. As he turns to leave, the writer shoots him in the back, apparently humiliated and hurt by the rejection. One of the final images of the film is the close-up of Andrew's face, with tears filling his eyes. This ending suggests that Milo, despite his apparent death, has proven the superior game-player thanks to his amorphous and ambivalent sexuality and that Andrew knows that he has been beaten. It appears, then, that, although it was Andrew who initially challenged Milo's sexuality and gender identity, in the end his own sexual integrity collapses as he surrenders to Milo's seduction. The remake repeats the dynamics of the original film's ending in which Milo wins the battle despite being shot, indicated by his reassured laughter before he draws his last breath.

The role-playing and role reversals in the remake of *Sleuth*, literally switching from scene to scene, recall the permanently fluctuating power dynamics in *The Servant*, which Walker calls 'a "dance" to destruction' ([1974] 2005: 214). This comparison equally applies to Branagh's film, which one IMDb user describes as 'a predatory mating dance designed to make the viewer wonder if one or both or neither of the men are closet cases as well as mental cases' (majikstl 2007). Unsurprisingly, Manohla Dargis of the *New York Times* titles her review of the film 'A Dance of Two Men, Twisting and Turning With a Gun That's More Than a Gun' (2007).

Now the predatory mating dance between Andrew and Milo becomes an on-screen duel between two opposite types of masculinity, as embodied by their respective stars. Even though Caine had previously played homosexual roles in *California Suite* (Ross, 1978) and *Deathtrap*, it is the iconic image of his 1960s and 1970s Cockney gangster and lover that remains imprinted on the popular imagination, especially following on from its endorsement by Lad culture in the 1990s. By contrast, Law's screen image is characterised by its more amorphous, malleable and experimental nature, questioning binary sexual and gender codes. In the remake of *Sleuth*, Law repeats his formula from the remake of *Alfie*, substituting Caine's heterosexual lover with metrosexuality, but here he takes it a step further. By exploring the performative nature of gender, the film also exposes the performative character of Caine's tough-guy screen masculinity, which Law deconstructs with gusto.

Discussing Hollywood franchise reboots, Kathleen Loock observes that they 'tend to follow a logic of generational succession in which continuity over many decades and into the future can only be maintained through legacy, inheritance and passing-of-the-torch rituals' (2020: 184). As a result, however, she notices that such 'nostalgia-driven reboots almost always promote a conservative politics of "reproductive futurism" (Edelman 2004) that normalises heteronormative gender scripts and perpetuates traditional notions of family, heterosexuality and biological reproduction' (184). *Sleuth*, which is not a franchise reboot as such, or even a typical Hollywood film, is a legacyquel with a difference. While it goes to great lengths to challenge the normalisation of 'traditional notions of family, heterosexuality and biological reproduction' within the film's narrative, its function remains inscribed within male rituals of heritage. Law becomes Caine's surrogate son in the acting profession, completing the rite of passage by emasculating his opponent. Despite negative reviews, *Sleuth* is a successful legacyquel as it 'gives old *and* young fans a movie they can claim as their own' and because 'in good legacyquels everything that's come before still matters and contributes to a larger narrative tapestry that's still being woven' (Singer 2015).

The remake follows in the footsteps of the original *Sleuth*, which, in retrospect, played a similar function for Caine as an actor, as did the remake for Law. Starring opposite Olivier allowed Caine to prove to any doubters that Michael Caine was more than just Alfie Elkins and that all his roles were carefully crafted performances. Walker observes:

> Though extraordinarily frightening in *Get Carter* (1971) as a vengeful racketeer [. . .] he still felt he ought to remove that vestigial cockney cloth cap to his 'betters' in the 'acting profession' till he appeared with Olivier in *Sleuth* (1972) and matched – and sometimes even mated – the senior actor move for move. Approached almost immediately afterwards to appear in a sequel to *Alfie* (for a very large fee indeed), he turned the offer down flat. *Alfie Mark II* could have added nothing to what he had achieved with *Sleuth*: a fulfilment of the Cockney boy's curiously dated yet still powerful aspiration to gain the 'respectability' of the class above him. ([1974] 2005: 308–9)

Caine often recalls that the greatest compliment of his career came from Olivier, who confessed that initially on the set of *Sleuth* he treated Caine as his understudy, to then realise that he had an equal partner. Of all the esteemed actors of the British stage and screen, Olivier chose Caine to carry his Oscar for Lifetime Achievements during his funeral service in Westminster Abbey, showing the measure of respect that the late thespian bestowed on his one-time co-star and on-screen rival.

CONCLUSION

It is believed that, together with Connery, Caine had a massive impact on the generation of British actors that followed, by paving the way for a new type of British masculinity on screen. Jonathan Stubbs mentions Tim Roth, Ewan McGregor, Gary Oldman, Clive Owen, Christian Bale and Pierce Brosnan, with Law thrown into the mix, who – thanks to their more explicitly heterosexual and heavily physical performance style inspired by Connery and Caine – all conform to the dominant Hollywood representation of masculinity (2002: 90–91). His inclusion of Law is problematic, however, as the actor stands out by questioning codes based on polarities such as 'masculine' versus 'feminine' or 'homosexual' versus 'heterosexual'. While hugely successful in supporting roles, when he takes centre stage, as in *Alfie*, or co-stars opposite Caine in *Sleuth*, Law invests the screen with so much sexually ambiguous tension as to produce polarised opinions. Caine seems to identify the problem by mentioning the actor's looks: 'I don't think he's got a great rap from critics actually for what he does. I think he's so pretty that it pisses people off. It pisses me off sometimes' (quoted in Weintraub 2007).

Although now cherished as the epitome of tough-guy masculinity himself, it is easy to forget that Caine was also an icon of style and fashion in the 1960s, photographed by Bailey in 1965 in a dark suit, horn-rimmed glasses and with a cigarette hanging nonchalantly from his mouth. Law, voted the sexiest man alive the same year that *Alfie* was released, reworks Caine's sexual appeal by extending his character's narcissism in *Alfie*, only to then destroy his pretty-boy image in the second half of *Sleuth*. While in *Alfie* Law not only seduces women within the story, but also charms male viewers via his address at the camera, in *Sleuth* he now not only seduces and replaces Caine, but also renders the older man impotent.

Unlike the remakes discussed in Chapter 2, with their newly devised upbeat endings and heterosexual pairings, the two remakes featuring Law in the lead refuse to offer clear resolutions. In this respect, they succeed in replicating their originals' open-endedness, more typical of British cinema, thus producing an interesting hybrid that draws on two cinematic traditions. As a result,

Alfie proposes more challenging material in terms of genre and gender representation, through reviving its connection with the original. The outcome is often confusing, however, such as when the remake at first appears to be a romantic comedy in the tradition of the Anglo-American cycle, but then goes on to contain relatively little humour, not to mention Law's fluctuating direct address that makes the identificatory strategy of the film problematic. Even *Sleuth* finishes with more questions than answers. We do not hear police sirens approaching the mansion, so it is impossible to say whether Andrew will be apprehended. The last shot of Milo may also raise some doubts about his demise since, despite the gunshot, there is no blood anywhere on his body.

However, what the two remakes succeed in doing via casting is a sense of seriality and continuity, not only across the originals and their remakes, but also across both remakes. Through the properties of their remakes, these two British classics become bound together in new ways, as Law's stepping into Caine's shoes was never intended to be a singular affair. Law's presence now defines the two films, turning them in effect into Part 1/Part 2 of a new series, which even overshadows the continuation caused by the casting of Caine in the *Sleuth* remake. With a new sense of continuity now spanning both films, Frank Kelleter and Kathleen Loock's observation about remaking as 'a more implicit practice of serialization' where 'a source text that was initially identified as a stand-alone story is re-activated, repeated, changed and indeed continued' (2017: 129) takes on a different dimension: the remake of *Alfie* becomes 're-activated, repeated, changed and indeed continued' into its second instalment – the remake of *Sleuth*.

In hindsight, it appears that Law always had (at least) two remakes of Caine's iconic works in mind to seal his image as the next generation's Michael Caine. That Law likes to toy with the idea is further shown by his appearance in Bailey's replica of Caine's 1965 classic portrait:

> Like Caine, now 71, Law wears a sharp, slim-fitting black suit, a narrow tie, simple white shirt and pouts on a cigarette. However, Law, 31, is not wearing the thick black spectacles Caine made famous in the Harry Palmer films: that, perhaps, would have been a tribute too far. (Leitch 2004)

Despite unflattering reviews of the two remakes featuring his 'surrogate son', two years after the release of *Sleuth*, when asked whether he thought it would be good to revive his Harry Palmer franchise, Caine appeared very enthusiastic about the idea. He said that he immediately knew who his successor should be: 'Jude Law can play Harry Palmer as long as he's got the glasses' (quoted in Warmoth 2009). Whether we will ever see the third instalment of the Law remake series remains to be seen. The fact that the actor was recently spotted wearing heavy-rimmed glassed at his London home while being interviewed by Jimmy Fallon gives that idea some hope.[21]

NOTES

1. At the end of the film, Robert Murphy finds Alfie 'confused rather than repentant' ([1992] 2008: 145). According to John Hill, the moralising conclusion is contrived. Rejected by Ruby, Alfie supposedly realises 'the hollowness of his existence', except 'the ending is itself hollow, undercut both by the complicity with Alfie's perspective that the film has maintained throughout and, as a result, the absence of any compelling alternative to Alfie's philandering' (1995: 165). Jeffrey Richards believes that, with Caine in the lead, Alfie becomes 'a role model rather than an object of condemnation' (1997: 163), while Christopher Bray is convinced that at the end he 'is up to his old tricks, charming his audience with whatever it wants to hear' (2006: 85).
2. His dream of a nuclear bomb blast that endangers his and his son Malcolm's life is the only indication of forces beyond his control that may affect his way of thinking. Naughton's novel includes one crucial detail missing from the film. Alfie was brought up by his father and a stepmother, suggesting that his mother either died or abandoned him as a child; this gives his commitment issues some validity.
3. Faced with the prospect of a physical confrontation with Frank (Sidney Tafler), Alfie loses his bearings and asks him not to punch him so as to spare his suit. Frank may not be a Northerner but is associated with the region through his frequent visits to Sheffield.
4. See Michael Caine's Oscars 2000 award-winning speech at https://www.youtube.com/watch?v=CuhXv2wBeiQ.
5. A similar idea occurred to Mike Hodges, who contemplated writing a sequel to *Get Carter*, featuring Carter's son: 'Jack Carter was dead, but I did suggest there was quite an interesting idea that Carter had a son with the Britt Ekland character and with all the knowledge since I made *Get Carter* of DNA and genetics, I thought it was quite an interesting thing for a young lad to be finding out that Carter was his father' ('Mike Hodges Discusses *Get Carter* with NFT audience, 23 September 1997' 1999: 125).
6. It is equally possible, following Nicola Rehling, to locate the remake within 'white masculinity in crisis' films (2009: 40). Hugh Grant's romantic comedies can also be seen as part of a larger cycle of films about male anxieties and alleged failings that contributed to the renaissance of British cinema in the late 1990s, becoming Britain's 'biggest cultural export'. Rehling notes how these stories of male insecurities mirrored similar concerns across the Atlantic (2009: 40). She mentions the remake of *Alfie* specifically, however, in the context of 'body anxiety films' such as *The Full Monty* (Cattaneo, 1997), *Human Traffic* (Kerrigan, 1999), *How to Kill Your Neighbor's Dog* (Kalesniko, 2000) and *The Real Blonde* (DiCillo, 1998) (2009: 97).
7. The screenplay features a reference to the Eiffel Tower instead.
8. Unlike the Hugh Grant romantic cycle, this one reverses the nationality of its lovers in that the woman is British and the man American.
9. Coincidentally, the film's release in the US occurred the same month when Law was named 'Sexiest Man Alive' by People magazine, beating, for instance, Johnny Depp, Brad Pitt and his fellow Brit, Colin Firth, who all represent a completely different type of on-screen masculinity.
10. *The Ipcress File* came out at the same time as *Thunderball*, the fourth instalment in Sean Connery's James Bond saga. Andrew Spicer believes it to be the only important rival to the Bond series at the time (2001: 76). *The Ipcress File*'s visual style was meant to juxtapose Bond's colourful fantasy world since it was filmed, as Peter Bradshaw observes, 'in a gritty, gloomy, decidedly non-swinging London of 1965' (2006). The film was advertised as 'the thinking man's *Goldfinger*' (Shail 2004: 71), or even 'the anti-Bond'.

Unlike her majesty's spy with a licence to kill, whose Scottish accent precludes any class identification, Palmer's Cockney accent quite clearly pins him down to one specific class and location. Angie Errigo observes that he was 'a fantasy figure for guys who wear glasses, people living in anonymous flats, driving unglamorous, functional cars and shopping for groceries after work. You can relate to Harry Palmer. He's capable and crafty. He's sexy. And he can cook' (2000).

11. As John Hill observes, '[a]s with many of the "new wave" films, the representation of husbands in the film is heavily marked by "castration": Harry is either bed-ridden or in a wheelchair, entirely innocent of his wife's infidelity; Sadie's cuckolded husband is drab and uninspiring (bold, bespectacled and pipe-smoking, given to a study of gardening manuals while his wife is out with Alfie), Humphrey, the surrogate father to Alfie's child, can only offer comfort and understanding to Gilda rather than a genuine excitement or passion' (1995: 164–65).
12. At the same time, however, it is important to note that, while Alfie focuses on his consumption of physically attractive women, there are scenes in the film that are equally complicit in using Law's white male body as an image for visual consumption.
13. For instance, Julie Christie, at the time regarded as the epitome of female modernity, was rejected for the part of a James Bond girl in *Thunderball*, since her cleavage was perceived to be too small (Chapman 2000: 117).
14. Liz is shown running around town, swinging her bag, whistling, smoking and laughing. On top of it, her 'simple bob, wide smile, muted makeup, and short skirts – when combined with her seeming independence, made for an immediate appeal to younger women, then without a contemporary screen icon of their own' (Gibson 2017: 135).
15. According to Lesley A. Hall, '[t]he single mother was still a stigmatised figure, making women reluctant to seek affiliation orders, which men could evade by alleging the woman's "bad character", or misrepresenting their income' (2000: 171).
16. The abortionist played by Denholm Elliott is an ambiguous figure, leaving one to wonder whether such procedures were 'undertaken by idealists who were also fighting for changes in the law' or functioned 'as purely commercial operations' (Hall 2000: 171).
17. Their rocky relationship on screen was then paralleled in real life, as the film marked the beginning of a highly-publicised turbulent affair that would continue on and off for almost a decade.
18. Reminiscing in the documentary *My Generation* (Batty, 2017) about how he landed his first big role, Caine notes that the only reason why he was even considered for the part of an officer in *Zulu* was because the director was American and, therefore, unhindered by any class prejudice.
19. For a discussion of remakes and re-adaptations, see Leitch 2002: 37–62.
20. This recalls a scene with Alfie on the bridge at the end of the novel, when he is reflecting on a 'kept' gay man.
21. In an online interview from his home office in London during the lockdown period in 2020, Law was seated with a enormous black and white photograph of Caine and Bob Hoskins – a publicity shot for Neil Jordan's film *Mona Lisa* (1985) – behind his back, which created an eerie effect of Caine looking over Law's shoulder for the duration of the entire interview (https://www.youtube.com/watch?v=ip7FmslxMWE).

CHAPTER 4

From Devilish Masters to Evil Dames: *Bedazzled* and *The Wicker Man*

Hollywood remakes featuring women in previously male roles have become quite prominent in recent years. The all-female *Ghostbusters* reboot (Feigs, 2016) attracted both a lot of attention and misogynistic hostility from the original's fan base (see Perkins 2020). The all-female requel *Ocean's 8* (Ross, 2018) escaped such harsh reactions, as it positioned itself somewhere between a remake and a sequel with its focus on generic and genetic continuation, while remaining safely on the fringes of the original franchise (see Forrest 2020). Another classic comedy, *Dirty Rotten Scoundrels* (Oz, 1988), was remade as *The Hustle* (Addison, 2019), also to mixed reviews, but showing that the trend is here to stay. This chapter examines two examples of Hollywood remakes, *Bedazzled* (Ramis, 2000) and *The Wicker Man* (LaBute, 2006),[1] which also transform previously male roles into modern female equivalents, before such practice became 'an industrial and political strategy for Hollywood at the end of the twenty-first century's second decade' (Perkins 2020: 158). Unlike the films mentioned above, here, however, the gender swapping applies to secondary characters only as the male protagonist's journey still dominates the plot.

As I will go on to show, although pertaining to different genres, both originals are now bound together retrospectively through the property of their gender-switching remakes and similar thematic concerns – such as the subject of the supernatural, counterculture and the idea of class difference. I will look first at Stanley Donen's satirical comedy, *Bedazzled* (1967), which is a loose update of the Faust legend, set in 1960s London, co-acted by the comedy duo Peter Cook and Dudley Moore and written by the former. Moore plays a working-class hero who gives away his soul to Cook's Devil in exchange for seven wishes to help him win over the woman he loves, with each wish representing a different fantasy and an opportunity to satirise an aspect of the 1960s scene. The remake by Harold Ramis (2000) shares its predecessor's loose episodic structure, but instead of taking on contemporary American society, it keeps more with the path of a conventional Hollywood romantic comedy. To that effect, the hero, played by Brendan Fraser, is now a socially awkward office worker tempted and misled by the provocative Elizabeth Hurley as the Devil.

In a way similar to Donen's comedy, Robin Hardy's cult horror classic *The Wicker Man* (1973) is also preoccupied with themes of counterculture, religion and fantasies turning into nightmares. The action takes place on a remote and privately-owned Scottish island whose pagan community brings to mind the utopian realisation of some of the 1960s ideals. In its controversial remake by Neil LaBute (2006), the original aristocratic leader played by Christopher Lee is replaced by a female Hollywood horror icon, Ellen Burstyn, who now rules over an isolated island in the contemporary United States, where men are used for breeding and slave labour. I will explore how both remakes show the ripple effect of a gender-switching adaptation strategy, redirecting the focus away from the class power games in the original films to the ongoing battle of the sexes in the updates. As a result, despite women being elevated to more prominent roles, the remakes also tend to depict them either as visual eye-candy or heavily drawn caricatures, as the upper-class masters from the originals become she-devils, female tricksters and even medieval witches in their Hollywood remakes.

BEDAZZLED (DONEN, 1967)/(RAMIS, 2000)

When discussing Swinging London films, certain titles always seem to spring to mind – for instance, *Darling* (Schlesinger, 1965), *The Knack . . . and How to Get It* (Lester, 1965), *Alfie* (Gilbert, 1966) and *Blow-Up* (Antonioni, 1966). So when in August 2018 the BFI compiled a list of the ten greatest films representing the period,[2] it included all the usual suspects. As an afterthought, however, the BFI then asked the public which films were missing from the ranking. This survey revealed quite a surprising result. Number one went to *Bedazzled*, a Swinging 60s London comedy, which had been largely neglected by critics, but not by audiences composed mostly of Cook's and Moore's devoted fans whose only chance to rewatch the film came through faded home recordings of its rare TV broadcasts. This could explain why William Cook commented in 2005 that it had taken nearly forty years for *Bedazzled* 'to acquire the status of a cult classic' (2005: 40). This remark was then confirmed by Eleanor Bron's[3] (Margaret in the film) observation in 2012 that the film had remained underappreciated in Britain.[4]

Bedazzled is loosely based on the Faustian myth about the infamous German necromancer and astrologer, perhaps explaining why Donen was drawn to the project. Donen had previously co-directed a modernised version of the myth as the musical comedy *Damn Yankees* (1958), in which a frustrated sports fan sells his soul to the Devil to regain his youth, become a baseball player and help his team beat the Yankees. Since its inception, which can be traced to the publication of the *Historia von D. Johann Fausten* in Frankfurt by Johann Spies (1587), the Faustian myth has been repeatedly adapted into numerous media, from opera, comic books, computer games to cinema, showing its potential for serial (re)invention and transmediality, its frequent appropriation as a tool for socio-cultural critique, as well as high entertainment value. In her book *Framing Faust: Twentieth-Century Cultural Struggles* (2005), Inez Hedges lists over eighty filmic reiterations of the Faust legend, including such diverse representations as *Phantom of the Paradise* (De Palma, 1974), *Mephisto* (Szabó, 1981), *Angel Heart* (Parker, 1987), *The Devil's Advocate* (Hackford, 1997), and *Ghost Rider* (Johnson, 2007). Cook, who penned the screenplay, drew ideas for the film from at least two sources. He mixed and mingled elements from Johann Wolfgang von Goethe's *Faust* (1833), such as the name of the protagonist's love and the fact that he escapes damnation, with Christopher Marlowe's tragedy *Doctor Faustus*, performed towards the end of the sixteenth century, such as the appearance of the Seven Deadly Sins or the relationship between Faustus and the Devil. In the play, the two discuss theology but mostly engage in pointless pursuits and trivial tricks. Faustus's final invocation when he is dragged to Hell – 'Oh, Mephistophilis!' – is ambiguous, but may suggest that he has formed a bond with the Devil against his better judgment. Thus, what is unique about Faust in comparison to other cultural 'types' that Hedges mentions – such as Hamlet, Don Juan, or Don Quixote – is that he is 'opposed by a single, formidable opponent' (2005: 1). In this respect, the story of Faust should be, and often is, seen as a double-act with the Devil, who has not ceased to fascinate since his first appearance on medieval frescoes and in mystery and morality plays, often stealing the show. This becomes a leitmotif for Cook and Moore's film, which focuses on the development of that unlikely bond.

Bedazzled's plotline turns on its head Robert Shail's claim that in the 1960s all that any man needed to succeed was to be young and working-class (2004: 75). Even though Stanley Moon (Dudley Moore) has all these qualities, he could not be further from enjoying the life of a 1960s Casanova. Not that his dreams are that extravagant either. He works as a short-order chef at Wimpy's and is in love with Cockney waitress Margaret Spencer (Eleanor Bron), who does not reciprocate his feelings. After the forlorn Stanley asks God for intervention, which meets with no reaction, he tries to hang himself, which becomes a cue for the Devil. Seeing the man's wavering faith and despair, he grants him seven wishes to help him seduce the woman he loves. Throughout the film, each wish seems to get him closer to achieving his desire of sexual fulfilment as either an intellectual with a Lolita-like admirer, a businessman with a trophy wife, a pop star with a besotted groupie, a young graduate with a mature housewife or even two nuns in love, before ending in frustration and failure. In Stanley's many visions and versions of Margaret, Cook's script reiterates what Marlow's play had already hinted at – the prevalence of male fantasies of the female ideal, in lieu of an almost complete lack of real female characters. The Devil appears in all of Stanley's wishes, playing different roles and sabotaging them in the process, often seducing the woman instead. Regardless, the two grow quite fond of each other, as they discuss many subjects, including faith, religion and class. The film finishes with Satan allowing Stanley to destroy the contract, since it appears that he has won the bet with God and managed to collect one hundred billion souls first. Stanley returns to his ordinary life to try to win Margaret's attention on her own terms. His adventures may not have led to a typical Hollywood conclusion of boy gets girl, but they have nonetheless made him older and wiser.

Figure 4.1 *Bedazzled* (1967): 'What sort of freedom of choice did I have about where I was born and what size I was and what a bloody awful job I landed myself in?'

Hedges notes how '[i]n Western culture, the Faustian metamorphosis has proven itself especially adept at expressing inner conflict as well as conflict between a character's inner convictions and the workings of the world outside', with the Faust theme being able to 'show how power collides with justice, and knowledge with happiness' (2005: 184). In adapting the Faustian myth to 1960s London, Cook and Moore used the opportunity to comment on contemporary topics. These range across the growing secularisation of British society, the sexual revolution, hippie movements, peace movements, Beatlemania, the British class system, and even political scandals of the day, such as when the Devil tells Lillian Lust (Raquel Welch as one of the Seven Deadly Sins) to go to the Foreign Office in a likely allusion to the Profumo affair of 1963. In fact, the film contains so many one-liners rich with references to the events and cultural icons of the period that this makes it enjoyable for some, but too dense and verbose for others. For example, whereas Roger Ebert found the film 'brilliant', 'intelligent' and 'very funny' (1967), Bosley Crowther of *The New York Times* complained that 'MAYBE the brand of British banter and buffoonery that Peter Cook and Dudley Moore bombard us with in Stanley Donen's "Bedazzled" would be very funny if it came in small bursts at not too frequent intervals in an expansive musical comedy or revue' (1967). According to reviewer W. Cook, '[a]s a stage play, Cook's script would have worked a treat. As a screenplay, it felt cold and stilted' (2005: 40). By contrast, the British comedian Eric Idle, whose Monty Python group owed a great debt of gratitude to the duo's comedy style, believes that Cook's and Moore's partnership 'came to perfection in their movie *Bedazzled* (which Peter wanted to call *Raquel Welch*, so they could bill it as Peter Cook and Dudley Moore *in* Raquel Welch . . .)' (2011).

The first wish starts with the magic words 'Julie Andrews' in reference to one of the biggest stars of the period, but also to show the Devil's mischievous sense of humour, since Andrews was mostly associated with good-natured characters. Stanley becomes an intellectual with a thick Welsh accent, parodying Richard Burton's Jimmy Porter from *Look Back in Anger* (1959), minus the anger, while a Lolita-like Margaret references Rita Tushingham's Nancy from *The Knack* (Lester, 1965), who also goes on to scream 'Rape!' when things get physical. The second wish opens with the magic words 'Jackie Kennedy'. These words transform Stanley into a wealthy businessman married to the sensual and sophisticated Margaret, whom he showers with gifts, possibly alluding to the US first lady's allegedly overzealous enjoyment of presents from foreign visitors. Since Cook was also rumoured to have had an affair with her while on tour with *Beyond the Fringe* in the US in 1963, this reference now acquires yet another coded meaning when the Devil seduces Margaret away from her husband.[5] Another wish alludes to Mike Nichol's *The Graduate* (1967), released the same year as *Bedazzled*, by depicting an exaggerated version of an adulterous relationship between a housewife and a young university student. Here, Eleanor Bron's hair and make-up resemble Anne Bancroft's as the famed Mrs Robinson. However, the couple is unable to consummate their relationship and weep uncontrollably at the thought of hurting Margaret's perfect husband, who is also Stanley's Oxford University mentor, played as the embodiment of virtues by the Devil himself.

The film would be incomplete without a comment on Beatlemania, and so the next episode, shot in black and white to emulate the popular TV show *Top of the Pops*, features Stanley as a new pop idol jumping all over the stage and imploring his fans to love him. Margaret is a groupie in the audience, besotted with the star whose fickle love-interest changes the minute a newcomer played by the Devil arrives with his group 'Drimble Wedge and the Vegetation'. His cold blank stare and passivity on stage stand in stark contrast to Stanley's act, provoking an even bigger case of hysteria when he calmly declares: 'You fill me with inertia' and 'I'm not available', with the chorus of girls chanting 'I'm bedazzled' in the background. The irony of the entire scene rests on the fact that, in reality, it was Moore who was a successful music entertainer, performer and composer, regularly featured on British TV with his Dudley Moore Trio, which established him as Britain's top jazz pianist. Moore also scored the music for *Bedazzled*.

Moreover, the episode parodying Beatlemania was not too far away from the comedians' real-life status at the time since their reported promiscuity often matched that of the film and pop stars of the day. According to Alexander Games, '[i]f sex officially started in Britain in 1963, as Philip Larkin claimed, Cook and Moore were among its most enthusiastic practitioners' (2012). In fact, Cook and Moore were often compared to the intellectual and sombre John Lennon and the cheerful and approachable Paul McCartney, respectively (Lennon would appear as a guest on *Not Only But Also*):

> Like Lennon & McCartney, whom they knew, and in some respects resembled, Cook's caustic wit was balanced by Moore's softer homespun humour. Cook, like Lennon, could be too acerbic to appease mainstream opinion, while Moore, like McCartney, was sometimes too saccharine to win critical acclaim. (Cook 2002: xvii)

The reference to the Beatles could not be more topical on one more account. It arrived only a year and a half after Lennon's controversial statement about the group being more popular than Jesus. The statement did not spark controversy in the already more secularised Britain, but it created an uproar in some parts of the US and resulted in the public destruction of the band's records by right-wing Christian groups and threats from the KKK.[6] As Danny Peary notes:

Considering that *Bedazzled* came out not long after John Lennon was forced to publicly retract his 'The Beatles are more popular than Jesus' remark in order to stop a boycott of Beatles records on many U.S. radio stations, as well as organized Nazi-like burnings of Beatles records and magazines, it's amazing Moore and Cook attempted and got away with using material I'm sure many people considered blasphemous. (quoted in Shreve 2014)

The material Peary refers to above is the subject of the next episode based on the duo's sketch from *Not Only But Also* (BBC2 1965), called 'Tramponuns'. After the fantasies of Margaret as a Lolita, a groupie, a trophy wife and a hot mistress all prove disastrous, Stanley asks to be 'far removed from the false glitter, the raucous music and the neon lights of this modern world'. He is transported to a convent where, as a novice, his 'sinful' and 'unnatural' love for Margaret allows the comedians to comment on the subject of homosexuality, made legal in the UK the same year *Bedazzled* opened in the cinemas. The episode also ridicules the abstract and obscure nature of religious rituals, which reaches its climax when, for Stanley's initiation ceremony, s/he is asked to bounce up and down on trampolines. *The New York Times* reviewer found the scene quite 'aggressive and unpleasant' (Crowther 1967). Fraser, the star of the remake, however, recalled being shocked and thrilled when he first saw it in 1979 as an eleven-year-old on Channel 13 in Seattle; he states: 'I love the nuns on the trampoline. I got a kick out of the movie because I thought, "You can't get away with doing these kind of things"' (quoted in Spelling 2000b: 64).[7]

Taking on the subject of religion also allowed the comedians to comment on social injustice. Stanley complains about the restrictions of his class and Satan about his reduced status as a fallen angel, who now resides in a run-down London club with the Seven Deadly Sins for company. Both are castaways and loners who talk of equality and need a miracle to change their circumstances, as they are rejected by the system and unable to rise in status. Cook's Satan never reveals his monstrous form. His clothes – an elegant black suit, a bow-tie and a black cloak with red lining – are reminiscent of another supernatural character: the vampire. The vampire was depicted as a sophisticated aristocrat in a black cloak by Bela Lugosi in Tod Browning's *Dracula* (1931) and then popularised further by Christopher Lee's aristocratic blood-thirsty villain in Terence Fisher's *Dracula* (1958) and its sequels. However, Cook's Prince of Darkness is a comical figure, never meant to inspire awe or fear as the King of Hell, but rather pity – his red socks are the only visual indicator of his otherworldly nature, an element of his disguise borrowed from *Damn Yankees*. Having been thrown out of heaven as punishment for wanting to be equal with God, he now struggles with his reduced circumstances and desperately wishes to return to his former glory. As one IMDb user observes: 'The Prince of Darkness is shown to be a mere beggar at the door after all' (angelynx-2 2000).

When Stanley asks whether God is English, Satan informs him that he is not only English but also very upper class. Complaining that God has never shown any interest in him, Stanley hears that the reason for this is our freedom of choice, to which he retorts: 'Freedom of choice? What sort of freedom of choice did I have about where I was born and what size I was and what a bloody awful job I landed myself in? [. . .] If we really had freedom of choice we should be able to decide who our parents are and what we look like and everything'. Over the course of the film, it appears that the Devil – who calls himself George Spiggott,[8] which further shows his paling rank – and Stanley may differ in intellect and background, but they both suffer from their reduced position, whether by choice or by birth. In the end, the strong sense of social injustice, the Creator's indifference to all misery and his malicious laughter at George's futile attempt to get back into heaven as the final credits are rolling leave the viewer feeling 'sympathy for the devil'. This notion acquired a new currency in the 1960s, with the release of The Rolling Stones' song by the same title (1968), apparently inspired by another version of the Faust myth, Mikhail Bulgakov's *The Master and Margarita* (published in English in 1967). God now symbolises the ruling upper classes and Satan, with his underground London club, a 1960s counterculture rebel dropout who opposes the establishment.

The theme of class is further accentuated by the film's casting, recreating some parallels between the actors' real lives and the unusual bond forged between a short-order cook and Lucifer who, despite their different backgrounds and agendas, end up becoming friends. It is tempting to see correlations between the characters and actors, who were often presented as 'a rags-and-riches partnership – Dudley from the mean streets, Peter from the gentry' (Cook 2014: 16). Yet, despite their apparent class differences, the two comedians, just like their movie alter egos, had more in common than it seemed. Dudley's family were respectable, and he won a music scholarship to Oxford, while Cook's upper-class family 'were comfortable rather than affluent' (16). In fact, W. Cook argues that, in their comedy acts, 'the proletarian and the patrician collided. In a decade where old class barriers were being rapidly demolished, it was a partnership that captured the spirit of its changing times' (2002: xvii). He quotes the producer of their *Not Only But Also* BBC series, Joe McGrath, who observed, 'If there is a class divide in Britain, they straddle it' (quoted in Cook 2002: xvii).

Unsurprisingly, then, Cook and Moore frequently relied on the theme of class for their BBC sketches which repeatedly featured Cook as an aloof and eccentric aristocrat. His eloquent and elegant Lucifer clearly follows in the footsteps of such upper-class losers:

His characters aren't rooted in our reality, but inhabit a bizarre hinterland, where a man can spend a lifetime trying to teach worms to talk, flowers to walk, or ravens to fly underwater. Nevertheless, there is one aspect of his output that is entirely realistic. Like him, his principal alter-egos [. . .] are typically, unapologetically English. And like all Englishmen, they're all helpless prisoners of that terribly English caste system called social class. (Cook 2002: xiii)

Similarly, the Devil in *Bedazzled* is shown wasting his time on meaningless pursuits. His petty mischiefs consist of, for example, scratching vinyl records, tearing out final pages of Agatha Christie's novels, scaring hippies with a swarm of wasps, or teaching pigeons to poop on passers-by, all of which Stanley finds pathetic, considering that they are orchestrated by the Prince of Darkness. By contrast, Dudley – who often played a son, subordinate or interviewer – represented the ordinary man with whom the audience could identify thanks to the fact that, as Jonathan Miller notes, '[t]here was a sort of sweet, proletarian cuddlesome quality about Dudley' (quoted in Cook 2002: xvii). Accordingly, in *Bedazzled*, Moore plays an everyman who, despite his numerous guises from Welsh professor to lesbian nun, remains first and foremost a quintessentially likeable underdog for whom we all want to root.

Figure 4.2 *Bedazzled* (1967): Unlikely friendship.

Bedazzled remains one of the best examples of the duo's winning formula, with Moore playing a 'cute and fragile character' with 'populist, sympathetic appeal' and providing a much needed 'contrast and an antidote to Cook's more aloof and condescending style' (Cook 2002: xvi). Its comedic appeal draws from the differences between wit and humour, the former being elitist, as 'a witty man is always in some way demonstrating his superiority', and the latter more inclusive and working-class (Leach 2004: 144). One of the IMDb users fittingly explains: 'Why is the movie so good? I believe the secret to the movie is that they played themselves, Cook cruel, but humorous, arrogant, intelligent but tragic, Moore full of good intention, seemingly one step behind, but with the brighter future; the combination is gripping' (Dave-1511 2004). It is no wonder, then, that this comedy can be, and often is, perceived in autobiographical terms, appreciated for its satirical take on the 1960s, but also as a reflection on the lives and careers of the two comic legends who redefined British comedy and inspired generations to come.

Before *Bedazzled* was remade by Ramis in 2000, it had spawned at least two continuations. In 1971, Cook played the titular hero in Kevin Billington's political satire *The Rise and Rise of Michael Rimmer*, co-written by Cook, Billington, John Cleese and Graham Chapman. Rimmer is a mysterious man who appears from out of nowhere, gets a job at a small advertising company and, applying his skills of manipulation and deceit, becomes the next Tory Prime Minister; he reminds one of Cook's Devil, who claimed that his greatest achievement was to have invented advertising. By contrast, Moore (or 'Cuddly Dudley' as he had begun to be called) became an unlikely international 'sex thimble' of the 1980s and, briefly, one of Hollywood's most bankable movie stars. From this perspective, his role in Blake Edwards' sex comedy hit *10* (1979), about his all-consuming obsession for one woman, could be interpreted as an American version of *Bedazzled*. However, now on American soil, Julie Andrews is no longer a comedy magic password into a fantasy world, as his character is already living the dream. He is a self-made successful composer, whose class background is completely immaterial, about to marry Julie Andrews' character, who finally accepts him in every way.

Ramis' remake similarly continues and develops the film's romantic angle above all else. To this effect, it follows the earlier film's episodic structure revolving around the protagonist's seven wishes. Instead of the buddy relationship that characterised the original, it moves the focus onto romantic entanglements. Finding American equivalents to Cook and Moore's double act would have been challenging, considering that such comic pairings are rare in contemporary American comedy focused predominantly on solo acts.[9] As Rob Young proclaims, '[s]adly, the era of the comedy duo has faded away' (2015).[10] Now, Brendan Fraser as Elliot single-handedly carries the comic burden of the film, while Cook's sarcastic Devil becomes a sexy villainess played by Elizabeth

Figure 4.3 *Bedazzled* (2000): Elliot and the sexy Devil.

Hurley. As the casting alone suggests, the remake's intent is to fit the original story within the confines of a Hollywood romantic comedy, replacing its satire with a coming-of-age teenage flick.

Whereas the first *Bedazzled* failed to attract a wide audience because it was very culturally specific, jokingly and grandiosely presenting London as portals to both Heaven and Hell, the remake's premise is more universal in order to achieve global appeal. This is already visible in its pre-credit sequence. The Devil's POV scans the entire planet via some modern satellite-like technology, before picking San Francisco and Elliot as her next victim. Elliot's wishes will then allow him to travel not only across time but also geographical borders, showing the Devil's powers and, by extension, the Hollywood remake's intention and ability to have a worldwide reach.

On a DVD commentary, Ramis claims that he enjoyed the humour of the original film but was confused as to what it was truly about. The remake can now be seen as his attempt at 'writing the wrong', adapting the earlier material as a coming-of-age story that involves adults instead of teenagers. The director explained the reasons behind his remake in the context of the Columbine massacre of 1999. Inspired by a few articles that suggested alienation and bullying as possible reasons for the attack, he decided to turn *Bedazzled* into a study of the insecurity of young people who find themselves under pressure to conform to magazine ads and to copy their favourite celebrities, trying to navigate through the turbulent time of adolescence (DVD commentary). Fraser's adult hero's multiple transformations embody different anxieties associated with puberty, such as extremely low self-esteem and unease with the opposite sex. Trying to forge an identity that will ensure peer appreciation has now become the driving force behind each of his wishes, as he pursues careers and identities commonly associated with power, popularity, privilege and success. While Stanley remained essentially the same person across all his wishes, consistently good-hearted, timid and gentle, Elliot starts off as an annoying and socially awkward character whose physical appearance and personality change wildly, allowing the actor to dazzle with numerous impersonations, but depriving the audience of the chance to build an emotional connection with the hero. Aided by a team of make-up artists and costume designers, Elliot's irritating character flaws disappear as he changes into a Colombian drug lord, a ginger-haired oversensitive guy, a gigantic basketball player, a successful author, a US president and, finally, in a deleted sequence – a heavy metal rock star.

On the surface, it seems that, in line with the original, Elliot's pursuit of love is identical to Stanley's. Upon closer scrutiny, however, it appears that Alison Gardner (Francis O'Connor) is now not only the object of his desire but, being a popular girl at work and quite a catch, also a status symbol. Each wish manifests Elliot's craving for peer acceptance and becomes an opportunity to not only possess the girl of his dreams, but also to impress and win the respect of his colleagues. Therefore, instead of the Devil, it is Elliot's co-workers who re-appear in each episode, impacting its development to a smaller or greater degree. Fraser aptly compares the two versions in the following way: 'That film was more skewed towards skewering church and state and British politics. It was very much a film that was in step with its times. This one is also about church and state, but more about interpersonal sexual politics, what it means to be attractive, to have power in society, what it is to be desirous of a better life' (quoted in Spelling 2000b: 64).

In a way similar to Donen's film, each instalment ends up with Elliot's symbolic castration, instead of helping him with his greatly diminished ego. In the first one, when he wakes up next to Alison in his beautiful Colombian mansion, the first thing he does is to jump out of bed to inspect his property, carefully adjusting his original Van Gogh's *Sunflowers* and rejoicing in the luxury of his home and estate. Alison is his fiery Hispanic wife, who not only despises him but also betrays him with her English-language tutor, causing his public humiliation. In the next fantasy, Elliot is the most sensitive ginger-haired and freckled man on the planet, who weeps at the sight of the setting sun on the beach and composes songs about 'our friend the dolphin' and a sonnet about his girlfriend's hair. It seems, however, that he is more in touch with his feelings than Alison's, who becomes so sexually frustrated that she leaves him for the first random man who comes along and is able to satisfy her physical needs. The episode with Elliot as a successful NBA basketball player predominantly focuses on his physical prowess and popularity with the crowd and only briefly features Alison at the end. She is a sports journalist who loses interest in him the minute it turns out that his massive height does not translate into a massive male appendage. Since his dreams of money, sensitivity and physical strength all prove disastrous, Elliot wishes to be educated, articulate and well-endowed. In some respects, this recalls Stanley's first wish, except, once again, Elliot's focus is placed on his rapport with others rather than on Alison. Here, he is an award-winning author at the centre of an exclusive dinner party whose guests, played by his co-workers, are in awe of his intellect. When Elliot and Alison do finally hit it off, it transpires that he is gay. Tired of asking for material things or amazing talents, he decides to become a US president next, only to realise that the Devil turns him into Abraham Lincoln on the evening of his assassination.[11] In the end, disappointed by his wishes, Elliot seeks solace in a local church. The institution is not mocked or criticised. The only irony comes from the fact that the priest calls the police to arrest him following his strange confession. In jail, he meets a mysterious African-American inmate who represents divine intervention and provides him with comfort. Once Elliot drops all pretence and accepts who he is, he is rewarded with a less glamorous and more down-to-earth version of Alison. His transformation from an unlikable office worker into a viable romantic lead at the film's closing shows how self-belief and integrity always pay off. The ending's 'grade school moralising and tacked-on feel' appears 'patronising, pat and pathetic, and it nearly ruins the whole film' (Spelling 2000a: 22).

When it comes to the Devil, the idea to replace Cook's intellectual and verbose character with Hurley seems to have been partly inspired by the promotional materials for the earlier film. The US marketing campaign focused on Raquel Welch as the film's main selling point, even though she had a relatively small role in the film. The poster features Stanley looking down at her impressive cleavage, totally mesmerised by her 'busty substances'[12] clad in a red bikini. The remake's poster design similarly centres on Hurley in a revealing red top. The previous relationship built on class contrast for comic effect now instead relies on gender difference; from the start, the Devil manipulates the hero with her devilish female charms, seducing him into signing a contract to part with his soul. If the original presented male fantasies of female attractiveness via Margaret's numerous impersonations, from Lolita to a hot housewife, the remake redirects these fantasies to the Devil. Indeed, throughout the film, she becomes a visual spectacle for the viewer, depicting stereotypical representations of male erotic desires, including a cheerleader, a nurse, a cop, a traffic warden, a Britney Spears lookalike from her 1999 hit album 'Baby One More Time' and the ultimate temptress – Eve with a serpent.

Casting Hurley had further consequences for the entire film, creating an unresolvable paradox in the story. Since the Devil's feminine charms overpower the conventionally less attractive Alison, numerous viewers found Elliot's decision to sell his soul for his co-worker unbelievable at best. Young explains it well:

> The banter and buddy aspect of the original is replaced by the sexual titillation of Hurley's temptress version. A problem with this approach is that Fraser's Elliot character enters into the agreement hoping to win over his dream girl Allison (Frances O'Conner) so the fact that he's being lured into his deal by the hotness of Hurley diminishes our belief that Elliot would sell his soul for this girl. (2015)

Whenever Elliot is returned from his dream-cum-nightmare with his tail between his legs, it is Hurley's Devil who welcomes him back in an outrageous and stereotypically sexy outfit, as if to rub in his failure while forcing him to get back on his feet. To what extent his actions are, therefore, motivated by his genuine feelings for Alison, as opposed to his lust for the Princess of Darkness, remains ambiguous. Unlike in the original, the Devil's manipulation of the hero is no longer based on intellect or class difference but physical attraction, shown best in their first encounter at a bar when Elliot is speechless and in awe of her beauty. This time, the Devil is intimidating because of her cover-girl attractiveness and overt sexiness, alongside her material status symbolised by her Lamborghini Diablo. The fact that Elliot is continuously kissed, stroked and patted by her, without ever being able to reciprocate, as he is upstaged on all levels by the sexually liberated and successful female devil, adds insult to injury and augments his sense of failure and emasculation.

In the original, Cook's red socks were the only symbolic visual indicator of his devilish nature. Hurley, by contrast, flaunts red in several figure-embracing and revealing outfits – bikinis, tight little dresses, fur coats and leather suits – with her female assets being served up so much on a plate that one wonders whether the film is not caricaturing her to-be-looked-at-ness. Significantly, a whole separate featurette on a DVD edition of the film is devoted to her wardrobe, with a designer praising the actress's strong fashion sense and devotion to brands such as Versace. For instance, Versace created the famous black dress held together by gold safety pins that catapulted Hurley into the mainstream media's attention when she wore it to the premiere of Hugh Grant (her then partner)'s film, *Four Weddings and a Funeral* (Newell, 1994). Hurley now owns a beachwear company, launched five years after *Bedazzled*, and to this day dazzles in her swimwear, promoting her label with her ageless beauty as if to prove that she has, indeed, some supernatural age-defying Satanic powers. Beyond identical sunglasses, the only similarity with Cook's Devil is her English nationality and accent. These serve as a tribute to the British original, but at the same time

Figure 4.4 *Bedazzled* (2000): The Devil wears Versace.

exploit two common movie clichés: having a Brit cast as the villain of the piece and using the English accent as a sign of class and sophistication. This motif is repeated in the recent Netflix series *Lucifer* (2016–21). In fact, it seems that Hurley's presence is less reminiscent of Cook than of Joan Collins' devilish Alexis from *Dynasty* (1981–89), becoming a contemporary stand-in for Collins' deep voice, elegance, regular facial features and villainous disposition.

Cook's Devil's rebellion and criticism of the system is gone from the remake. At the end of the film, Hurley's Devil plays chess with God and looks approvingly at Elliot's newfound happiness. The American remake implies that good and evil are complementary forces whose agents, operating amongst humans, work towards achieving balance and the greater good. This spiritual and moralising dimension is significantly at odds with the premise of the original *Bedazzled*, which was highly suspicious of any doctrine and anti-establishment in nature. Instead of rebelling against God, Hurley's Devil does not challenge or subvert the old order but seems to sustain and support it.

Thus, looking at all the modifications that the remake underwent shows how the new version tries to have a global appeal by feeding into the popularity of romantic comedies, teenage films and masculinity-in-crisis films of the time, such as *American Beauty* (Mendes, 1999), released only a year earlier. *Bedazzled* tackles the subject of male insecurities, re-inventing its comedic potential to suit the youth market. Instead of the controversies of *American Beauty*, we have the uplifting story of Elliot's self-discovery and growth, while also being titillated by the presence of Hurley's alluring Devil. Compared to the earlier version, the new one, as Bob Aulert observes, is 'a little too Politically Correct for its own good. It takes far fewer chances and potshots, and as a result both offends and entertains less than the original did' (n. d) – all in an effort to stay within a PG-13 certification, unlike the original's adults-only rating.[13]

THE WICKER MAN (HARDY, 1973)/(LABUTE, 2006)

Because of its patchy release and sketchy distribution deal, *The Wicker Man* (Hardy, 1973) was forgotten for many years. Upon its rediscovery in 1977 during its second US release, it received generous coverage in *Cinefantastique* magazine, which pronounced it to be the 'Citizen Kane of horror'. Since then, it has literally managed to rise from the ashes and to become continuously adapted and referenced in various forms and formats, thus slowly infiltrating popular culture. In 1978, Robin Hardy turned it into a novel. In 1986, The Burning Man Festival was established in Nevada, which continues to attract thousands of participants every August to witness the burning of a huge human effigy, although its creators deny any connection to the film. In 2000, the British heavy metal group Iron Maiden released a song called 'The Wicker Man' in a tribute to the film, and in 2016, another British band, Radiohead, premiered a stop-motion animation video 'Burn the Witch', which closely mirrors its plot. In March 2018, the UK's largest amusement park, Alton Towers, opened a wooden Wicker Man rollercoaster ride, featuring a burning effigy through which visitors pass on their way to a sacrificial ceremony. The theme of a cop investigating murders in a quiet English village was also parodied in the BBC comedy series *The League of Gentlemen* (Bendelack, 1999) and then later in Simon Pegg and Edgar Wright's now-classic comedy *Hot Fuzz* (Wright, 2007) (see Archer 2017: 151–60). Aside from parodies, the idea of a cut-off village practising pagan rituals has recently resurfaced in the HBO horror series, *The Third Day* (2020–), starring Jude Law. This reveals that *The Wicker Man* to this day functions as an important point of reference in the genre and that its appeal still holds.

All these examples indicate that, when in 1999 the BFI finally included *The Wicker Man* in its list of 100 best British films at number 96, they were only stating the obvious.[14] At the turn of the millennium, *The Wicker Man*'s established position made it a likely contender for Hollywood remaking, which could not only improve on its forerunner's imperfections caused by budgetary restraints, but also update its conflict for the new millennium. In March 2002, *The Guardian* announced that Nicolas Cage was 'keen to land the lead role in Neil Labute's [sic] remake of cult British horror classic' ('In Brief: Cage in

The Wicker Man'). The same month, during a press conference at the Brussels Fantasy film festival, Lee also mentioned the possibility of the remake with Cage, provoking a few uneasy chuckles from within the audience. Lee revealed that he might be approached to play in the update, which he found unfathomable because it was to be located in America and feature an American hero, leaving no room for the return of his Scottish villain. As one fan stated on IMDb in 2004, '[r]umours that Hollywood is going to give this superb film its remake treatment are a cause for real concern' (penseur 2004). When the new version finally entered the production phase, *The Guardian* reminded its readers that '[b]oth Hardy and Christopher Lee, who played Lord Summerisle, have previously expressed doubts over a new version of the pagan horror, questioning efforts to update the classic' ('Cage to Rekindle *Wicker Man* Remake' 2005). The title of *The New York Times* article – 'Remake "The Wicker Man"? Now That's Scary?' – written a month before the film hit the screens, conveyed well the atmosphere surrounding the project, with fans and director Hardy reportedly watching 'warily from the sidelines' (Lyons 2006).

Before analysing whether any of these trepidations were well-founded, I will first look at the original to see what makes it so unique and loved to this day while posing a possible challenge for its remake. Three issues will be scrutinised: the film's topicality, making it very much a product of its times; its generic originality; and, finally, its conflict based on two different belief systems at the roots of which lies a hidden class power structure.

Similar to Donen's *Bedazzled*, Hardy's *The Wicker Man* was a thoughtful response to society at the time. However, rather than focusing on the capital and its Swinging mythos, it moves the action out onto the fringes by depicting an isolated Scottish island. The island's inhabitants resemble a hippie commune that has not only rejected industrialisation in favour of pre-industrial agrarian culture but also returned to pagan practices. The film serves as an excellent example of how 1960s counterculture came to manifest itself through 'hippy environmentalism and back-to-nature rhetoric' (Smith 2009: 59). It also shows the backlash at that time against 'the blind faith in technological and economic progress that had evolved since the end of World War II', which in the 1960s was replaced by scepticism and pessimism, with youth culture embracing utopian alternatives (Fahlenbrach 2014: 83). To many, the film 'questions the hegemonic values of Christianity, sexual repressiveness and capitalist modernity – values frequently challenged in the countercultural climate of Britain in the early 1970s, particularly among "hippies" and "pagans"' (Harper 2012: 155).[15]

Generically, *The Wicker Man* has caused some confusion to critics and viewers, because it blends numerous conventions, from the detective genre and folk musical to horror, showing that much of British cinema in the 1970s 'was marked by a distinct hybridity' (Newland 2013: 23). It is only quite recently with the growing popularity of a new horror subcategory – folk-horror, also known as rural-horror and even rural-gothic (see Murphy 2013: 77) – that, finally, the film began to fit in somewhere. Chloé Germaine Buckley believes that the name 'originates with British director, Piers Haggard, in an interview for *Fangoria* magazine, as a description for the 1971 film, *Blood on Satan's Claw*' (2019: 23). But, in fact, it only really came to prominence in 2010, when Mark Gatiss used it as an umbrella term for several British films in his BBC4 documentary *A History of Horror*. According to Peter Hutchings, rural horror consists of the following features:

> Borders and peripheral settings loom large in this type of horror, among them deserted beaches, inaccessible islands, and isolated woods and marshes. However, so do apparently more reassuring settings such as, most of all, the village. Indeed it is probably here that British rural horror is at its most unsettling, rendering strange and dangerous what many think of as the ideal community. (2015)

The Wicker Man – 'in which a remote regional community, and ancient customs and archaic superstitions, dismissed or marginalised by clever-clogs city folk, wreak havoc upon forces of modernity, order and authority' (Pratt 2016) – is now regarded as the genre's most splendid representative.

The film is based on Anthony Shaffer's screenplay; similar to *Sleuth* (1972), it is also structurally based on the detective story, while revolving around class power games that prove to be at the root of the conflict. The idea was loosely inspired by David Pinner's novel *Ritual* (1967) and Sir James George Frazer's *The Golden Bough: A Study in Comparative Religion* (1890). However, by directly linking pagan rituals to the 1960s counterculture movement, it differs from most other examples of folk horror, such as *Witchfinder General* (Reeves, 1968) or *Blood on Satan's Claw* (Haggard, 1971),[16] as it is firmly set in the present and devoid of any medieval or period elements. To emphasise its contemporality, the film begins with the following introduction: 'The producer would like to thank the Lord Summerisle and the people of his island off the West Coast of Scotland for this privileged insight into their religious practices and for their generous co-operation in the making of this film'. According to Paul Newland, the title card poses a fundamental question about the film's relationship to the contemporary moment (2008: 120).

The film starts with a bird eye's view of the island, from Sergeant Howie (Edward Woodward) 's plane.[17] According to Shaffer's screenplay, '[n]o terrain since Arcadia was ever so fecund. The meadows are dense with spring field flowers and everywhere, standing in long orderly ranks, are fruit trees heavy with blossom' (quoted in Brown 2000: 152). The film captures that feeling, portraying the island's 'lush vegetation and tropical flora' that 'evoke an exotic mysteriousness' and create the image of a rural folk idyll and a hippy commune in one (Newland 2008: 120). The community appears to be prospering through growing apples for export. However, just as in the case of the remake of *Bedazzled*, which features the fruit in many scenes to suggest deceit and corruption, here the island's apple-growing business in unfriendly climatic conditions raises suspicions, suggesting that most of our initial assumptions might prove false.

When Sergeant Howie starts his investigation into the disappearance of a teenage girl, Rowan Morrison, to his surprise nobody gives any acknowledgement of her existence. As he wanders around the village looking for clues, he also discovers that the villagers practise pagan rituals, such as naked girls jumping over a bonfire or couples mating on the village green at night. This upsets his deeply held beliefs, as we find out that he is a devout Christian and a repressed virgin. The island is governed by an aristocratic leader, indicating that class is a significant factor in the creation, propagation and sustenance of its belief system and the mystique surrounding its Lord, played with aplomb by Christopher Lee. Since the islanders insist that they cannot cooperate unless he obtains Lord Summerisle's authority, the pious sergeant visits the mysterious figure in his grand mansion overlooking the village. There, he finds that his harsh criticism of the island's 'degenerate practices' that combine 'aspects of traditional, pagan folk culture with the contemporary counter-culture' (Newland 2008: 119) meets with Lord Summerisle's calm and erudite explanations. Of course, they are jumping naked over a fire; it would be foolish to do so in clothes – so he proclaims and then goes on to calmly explain that God had his chance and quite simply 'blew it'.

Figure 4.5 *The Wicker Man* (1973): Sergeant Howie meets Lord Summerisle.

However, the idyllic presentation of the island, whose inhabitants are unfamiliar with the concept of sinning, as they live outside of social norms and constraints, is gradually put into question, just as the film begins to sabotage genre conventions. When Howie rejects sexual advances from the innkeeper's enchanting daughter Willow (Britt Ekland), he does not realise that his actions have inadvertently sealed his fate. As Allan Brown observes, *The Wicker Man* subverts conventional horror tropes, because rather than lead to death, sex is Howie's only chance to survive (2000: 67–68). In the final moment of the film, the real purpose of his visit is finally revealed. Suspecting that Rowan is going to be sacrificed during the May Day celebrations to prevent another failed apple crop, Howie joins in with the procession dressed up and masked as Punch, the fool. When he spots a girl dressed in white with a garland of flowers around her neck and hands tied, he instinctively runs to try to save her. However, it is all an elaborate charade to mislead him, revealed as the Lord congratulates Rowan on her performance and Howie for splendidly fulfilling his role of a perfect human sacrifice – king-like, virginal and foolish. In the final gruesome scene, almost Christ-like, Howie is dressed in a white sacrificial robe and carried into a huge wicker man effigy at the top of the cliff where he is then burned alive. If throughout the film, his conservatism, repression, narrow-mindedness and patronising attitude towards the islanders turn him

Figure 4.6 *The Wicker Man* (1973): The perfect sacrifice.

into 'a flawed and essentially dislikeable character' (Newland 2008: 119), in the end Howie becomes a victim as we realise the precariousness of his situation. In his final moments, his behaviour also diverges from that of a typical male hero of the horror genre. As he is about to meet his end, Howie exhibits emotions that Carol J. Clover classifies as feminine such as 'crying, cowering, screaming, fainting, trembling, begging for mercy' (2000: 157). Whereas in slasher films men tend to be killed quickly or off-screen, this is not the case in Hardy's film, whose last few minutes depict Howie's growing physical and emotional terror, typically associated with female characters (see Clover 2000: 157). As his composed recitations of biblical verses turn into howling screams, the islanders, men, women and children chant, joyfully looking on.

Examining the ending, Justin Smith finds that it reveals the inherent dangers of 'the seductive power – and the repellent violence – of alternative systems of belief presided over by symbolic "bad fathers"' (2009: 59). Howie's final warning ultimately resonates the longest as he cries out: 'If the crops fail, Summerisle, next year your people will kill you on May Day'. This recalls another British horror, *Eye of the Devil* (Thompson, 1967), where a ritual sacrifice of the marquis (David Niven) sustains the community's prosperity. It also indicates that Howie, with his policeman badge, is only a stand-in for the island's true ruler, giving the ending a sense of foreboding irony. As it turns out, Lord Summerisle inherited the island from his free-thinking Victorian grandfather, who purchased it back in the nineteenth century, banished Catholic religion and restored its old pagan beliefs. This distorts the idea of a contemporary hippy community and suggests that under the veneer of counterculture comradery Lord Summerisle is using the locals for his own benefit. As David Bartholomew observed in *Cinefantastigue* in 1977:

> We wonder if Summerisle, as Howie suspects, is not using these people as pawns – as his grandfather did, to a certain extent, in reintroducing 'the old gods' to the island to allow him to continue his botanical studies – for more conventionally criminal purposes, like a pot of gold in the basement, or for personal selfishness.

Even though, as Paul Newland argues, 'the people of Summerisle are freely operating beyond the reach of a modern culture industry' and 'enjoy a measure of socio-cultural freedom', as they 'can still be seen to be producing their own culture "from below"' (2008: 121), it soon becomes clear that Lord Summerisle runs the place like a feudal lord. He yields power over the entire community by self-appointment as its spiritual leader. Benjamin Franks also agrees: 'Whilst the Summerisle community is presented in the film as superficially idyllic – there is sexual licence, a strong sense of social solidarity and an approach to the natural world that fears neither death nor guilt – it is nonetheless governed by a rigid and unequal power structure' (2005: 67). He claims that there is a clear division between the governor and the governed on the island, as well as 'a rigid division of labour, with characters assigned roles by occupation ("doctor", "fisherman", "librarian" and "school-teacher")' (Franks 2005: 74–75). Lord Summerisle is no Stephen Gaskin with his hippie 'farm' community project founded two years before the film's release; rather, as Lee observes, he is a 'benevolent tyrant' who is 'both king and priest in one' (quoted in Bartholomew 1977). The layout of the village continuously reminds it inhabitants of the Lord's total control over the island. Its hierarchy is dominated by his imposing mansion located on the outskirt and overlooking the village from a hilltop, shot on location in the impressive Culzean Castle, once the seat of the Chief of Clan Kennedy. Thus, it appears that, as Leon Hunt observes, 'it is aristocracy who really keep the old religions going' (2002: 96), using it, according to Brown, as 'a method of social control' (2000: 69).[18]

There is no doubt that Lee's earlier Hammer roles as Count Dracula (1958–76) also feed into our perception of this character as a potentially dangerous aristocratic villain, in addition to Lee's strong identification with the role. Lee, the son of a Countess whose lineage could be traced back to Charlemagne, claimed that Lord Summerisle had been modelled on him and considered it his best and favourite role: 'And I know that Tony had me in mind when he wrote it. He knows me and my career. You can say that Summerisle is an amalgam of many roles I have played on-screen. Figures of power, of mystery, of authority, of presence' (quoted in Bartholomew 1977). The actor even admitted that his delivery of the lines was identical to the way he spoke and that he could be equally dangerous when crossed (quoted in Bartholomew 1977).[19] His strong association with the role could explain why the Lord who looks like an island native in his elegant kilt makes no effort to speak with a Scottish accent.

Hardy's film is usually discussed in terms of a conflict between two forces – one represented by the policeman, who stands for repression, and the other represented by Lord Summerisle, who stands for permission (Smith 2009: 59). Franks offers another possibility, however, claiming that the former represents 'liberalism, modernity and democracy', while the latter stands for 'tradition, pre-modernity and authoritarianism' (2005: 70). When looked at from this perspective, *The Wicker Man* reveals, as Tanya Krzywinska argues, a 'suspicion of, but also fascination with, "the mad, bad and dangerous to know" aristocracy' (2008: 80). Made four years after the brutal Manson Family attacks in California, which heralded the end of the 1960s and its hippie counterculture, *The Wicker Man* shows the collapse of that same dream as it degenerates into a nightmare. But whereas in the US the infamous cult was in the thrall of an unemployed ex-convict, on British soil the islanders are mesmerised by a sophisticated aristocratic landowner, whose hippie commune is a cleverly run fiefdom.

As Ethan Alter observes, to remake the original conflict successfully, LaBute would have had to find a contemporary equivalent that could deliver 'an equally potent punch' (2006: 50). Considering that the original film depicted a conflict between two different and irreconcilable belief systems, the idea of LaBute directing the update for the modern audience seemed like an interesting choice. He had converted to Mormonism in the 1980s, only then to be disowned by the church in 2004. However, there was to be another surprising turn of events. As Charles Lyons of *The New York Times* explained, '[w]hen they finally catch up with the remake, Mr. Hardy and devotees of the original will learn that Mr. LaBute – the 45-year-old playwright whose debut film "In the Company of Men" examined male cruelty towards women – has rediscovered the gender wars in his new version'. According to Lyons, the director 'was interested in probing the assumed white male authority position that Mr. Cage's character represents, and the inevitable power struggle between men and women' (2006).

The film reveals LaBute's insecurities as a director new to the horror genre, which explains why he includes more numerous visual and thematic allusions to other horror classics than in its immediate predecessor. As Jenny McDonnell claims, this makes the remake look 'like a hodgepodge of any number of better films' (2006: 122). Starting with paratextual materials, the poster shows a girl in a white dress with a garland of flowers on her head. This image alludes to the original film, but at the same time places the remake firmly within the tradition of such American folk horror classics as Stephen King's *Children of the Corn* (1977), first adapted in 1984 by Fritz Kiersch, whose success then spawned a series with ten more instalments. The poster also references the British version of *The Village of the Damned* (Rilla, 1960) and its American remake (Carpenter, 1995), by making the child's white pupils its central image. It thus shifts the attention away from the original poster featuring the wicker effigy to the girl's eerie look, becoming an important indicator of how the remake will twist and transform the original film's premise.

The idea of the battle of the sexes seemed to take *The Wicker Man* in a new direction. According to Alter, '[t]hroughout his career, LaBute has regularly been accused of being a misogynist, a charge he's often managed to dodge by maintaining that the men in his work are as unlikable, if not more so, than the women' (2006: 50). Therefore, it was intriguing to see how he would now play out this gender conflict, and to what extent the remake would confirm or challenge the perception of LaBute as a provocateur 'accused of misogyny, misanthropy and obscenity' (Bigsby 2007: 251). When the film was finally released on 1 September 2006, it became evident that Warners had a good reason for concern. Leydon argues:

> When a major studio release with two Oscar-winning stars opens without press previews, one assumes the distrib is trying to hide the pic

from critics. In the case of Neil LaBute's remake of 'The Wicker Man', however, it's entirely possible that Warners indeed wanted to conceal a ludicrous misfire from auds as well. Once derisive word of mouth starts to spread, only connoisseurs of high camp and curious devotees of disasters will be queuing up at the box office. (2006: 8)

Now it appeared that the remake could be bound to follow in its predecessor's footsteps, repeating Warners' distribution nightmare from 1973 and, even more uncannily, replicating the original's fate by becoming a cult classic, but for entirely different reasons.

Unlike other cult British films discussed in this book, which are all male-centred with women serving a more decorative function, Hardy's *Wicker Man* gave them more substance. This, together with the original's denouement which featured Lee's Lord Summerisle dressed up as a woman for May Day celebrations as he becomes 'transformed from patriarchal power to matriarchal priestess' (Claydon 2010: 138), may have inspired LaBute's gender-reversed casting.[20] The remake also continued the theme of male/female relations and betrayal explored in his earlier cinematic and theatre works. Having grown tired of the continuous religious conversation around his films and his persona, LaBute explained his idea to the studio executives in the following way: 'I would, for the most part, strip out all the religious discussion, because they did it quite well in the first one'. He then added that he was 'much more interested in this even deeper-rooted male/female theme. It is almost like the white American male nightmare [. . .] the idea of women ruling the world. Let me give you a taste of what that is' (Bigsby 2007: 251).

The film opens with a motorcycle cop by the name of Edward Malus (Nicolas Cage), who witnesses a traffic accident and unsuccessfully tries to save a pretty little girl in a red cardigan and her mother from a burning car. Thus, whereas the original finishes in a blaze, the remake opens with the theme of death by fire. Plagued by guilt, the cop takes anti-depressants and hallucinates, repeatedly seeing the girl in red. This alludes to another British horror classic, Nicolas Roeg's *Don't Look Now* (1973), with which the original was associated not only via genre but also because they were released as a double bill in the US.[21] It also introduces one of many in a long list of cinematic allusions to other horror classics from the 1970s and beyond. To recuperate his nerves, Malus is granted leave of absence during which he unexpectedly receives a letter from his old flame, Willow (Kate Beahan), who asks him to help her find her missing daughter, Rowan (Erika-Shaye Gair). Malus travels to an isolated island off the coast of contemporary Washington State to look for her, motivated by guilt and romantic feelings towards his old girlfriend. As Malus is approaching the island on a plane, the scene is less reminiscent of Hardy's film than of Christopher Nolan's remake of the Norwegian crime drama *Insomnia* (2002), which equally draws 'on well-established tropes of the outsider lawman arriving at a remote frontier town to bring law and order' (Herbert 2009: 151). Unlike the Scottish island seductively portrayed as a land of fruitful harvest and exotic beauty, this one is a hostile place whose inhabitants keep bees rather than grow apples (quite conveniently Malus is allergic to bee stings). It resembles an Amish village with the women's clothes and the dwellings recalling old westerns and colonial times. LaBute draws from the Hollywood western tradition with its classic oppositions between civilisation and wilderness. Once on the island, Malus comes across three older women who reference Shakespeare's *Macbeth*'s Weird Sisters, which is meant to unsettle the audience by showing that the hero's future in the new location is predetermined by forces beyond his control. It also hints at the idea that these hippy-looking islanders are not really committed to ecological conservation or practice 'good' witchcraft, but are in fact agents of evil and destruction, perpetuating the witch stereotype of the Early Modern period (Germaine Buckley 2019: 34). Some islanders look disfigured as a result of in-breeding, and a pair of spooky old blind twins references Roeg's classic. In the end, it turns out that Willow purposefully seduced Malus ten years earlier to get pregnant so that she can now trick him into coming to her island to be sacrificed. Willow is the future queen bee of the colony, and Rowan, who is now not only the bait but also Malus' daughter, sets her dad on fire in the wicker effigy. Where Sergeant Howie made a perfect victim thanks to his virginity and religious zeal, Malus is sexually active and does not seem to follow any religious creed. Having fulfilled his mating function, just like a drone bee, he now must die. Before he is carried into the wicker effigy, however, his kneecaps are broken, recalling Rob Reiner's *Misery* (1990); a helmet full of bees is shoved on his head, and then he is brought back to life with an epinephrine shot for the final ceremony. There is no explanation for this unnecessary cruelty, which seems largely decorative and serves no narrative function. His screams in the wicker effigy send the women into an almost orgasmic trance as they all chant: 'The drone must die'.[22] They are joined by the girl from the traffic accident and her mother, who miraculously re-appear at the site.

While this plotline seems to succeed in following Hitchcock's call for more tortured women on screen (quoted in Clover [1992] 2015: 42), it also subverts that convention since all females in distress are pretending and the only person in need of saving turns out to be a white patriarchal figure. This upset those audience members who had believed that casting Cage would lead to a different conclusion, such as one IMDb user who observed: 'Nicky Cage is remaking this movie, and hopefully at the end of it he doesn't sit in the wicker statue and cry while he is burned to death, while and [sic] 10 year old boy could easily break the door that is made of little sticks the diameter of a quarter' (DarekH 2006). By contrast, our hero is from the start presented as a failure, subverting any expectations created by the casting. First, he fails to save the girl and her mother from the burning car, and this trauma leaves him so scarred that he is unable to return to work. He continues to take numerous pills to alleviate his emotional pain and help him deal with the constant hallucinations of the tragic event. Once on the island, his behaviour becomes even more erratic: he repeatedly dozes off in unexpected situations, further indicating that he has lost all control. This stands in stark contrast to another Cage star vehicle released the same year – *World Trade Center* (Stone), which focuses on his cop character's survival skills and mental resilience under duress.

Instead of addressing the collision of two religions, LaBute uses the beehive analogy to depict a primal conflict between men and women. Films depicting matriarchal societies and female predators are nothing new. Even the beehive analogy has been previously explored, suggesting that LaBute may have in fact remade more than one film. His inspiration for the women's cult seems to have derived from another British picture, *Bees in Paradise* (Guest, 1944). This Gainsborough musical comedy is about a mysterious female island governed by a queen whose inhabitants refer to men as drones and use them for breeding purposes only. When a military plane with four British men crashes on its shore, it first appears that they have landed in a paradise full of scantily clad beautiful women, whose clothes and housing all bear beehive insignia. Then, it transpires that the island's law requires men to marry and two months later commit suicide by jumping off the cliff. The comedy finishes with the men waiting for a rescue operation joined by two women who are not happy with the island's cruel ways. Its story serves as an amusing response to the public's growing anxiety concerning the long-term consequences of women's increased integration into the workforce during World War II. But while comedy may allow filmmakers to get away with confronting any risky material, LaBute's beehive cult belongs to the realm of the horror genre, which tends to be particularly effective in illustrating current fears, paranoias and anxiety. When he resorts to 'another one of his patented battles of the sexes, in which naive men routinely find their lives destroyed by coldhearted shrews' (Alter 2006: 50), the women's caricature-like villainy provokes an adverse reaction and LaBute's beehive metaphor quickly transforms into a veritable hornets' nest.

In the original, Lord Summerisle was a charismatic spiritual leader whose pagan ways served as counterpoint to Howie's strict puritan beliefs. In the remake, Burstyn's Sister Summerisle represents the mother goddess of the island, introducing an entirely new power dynamic, with the island now populated and ruled by women and a handful of men used for labour and procreation. Leydon observes: 'Sister Summersisle (Ellen Burstyn), the serenely self-assured local leader, is a high-priestess type who runs the place as matriarchal fiefdom with an absolute minimum of 21st-century technology' (2006: 8). Burstyn's presence additionally creates strong associations with the horror genre, due to her role as the mother of the demonically possessed teenager in *The Exorcist* (Friedkin), released the same year as the original *Wicker Man*.

Figure 4.7 *The Wicker Man* (2006): Ellen Burstyn as the queen bee of the colony.

Thus, if the first *Wicker Man* depicted a society ruled by a calculating patriarchal lord, in LaBute's version the women unleash their primal instincts encouraged by their irrational, post-menopausal leader. Malus' ritual killing induces ecstatic reactions from the female crowd, implying that they have lost all reason. Krzywinska mentions that, according to classical Greek discourse, such enthusiastic worship of rural deities was believed to be unreasonable and the domain of women, slaves and rural people who were considered uncivilised. By contrast, male citizens' relation to the gods was characterised by scepticism and rationality (2000: 41). She points out that this gender division 'threads its way through Western history to the present day' (42), with LaBute's *Wicker Man* serving as its excellent example. Marion Gibson also argues that LaBute's adaptation draws from classical Greek discourse, as it seems based on

> the first century CE geographer Strabo's description of an island of Bacchus-worshipping women somewhere off the mouth of the Loire in his *Geographica*, rather than the passage of Caesar that inspired the 1973 *Wicker Man* [. . .] His Dionysian women allow no males on their island, travelling to the mainland once a year to find men with whom to procreate. They ritually murder one of their sisters annually, too, in a rite which includes rebuilding their temple. (2012)

By substituting the male leader with a female, LaBute swapped reason and rationality for primitive forces coded as feminine, perpetuating many-century-old gender stereotypes.

The film depicts women as deliberately cruel, enjoying inflicting pain on the protagonist without any logical explanation, except for the story that Sister Summerisle shares with Malus about her seventeenth-century Celtic ancestors who 'rebelled against the suppression of the feminine' and fled to America. As luck would have it, they settled near Salem. Witnessing persecution still being continued in the New World, they decided to migrate west and eventually set up a self-sufficient commune on an island, isolating themselves from the rest of the world. LaBute's female cult is, therefore, sustained by its fear of persecution and desire to avenge the wrongs done in the past, which is possibly why they subjugate all the men on the island, cut out their tongues and abort male foetuses. Unlike in the original film, the rebirth of the old religion is not in any way the result of economic expediency.

LaBute's idea of women becoming the dominant gender would have been interesting to explore, had it been done without resorting to a cliché. For example, Naomi Alderman's latest novel, *The Power* (2016), describes women's gradual takeover of the world. Initially excited about their newly acquired skill to send through their fingertips electric shocks that can be pleasurable in small amounts but lethal in large ones, women end up subjugating men, inflicting on them much physical and emotional pain – this leads to a global gender war. Thousands of years after the cataclysm, a new world order emerges, according to which men are the weaker and meeker sex and women are believed to be inherently strong and aggressive to protect their offspring. Where Alderman takes great pains to explain the process of power and gender reversal, drawing from Judith Butler's notion of gender performativity as well as Margaret Atwood's canonical *The Handmaid's Tale* (1985), LaBute resorts to the age-old notion of the powerful woman as an evil witch, reinforced by the islanders' disfigured appearances and references to the Salem witch trials.

The 1973 Summerisle community's religious customs were believable because the island was geographically removed, with little or no contact with the outside world. The same idea is nowhere near as convincing in modern America. We see some female islanders travel to a big city where they mingle with the rest of society, which means that they should also absorb influences from the outside world. Instead, the film shows how their actions penetrate and infiltrate the mainland. Like a sleeper-cell terrorist organisation, the women wait for the right moment to attack. The female police officer who consoled Malus after his failed attempt at rescuing the girl in the traffic accident is present at the final sacrifice. Her presence implies her involvement in the conspiracy from the beginning and proves that the islanders have influence and allies in positions of power and authority on the mainland working under cover.

Moreover, Malus' death is not only a carefully orchestrated long-term endeavour but also part of a much bigger plan. Thus, where Howie's death was unprecedented, in LaBute's update the sacrifice is not a matter of some temporary drastic measures to ensure the prosperity of the island, but rather the beginning of the women's serial project of killing men, creating the possibility for both a sequel and imminent apocalypse. Unlike the original ending, LaBute's finishes with a typical sequel hook, a card announcing 'Six months later', which shows Willow and her recruit, Sister Honey (Leelee Sobieski), seducing potential new male victims. The enchanted is a young policeman (James Franco) who is now bound to follow in Malus' footsteps as a growing non-diegetic sound of buzzing bees mixed with Cage's screaming indicates.

Examining reviews and IMDb user comments reveals that LaBute's depiction of women is perceived as misogynistic and offensive. Some even wonder whether his over-the-top portrayal of women's villainy towards their hapless victim was not actually meant as a comedy, especially when Cage's immaculately dressed cop in a white shirt and black tie suddenly karate-kicks a woman in the head and punches others in the face, knocking them out cold. Such moments of unexpected hilarity also include Malus' torture scene during which his character repeatedly screams: 'Not the bees!' Not surprisingly, the excerpt soon found its new rightful home on YouTube, featuring in numerous compilations and turned into mash-up videos, such as the one entitled 'Not the bees!' where Winnie the Pooh is chased by bees and screams 'You bitches!' in Cage's voice. As Ryan McDearmont explains:

> Oh yes. The bees. The bees, the bees, the bees. Picking up on what's now one of the most infamous bee related film sequences of all time, the internet quickly harvested *The Wicker Man* as fodder for endless memes and video gags in the 12 years since release. Anyone who's watched an 'Ultimate Bad Acting Compilation', or perhaps a 'Nicolas Cage Best Moments!' video on YouTube will surely recognize the scene: hundreds of agitated honey bees pour onto Cage's face as he screams like a banshee and writhes as if electrocuted. 'Not the bees!' he proclaims, jerking his head to shake off the invading insects. His intense movements and exclamations are answered only by the comically stony-faced onlookers, a set of actors and extras privileged enough to experience one of the greatest film freak-outs of all time. Carried by Cage's absurd energy, the scene is monumental in both stupidity and unintentional hilarity. (2018: 65)

Where in his final hour in order to retain his dignity Howie appealed to his Christian God, unwavering in his faith, Malus faces directly his perpetrators, repeatedly calling them 'You bitches!!!' and screaming 'Killing me won't bring your goddamned honey back!' These women are portrayed as

Figure 4.8 *The Wicker Man* (2006): 'The drone must die'.

witches and then dismissed as bitches, preventing any ground for a serious gender clash debate. If in his final moments, just like Howie, Malus expresses his deep convictions, then it appears that this supposedly good law-enforcing American cop – whose name stands for a breed of apples, an amalgam of 'male' and 'phallus', but also Latin for 'wicked' and 'evil' – also reveals his true misogynist face. It is perhaps for this reason that the torture scene and Cage's screams in the wicker effigy are perceived as comical by viewers who have been prevented from forming any kind of emotional connection with the character whose antics are so out of place.

In his defence, LaBute seems to imply that his version is a satire (see his interview with Kim Morgan [2017]). If its function is, in essence, to be a reaction to current trends, pinpointing the flaws ailing contemporary society, then what global anxieties could his nightmarish island microcosm represent? As Germaine Buckley observes, the early decades of the twenty-first century saw an increased post-feminist backlash against women in power. US rightwing commentators dismissed Hillary Clinton as a presidential candidate in 2016, claiming that she dabbled in magic, and in 2018 critics of former UK Prime Minister Theresa May portrayed her in a witch's hat in internet memes (Germaine Buckley 2019: 22–23). Such analysis, however, when applied to LaBute's remake, would require taking the film's premise seriously, but the majority of viewers, as seen from the analysis of IMDb comments, has chosen to laugh along instead. From this perspective, LaBute's project is now a disaster film deserving of its cult following for how the audiences responded to its concept, acting and dialogue. Jenny McDonnell finds that, 'read in relation to its obvious influences, *The Wicker Man* almost feels like four bad remakes: they add up to one farcical folly' (2006: 122).

CONCLUSION

The originals of *Bedazzled* and *The Wicker Man* show the collapse of a world built on fantasy. In *Bedazzled*'s case, it is the belief in women's sexual availability and promiscuity promoted in the 1960s; in the case of *The Wicker Man*, it is the aristocracy's dream to be able to construct a new belief system to retain their wealth. While Stanley is desperate to lose his virginity, Howie tries his hardest to keep his, as both battle their sexual frustrations when confronted with the sexual license around them and ask the divine to intervene. Both films take religion and Swinging 60s ideals for a satirical spin to offer insightful critiques of different oppressive systems. *Bedazzled* expresses sympathy for the Devil, who has lost his status in 1960s London where taboos are now the norm. *The Wicker Man* exhumes pagan gods to reinforce 1960s liberal views to tighten the ruler's grip over the community. But where Stanley and the Devil recognise their shared commonalities, Lord Summerisle's confrontation with Howie only fuels a conflict that is to continue unresolved.

Retaining the skeleton of the original stories but changing the gender of the key characters in the remakes resulted in creating a new power dynamic with often ambiguous results. Although on the surface the remakes of *Bedazzled* and *The Wicker Man* have little in common, as one is a romantic comedy and the other a horror film, both reduce female power by employing gender stereotypes while moving the stories into the twenty-first century. Significantly, where Cook's intellectual Devil challenged the old order and criticised his master, Hurley's sexy villainess works at his service, reducing her badness to an empty show. Cook's Devil was no longer a villain due to his depreciated social status. Hurley's, however, is not to be taken seriously due to her gender. In *The Wicker Man*, the women are portrayed as evil bitches and crazy witches dressed in old-fashioned colonial robes to hide their feminine charms, as LaBute looked to update the power games of the original film by using century-old gender stereotypes. As a result, his remake is strangely anachronistic when compared to the original film, whose story about an aristocrat manipulating a whole island for his benefit has never lost currency and rings especially true in contemporary Brexit-torn Britain (see Scovell 2017).

Last but not least, the *Bedazzled* and *The Wicker Man* remakes have one more thing in common. Where the original films asked some difficult questions and often provoked mixed reactions, the remakes, despite pertaining to different genres, both mainly succeed in providing their audiences with light-hearted laughs. While *Bedazzled*'s humour relies on heavily drawn caricatures of male inadequacies, *The Wicker Man* has gone on to gain a cult comedy following, becoming an unintentional disaster film, not unlike *The Room* (Wiseau, 2003). It is mostly remembered for Cage's meltdowns and histrionics. Both remakes offer absurd escapist humour, but neither seems to engage with the times in which they were made in productive or thoughtful ways.

NOTES

1. In 2004 and 2007, there were two other remakes (incidentally both starring Nicole Kidman), which cast women in formerly male roles. In Frank Oz's *The Stepford Wives*, Glenn Close plays a mad brain surgeon and genetic engineer who tries to create an alternative pre-feminist world, and in Oliver Hirschbiegel's *The Invasion*, Kidman plays a psychiatrist who saves the world.
2. See https://www.bfi.org.uk/news-opinion/news-bfi/lists/10-great-films-set-swinging-60s.
3. Bron was the first woman to ever appear in the Cambridge University Footlight's Revue and in The Establishment, a satirical cabaret set up by Peter Cook.
4. Bron interviewed by Peter Serafinowicz on stage at the BFI Southbank on 26 November 2012, to introduce *Bedazzled* for the Screen Epiphanies series produced in partnership with American Express.
5. See https://www.telegraph.co.uk/news/celebritynews/6759497/Peter-Cook-had-affair-with-Jackie-Kennedy.html or https://www.independent.co.uk/voices/columnists/david-lister/david-lister-peter-jackie-and-questions-never-asked-1836077.html.
6. In 2008, the Vatican officially absolved Lennon, blaming his lack of judgment on his class belonging: 'After so many years it sounds merely like the boasting of an English working-class lad struggling to cope with unexpected success'. See https://www.telegraph.co.uk/news/newstopics/howaboutthat/3497623/Vatican-forgives-Lennon-for-more-popular-than-Jesus-remark.html.
7. The film's provocative take on religion comes in many forms. For example, in the Devil's London headquarters, one of his party guests is a drunken cardinal who asks Stanley, still dressed up as a novice, for a dance. When Stanley wonders why Lucifer does not tempt a vicar in the street, the latter nonchalantly explains: 'He's one of ours'. At another point in the film, they discuss God's omnipresence and, to explain it, the Devil unexpectedly kicks Stanley's rear, saying that he saw God nestling in his trousers. He also contemptuously refers to the Biblical Eden as 'a boggy swamp just south of Croydon' and provocatively rewrites a newspaper headline from 'Pop stars in sex and drugs drama' to 'Pope stars in sex and drugs drama'.
8. This is the name of a character from one of their most popular sketches, 'One Leg Too Few', authored by Cook and performed by the duo.
9. The tradition may have faded in the US but is still strong on UK soil with Mitchell and Webb, Little Britain, Fry and Laurie, French and Saunders, and Gervais and Merchant, to mention the most obvious examples.

10. Young suggests that '[t]he only people today who could probably replicate that kind of chemistry would be Simon Pegg and Nick Frost. Those two could have done justice to the source material, and considering they're Brits, they would fit into the mould of Pete & Dud properly' (2015). Except, of course, that the remake of *Bedazzled* came out four years ahead of their first debut international hit *Shaun of the Dead* (Wright, 2004). A much more convincing update could involve Ricky Gervais as the Devil and Karl Pilkington as Stanley, since their comic interactions heavily rely on the aspect of bullying and intellectual difference.
11. The part where the remake treads closest to the original is in a deleted instalment that can only be watched on the DVD bonus materials. It is a *This Is Spinal Tap* (Reiner, 1984) spoof of sorts, in which Elliot is a heavy metal rock star in a contemporary equivalent to Stanley's and George's competing 1960s pop musicians in the original. Here, he is a blend of Ozzie Osbourne and Sid Vicious, with O'Connor as a Nancy Spurgeon caricature, whose dialogues are bleeped continuously for further comic effect. Their sex, drugs and rock'n'roll lifestyle is a perpetual emotional rollercoaster, photographed and filmed continuously by an ever-present film crew. The two have more physical contact than in any other episode, interchangeably kissing and hitting each other and finally making out on a table in front of everybody. As a rock star, Elliot is finally able to assert his masculinity and get the girl, albeit briefly, as he suffers from a cardiac arrest. However, thanks to an oxygen mask, he comes to and, true to fashion, lights a cigarette, igniting the oxygen and blowing everything up before going back on stage. The scene did not make it into the final cut, possibly because it was considered too risky or could have cost the film its PG-13 rating, thereby losing a large segment of its target audience.
12. This is a phrase often employed by Pete and Dud in their comedy sketches.
13. It has now been downgraded to GB-12 for a modern audience.
14. At the time of the ranking's publication, Shaffer was busy trying to get his own sequel filmed, and Canal +, who held world rights to the original, announced that they were looking to remake it with either Liam Neeson or Robert Carlyle as Sergeant Howie (Brown 2000: 180). In 2002, Hardy failed to raise funds for his new feature about a cult in Scotland and turned it into a novel, *Cowboys for Christ* (2006), before filming it under a new title, *The Wicker Tree* (2011), in an apparent reference to his earlier venture.
15. Yet, the film can equally function as an upholder of Christianity, as reported by Lee, who claimed that it was greatly enjoyed by Christian congregations in the very religious American Bible Belt (quoted in Brown: 2000: 122).
16. However, *The Wicker Man* shares a few surprising similarities with another cult horror film that was also released in 1973 – *Psychomania* (Sharp). The latter transplants American biking subculture onto British soil and in the process mixes ancient Druid stone circles, frogs, hippie elements and aristocratic roots with the belief in life after death. The protagonist is a member of an aristocratic family who commits suicide, returns to the living and becomes the leader of a motorcycle gang called The Living Dead, who go on a killing spree around the neighbourhood.
17. Even though the film was shot in autumn instead of spring, the island's unique microclimate was still perfectly rendered on screen, thanks to the ingenuity of the production team working on a very tight budget.
18. The island's religious practices have infiltrated all aspects of its life, from education and procreation to the system of governance that determines its economic prosperity. Significantly, the schoolteacher (Diane Cilento) is not only in charge of education, but also serves as the high priestess of the order and, quite conveniently, Lord Summerisle's lover. Hunt comments: 'This pagan revival begins as a matter of expediency, as a way of encouraging the islanders to make the land fruitful again, exploiting the volcanic soil

and warm Gulf stream' (2002: 96). Krzywinska shares this viewpoint, claiming that reintroducing paganism was at source driven by the requirements of a business venture (2000: 80). Franks also argues that Summerisle's 'irrational religious superstructure was constructed to maintain a rational entrepreneurial exercise. As Lord Summerisle explains to Howie over a sample of one of his cultivars, the "joyous old Gods" were reconstituted to increase economic efficiency and "rouse them [the workers] from their apathy"' (2005: 75).

19. Lee would also hold grudges. Over the years, he systematically blamed the producer Michael Deeley for *The Wicker Man*'s re-edit and loss of the film's negative.
20. Bartholomew found the actor's costume ludicrous, describing it as a 'frumpy housewifely frock, sneakers, and a wig that looks like the '60s Cher' (1977). My students, however, read Lee's long black hair as an uncanny foretelling reference to his later impersonation of Saruman in the *Lord of The Rings* (Jackson, 2001, 2002, 2003) trilogy.
21. An alternative poster design for the remake's DVD 'Director's Cut' features Cage holding the girl dripping water, in a stark visual reference to Roeg's haunting imagery.
22. There is an analogy here between Malus' function as the drone in the film and medieval reports of witches removing penises from their unsuspecting victims, both playing on men's castration anxieties and performance (see Asma 2009: 110–12).

CHAPTER 5

Remaking, Cultural Exchange and Personal Legacy: *The Limey*

Looking at the BFI list of 'Top 100 British films' of the last century reveals the importance of the 1960s in British film history, with twenty-six titles from the period dominating the ranking (and ten titles from the 1970s). This provoked Robert Murphy to conclude that 'the 1960s saw a greater number of significant and exciting films made in Britain than at any time before or since' ([1992] 2008: 278). Many of them are representatives of the British New Wave or Swinging London films and were made by such key British filmmakers as Nicolas Roeg, Ken Loach, Karel Reisz, Lewis Gilbert, Tony Richardson, Lindsay Anderson, John Schlesinger, Peter Collinson, Thomas Hardy and Mike Hodges. Of the twenty-six titles, some were also made by American directors who found their way to Britain at the time and even decided to make it their permanent home – Stanley Kubrick, Richard Lester and Joseph Losey. Most of these titles were financed by Hollywood majors, showing their undisputable impact on the visibility, global reach and creation of the British classics. Undeniably, something stirred in British cinema at the time of its brief international cultural dominance and, looking at the above names, it is no wonder that the so-called 'Long 60s' have become a subject of fixation for film scholars, critics and filmmakers alike, casting a shadow over generations of filmmakers to come.

It is to some of the period's iconic titles made by British and American filmmakers working in London that Hollywood would return three or so decades later during the period of rejuvenated interest in British cinema stateside. They did not discriminate against any genre, but rather chose films for their iconic status and cultural cachet. Another motivation was undeniably also a search for fool-proof stories and stock characters that could easily travel across the Atlantic and appeal to a global viewer once they became adequately transformed. While giving the old films a new spin, at the same time, the remakes provide the viewer with enough continuities, variations and repetitions to create interest in their makeovers and to satisfy many audiences, whether on a national, generational, gender or other level. The variety of adaptation strategies that they employ reveals a wide arsenal of tools developed to form and sustain the connections with the original works, while trying to rejuvenate them to close the gap of thirty years.

To this effect, narrative repetitions and continuities are most often achieved via similar plotlines which follow the originals quite closely. This allows viewers to compare and contrast their favourite car chase with its modernised rendition (*The Italian Job*), or characters' romantic entanglements as they are transformed from their 1960s equivalents to the present day, in the process undergoing class and gender modifications (*Alfie, Sleuth, The Italian Job, Bedazzled*). Any narrative extensions and reformations thus become most strikingly visible in the final moments of the remakes, where they assert their independence from the original works, while also succumbing to the requirements of traditional Hollywood masculinity heroism (*Get Carter, The Italian Job, The Wicker Man*) and its heterosexual normativity (*The Italian Job, Bedazzled, The Wicker Man*). This is very much at odds with what the British originals often offered. Where the remakes tread closest to the original British endings, rejecting upbeat moments, we get ambiguity and open-endedness instead of narrative closure, while additionally often positing a question about the protagonists' gender and sexual identity (*Alfie, Sleuth*). And when American protagonists mirror the fate of their British counterparts against generic conventions and casting expectations, their inability to save themselves and the world from impending doom seats uneasily with the audience, which accordingly translates into poor box office receipts (*The Wicker Man*).

Casting becomes another powerful tool with which to ascertain the remake's independence while forming a continuation with the previous works to show their mutual cross-cultural roots. Thus, as these remakes are involved in a cross-Atlantic journey that has been part and parcel of British-Hollywood film industries since at least the 1920s, most of them contain some level of cross-cultural casting to appeal to multiple audiences. These vary from token gestures of celebrity intertextuality cameos (*Get Carter, The Italian Job*) to becoming integral elements of the stories themselves, particularly when the main character is again British (*Alfie*). Whether cast in the main or secondary parts, such appearances function not only as veiled tributes to the original films, but also as references to and rejuvenated 'cultural replacements' of the original iconic British stars. Such is the case with Jason Statham in *The Italian Job* (Gray, 2003) as a stand-in for Michael Caine's cool working-class Cockney gangster, although Caine appears more inclined to endorse Jude Law as his new alter ego (*Alfie, Sleuth*). Even if a secondary character's Britishness follows on from the well-established cliché of casting a Brit as the villain of the piece, as in the case of Elizabeth Hurley in *Bedazzled* (Ramis, 2000), it still clearly channels Joan Collins as another famed British cultural export that became part of American cultural legacy.

Moreover, in choosing these films over others, Hollywood also often found ready-made generic blueprints that could easily be transformed back into Hollywood settings. Some of the originals themselves were already heavily influenced by such classic genres as gangster or western, allowing for a smooth and natural transition (*Get Carter*). In other cases, however, genre tweaking was required and demonstrates that the creators of these Hollywood remakes were less interested in responding to the current societal concerns, unlike their originals, than to the recent trends in the industry. As a result, *Bedazzled* (Donen, 1967) was transformed from a satire into a teenage romantic flick, whose popularity has not wavered since the1990s. *Alfie* (Gilbert, 1966; Shyer, 2004) was reshaped from a kitchen-sink comedy/drama into an Anglo-American romantic comedy to place it within a successful cycle of cross-cultural romance. The original *Italian Job*'s (Collinson, 1969; Gray, 2003) caper was modified as a heist film at the peak of its popularity at the beginning of the 2000s. In some instances, such genre modifications resulted in producing interesting hybrids between the two film cultures and traditions, such as when *Alfie* at first promises to be a romantic comedy, similar to a Hugh Grant vehicle, and delivers a morality tale instead.

Other than blending the two film cultures and cinematic traditions, the remakes often extend their boundaries in other ways, displaying the complexities of this form of narrative repetition that blends and crosses borders with other types of narrative continuation and renewal, such as the sequel (*Alfie*, *Sleuth*) or the reboot (*Get Carter*). The remake can, therefore, be seen as having a broad and encompassing function. Its boundaries extend, include and overlap not only with the sequel and reboot, but also with the re-adaptation (*Sleuth*). Some remakes operate via complex and extensive cinematic allusions, visible in *The Wicker Man*'s (LaBute, 2006) multiple tributes to horror classics whose function is to validate the director's venture into a new genre. The reboot can also acquire a new purpose other than kick-starting a franchise or series. Instead, it becomes an opportunity to redirect the route of a star's trajectory, as in the case of Sylvester Stallone's 'body reboot' in *Get Carter* (Kay, 2000), returning him to full functionality after his critically underappreciated effort at method acting in *Cop Land* (Mangold, 1997). The remake thus becomes a second chance in more ways than one. It offers an opportunity not only to iron out narrative ambiguities (*Alfie*), improve on unsatisfactory conclusions (*The Italian Job*, *Get Carter*, *Bedazzled*) or budgetary constraints (*The Wicker Man*), but also to smooth out a path in one's acting journey, clearing one's name, or returning to one's roots (*Alfie*, *Sleuth*, *Get Carter*). These Hollywood remakes of British films demonstrate, following Constantine Verevis, that the film 'remake has never been a static thing but a concept that is always evolving' (2017: 164).

In its effort at cultural, racial and gender diversity, the remake can also become a second chance at updating the gender and class representation of the earlier films, giving voice and agency to previously muted or insignificant characters. The main strategy of dealing with the previous class dynamic visible in all of the British originals lies in replacing it with gender conflicts and/or gender power games based on sexual frustration and desire (*Alfie, Sleuth, Bedazzled, The Wicker Man*). Here, the efforts vary and point to an uneasy balancing act between wanting to give women a more central role within the story, while continually objectifying them visually (*Alfie, The Italian Job, Bedazzled*). In the case of *The Wicker Man* remake, the portrayal of women resorts to clichés and offensive stereotypes, leading to accusations of misogyny. In such instances, the original film appears more progressive than its millennial counterpart and points to a worrying trend, not only within the industry, but also in society and politics at large, as these seem to take the gains of feminism for granted and thus assume that they can now be easily mocked and ridiculed. Here, it is important to note that even the so-called bad-ass female characters in the remakes that replace previously male roles or improve on their earlier dolly-bird versions still act on behalf of male authority (*Bedazzled*) or function as a reward for the all-conquering hero (*The Italian Job*). Racial diversity and inclusion, while mostly delegated to background characters (*The Italian Job, Bedazzled, Alfie*), nevertheless provide a powerful contrast with the earlier versions. However, despite a more democratic and politically correct representation in the 2000s, the white patriarchal figure's journey continues to dominate in all of the remakes, revealing certain limitations to their revisionist politics and their inherently conservative nature.

All the remakes were made from 2000 onwards, and it is useful to check their characteristics against a list of five provisional features that Verevis identifies in relation to new millennial remakes. These include their intermediality, transnationality, post-authorial character, as well as their coexistence with other versions and variations due to their 'proliferation and simultaneity' (2017: 158). The close analysis of all the case-studies supports his proposition. Their intermediality is noticeable, for instance, in the proliferation of user-created online content surrounding their release, particularly amateur mash-up videos that mushroomed in response to LaBute's controversial effort. Their transnational character is manifest in their complex and multiple cross-cultural transactions and influences, seen in casting choices and generic mutations. The importance of the figure of the post-auteur can be explored, among others, using LaBute's remake, which is not only discussed in the context of the original canonical text, but also understood as 'a filmmaker's desire to repeatedly express and modify a particular aesthetic sensibility and worldview' (Verevis, 2017: 156–57). And in the case of the *Bedazzled* remake, Harold Ramis' reputation as a comedy genius is a crucial factor in the reception and promotion of the new version, superseding the importance of the original's cult status. Finally, all of these remakes are available alongside the originals, allowing both to enjoy 'a more complementary relationship' (Verevis 2017: 159). Except for Ramis' *Bedazzled*, DVD reissues of the old classics accompanied, preceded or immediately followed the release of their remakes, becoming promotional materials for both films and opening them up to new interpretations. Numerous supplemental features contained within them encourage self-reflexive and interactive viewing. Through their multiple intertextual gestures, they invite audiences to compare and contrast both versions.

Summarising the adaptation strategies and features of Hollywood remakes of British films shows that in many ways it was Steven Soderberg's *The Limey* (1999) made at the turn of the millennium that can be traced as a precursor to this cycle of films. It not only precedes them chronologically but, more importantly, already exhibits most of the characteristics of the new millennial remakes and, in particular, their Anglo-American variant. Among them, one can include its balancing act between two forms of narrative repetition and continuation, the sequel and the remake, its multiple cinematic allusions, its heavy self-referentiality, its substantial reliance on cross-cultural casting, its post-authorial nature, its generic mutations and, finally, its gender, racial and age diversity. It is for this reason that Soderbergh's unofficial remake of Hodges' *Get Carter* (1971) stands out and, at the same time, becomes a perfect film with which to conclude the discussion on Hollywood remakes of iconic British films.

In hindsight, Soderbergh's film appears to sit between two important developments in the remake discourse and practice. On the one hand, it precedes the Anglo-American remake cycle, as mentioned above, and suggests ways and directions in which future remakes could tackle the legacy of the earlier films and their cross-cultural heritage. On the other hand, it follows on from a highly-publicised and criticised remake attempt, Gus Van Sant's *Psycho* (1998), which antagonised critics and viewers alike (see Verevis 2006b; Zanger 2006; Leitch 2003; Naremore 1999–2000). While it is impossible to know what Soderbergh thought of Van Sant's shot-for-shot concept, a comment he made on his website in 2014 about its religious faithfulness gives us some clues and explains why he decided to mash it up with Alfred Hitchcock's famed classic (1960). This edited video does not ask us to see both versions in a linear progressive order from some superior original vantage point to its debased copy. Instead, placing them side by side creates an opportunity to engage with them simultaneously and equally, obscuring chronology and creating a more hypertext-like experience. This personal homemade project reveals that Soderbergh's approach to remaking involves creative sampling, already visible in his 'mash-up' of Hodges' *Get Carter* with other classic British and American films from the period.

Despite there being no mention of *The Limey* as a remake outside of Soderbergh's comment that 'if we do our job right this is *Get Carter* as made by Alain Resnais' (quoted in Palmer 2011: 69), the film's affinities with Hodges' work and other iconic British and American titles from the period are writ large all over the film from start to finish. They reveal his fascination with 1960s and 1970s American and British cinemas, which, according to Mark Gallagher, is visible in his oeuvre (2013a: 84) and proves, as Verevis puts it, the 'unprecedented awareness of film history among new Hollywood filmmakers and contemporary audiences' (2004: 94). What differentiates this remake from the others discussed in this study, however, is an overt consciousness with which it not only samples the films from the past, but also engages with the period in which they were made on a thematic level.

Significantly, Jason Wood claims that *The Limey* was made during a time when Soderbergh was editing a series of interviews with Lester for the book *Getting Away With It* (1999). This makes it tempting to assume that, when he was directing the film, Soderbergh was also trying to 'put the 1960s into perspective, specifically the shift from optimism to disillusionment post 1967' (Wood 2002: 67). Thus, while *The Limey* is on one level quite simply a revenge story, on another level it is also about Soderbergh's own artistic journey, returning to his fascination with 1960s and 1970s cinema.[1] This period coincides with his teenage years, before he became a contemporary auteur with remaking sensibilities as one of his signature characteristics where 'his originality (if we can be permitted to use the word) consists in recycling, reiterating, repeating, and remaking the works of his cinematic predecessors' (Moses 2011: 283). Soderbergh's *The Limey* is thus a deeply self-reflexive work that comments on filmmaking, remaking, cultural exchange and personal legacies. For any filmmaker born too late to witness the revolutionary changes that occurred in society and art in the 1960s first-hand, yet deeply influenced by the period's achievements, these films, and remaking them, can become a window to that world. The originals often shocked the public with their new heroes and themes whose authenticity was aided by location-shooting, natural lighting and regional accents. Now, any filmmaker interested in remaking them has the opportunity to revisit some of the most creative and imaginative narratives while also exploring their own cinematic and cultural roots and artistic heritage. *The Limey* forges a link between the old and the new, the past and the present, and participates in a continued cultural dialogue between British and American cinemas with their unique but at the same time interconnected film cultures and histories. In this respect, Soderbergh's 'use of allusion and remakes demonstrates his knowledge of film history [. . .] not only to attract audiences with the familiar but also to take advantage of the assumption that the invocation of earlier movies has given him license to modify them' (Baker 2011: 124).

Unlike all the other remakes whose protagonists were updated and rejuvenated to fit in with the twenty-first century – a strategy that allows the original characters to live on, forever young through new incarnations – *The Limey* does something unusual: it places the character from the original story in a similar situation, but twenty-eight years later. The idea for the film was first conceived around 1977 by the then nineteen-year-old Lem Dobbs, who wrote it specifically for Caine at the height of the actor's career. It was forgotten and not picked up until two decades later, then finally filmed in 1999. This delay from conception to realisation had many consequences, as over time the script 'matured' alongside the characters contained within it and the lead for which it was initially intended. Come 1999, its main protagonist was no longer a thirty-something Cockney gangster but an ageing criminal, which both Dobbs and Soderbergh found very appealing. They comment on the DVD track how Hollywood films tend to avoid featuring mature protagonist and how they were pleased to break with that convention.

The Limey revisits *Get Carter*'s revenge motif, melancholy tone, the journey across two geographically and culturally distinct locations and many more nuanced plot details. At the same time, it continues and extends Soderbergh's authorial preoccupations, which Wood identifies as 'the difficulties of communication, the betrayal of trust and the spectres of the past' (2002: 11). As a remake, it reuses key motifs of the earlier film. At the same time, as a sequel, it picks up where the first film left off, as if resurrecting Carter and altering the original film's conclusion. Thus, the titular limey, Wilson (Terence Stamp), is now not only in his early 60s but also firmly rooted in the 1960s. This is established through casting an ageing star associated with the period and through the film's integrated sampling of Loach's British New Wave debut – *Poor Cow* (1967). Used for Wilson's flashbacks, these fragments serve to provide the character's backstory. Because of their sepia-tinged quality, they also add to the pervasive feeling of nostalgia present throughout the film, alongside creating a chance to explore Wilson's unrealised potential at creating a happy family life. Unlike other remakes analysed so far, whose protagonists had to be adjusted to changes in class and gender representation at the turn of the new millennium, Wilson's values remain the same as he is time-warped in the 1960s, having spent most of his life behind bars.

In the original, Carter is indirectly responsible for Doreen's downfall by working for a London porn lord whose activities spread to Newcastle, where she appears in one of his nasties. This then leads to his brother's murder when he discovers the truth. In the remake, Wilson's daughter replaces the brother, which gives his revenge even more impetus and also implicates him more deeply in her death. Jenny (Melisa George) ran away from London to California because she was fed up with her father's immaturity and unremitting criminal tendencies – only to, ironically, end up in a liaison with a man her father's age, Terry Valentine (Peter Fonda), who himself is also descending into criminality. When she reproaches him and pretends to call the police, a gimmick she used on her father to dissuade him from his illegal activities, Valentine panics, pushes her against the wall and accidentally breaks her neck. To cover it up, her body is then placed in a car and set on fire. Again, the official story goes that the accident was caused by reckless/drunk driving, which Wilson, just like Carter, refuses to believe, determined to solve the mystery of her death.

In both films, the final confrontation between the two antagonists takes place on a beach and is infused with irony. In the original, after fulfilling his revenge, Carter is shot by an anonymous assassin first seen during the opening credits. Thus, despite his agency, Carter is in the end presented as pawn in a bigger game that he never quite understood. The twist in *The Limey* derives from the fact that the villain whom Wilson is trying to apprehend all along is actually himself, placing the remake within the neo-noir tradition even more firmly than its predecessor and recalling such works as *Angel Heart* (Parker, 1987). In the final scenes, instead of administering justice, and in the process losing his humanity and possibly his life, Wilson spares Valentine, recognising that he himself is equally responsible for his daughter's death. This allows him, as Barton R. Palmer notes, to 'reconcile his past and present, in the process perhaps achieving both moral and psychological wholeness' (2011: 74). The remake also returns to the key native issue behind *Get Carter* about one generation's pursuits of freedom and lifestyle outside of social norms and their repercussions for the next generation. In this respect, Soderbergh's film mirrors the sadness of the original story about past mistakes that cannot be repaired. As Wood comments, 'there's a pervading sense of regret, of misplaced time and a desire to exorcise ghosts and actions from the past' (2002: 66). This is common for Soderbergh's protagonists who, according to Andrew deWaard and R. Colin Tait, need to 'move through their memories, battling with the ghosts that still haunt them' (2013: 78) in order to understand the impact of their past traumas on the present.

Valentine and Wilson are thus connected through loving and hurting the same woman. They both are also past their prime, repeatedly revisiting their past. Palmer notices how they are 'obsessively backward-looking' (2011: 72), and it is this nostalgia for the 1960s that causes Valentine to desperately cling to dating younger women and Wilson to still refer to his London cronies as 'lads'. Paradoxically, then, *The Limey*, whose title alone stresses foreignness and divisions, ends up re-affirming similarities over differences between the two ageing men unable to move on and retire, trapped in a value system that is increasingly becoming unsustainable and out of place.

The similarity between Valentine and Wilson is further emphasised as both 'made their money from rock music: Valentine by selling the tickets, Wilson by stealing the receipts of a Pink Floyd concert' (Ebert 1999). This blends the criminal underworld and the music industry and recalls another late-1960s cult British film, *Performance* (Cammell and Roeg, 1969).[2] The song chosen as each of the character's theme by two British bands from the period is an additional indication of points in common. The Hollies' 'King Midas in Reverse' (1968) introduces Valentine, and in the opening sequence of *The Limey*, The Who's 'The Seeker' (1971) is used to comment on Wilson's predicament with the appropriately titled song mirroring his situation.[3] In the song, the protagonist calls himself a desperate man who seeks everywhere for answers to unspecified questions that appear to be spiritual in nature. In despair, he even reaches out to Bobby Dylan, The Beatles and Timothy Leary, who all fail to give him any direction. The lyrics remind us of a crucial moment in history when the difference between modern British and American cultural icons was blurry, with each influencing the other. In this sense, it not only brings to mind the British invasion of American music charts in the 1960s but also of Hollywood's 'invasion' of British cinema at the time.

Figure 5.1 *The Limey* (1999): 'King Midas in reverse'.

Moreover, remaking a film from and about the period which produced not only many iconic bands, but also actors that are still actively working today offered Soderberg a unique opportunity to make a marketing connection, as well as an authentic cultural connection. This possibility was barely touched upon by the casting of Caine in the Stallone version of *Get Carter*; one can only speculate how the presence of Christopher Lee could have reshaped *The Wicker Man*'s remake. In Branagh's remake of *Sleuth* (2007), there was a clever use of recasting Caine. It allowed for some of the values of his previous character to resurface and then be challenged as the former film's class conflict transforms into gender wars. In the case of *The Limey*, through ingenious casting choices, Soderbergh manages to establish a link not only to Hodges' film, but also to the entire 1960s Zeitgeist, creating his characters' backstories and provoking one to explore alternative scenarios.

By packing the film full of iconic actors from the period to form authentic connections with the 1960s, unlike the other remakes discussed in this book, this one allowed Soderbergh the satisfaction of recreating the world of the original almost three decades later, with the actors happily carrying all their past baggage. On the DVD commentary track, rather amusingly, Dobbs repeatedly voices his frustrations with Soderbergh's decision to cut out most of the characters' backstories. He believes that viewers now would struggle to understand their motivation without some of the crucial details he included in his screenplay. In response, Soderbergh reassures him that they come through, thanks to the actors' nuanced performances. What he omits to add, however, is that each backstory is provided not only by what the performer does or says, but also by the casting itself, as the audience aware of their previous work can add all the necessary complexity and background to their actions.

Once again, casting a British actor creates a strong sense of continuity, as seen in the examples of the *Alfie* and *Sleuth* remakes. Instead of Caine, Terence Stamp functions as his nearest possible replacement as another icon of the 1960s whose persona was equally associated with the figure of the hedonistic working-class playboy and rogue, characterised by 'a conspicuous consumption and a freer attitude towards sexual morality, combined with a new form of democratic accessibility' (Shail 2008: 154). Both actors not only started their careers at the same time, but were also from similar backgrounds, and throughout the 1960s remained close, even sharing a flat. It is not without significance that it was Stamp who was first approached to star in the original *Alfie*, an obvious choice considering that he had already played the part on the stage. He refused the role, however, and passed it on to his roommate, thus gifting him his biggest career breakthrough. Three decades later, Stamp takes on a part previously written for Caine, which again shows the close association between the two stars and their ability to effortlessly interchange starring roles. However, despite similarities, Stamp manages to make the role his own by giving it a novel reflective quality that was absent in Caine's Carter.

Figure 5.2 *The Limey* (1999): 'They call him the Seeker'.

Except for Stamp, other icons associated with the 1960s make smaller or bigger contributions – all, however, leaving the viewer with some lasting impressions. The main villain from the original *Get Carter* played by John Osborne is replaced by Peter Fonda in an equally ironic and meaningful casting choice, as the *Easy Rider* (Hopper, 1969) star remains to this day an iconic rebel associated with 1960s counterculture values. In the film, he plays an ageing music producer still in awe of his past, intent on 'swinging' along forever, even if that means dealing drugs to continue his fading rock-and-roll lifestyle. When Osborne and Fonda are transformed into underworld criminals, in many ways it becomes difficult to offload their previous artistic achievements and status as icons of liberal 1960s values and to accept them in their new roles. In this respect, both films remind us that, in the 1960s, the difference between artistic and criminal activities was often blurry (see *Performance* and the frequent employment of real-life criminals in film, for example, John Bindon's appearance in *Performance*, *Poor Cow* and *Get Carter*) and toy with possible alternative scenarios, recalling Caine's and Stamp's proclamations that, if they had not made it as actors, they probably would have ended up as professional crooks.

Other casting choices also speak volumes and create further backstories and alternatives. Barry Newman, famous for the cult film *Vanishing Point* (Sarafian, 1971),[4] is cast as Valentine's security expert, Avery, who introduces him into a criminal underworld before being betrayed by Valentine and paying the price with his life. Newman's former role as an unruly ex-cop, Kowalski, made famous for his maniac driving skills, is now re-enacted when Avery jumps behind a wheel and chases Wilson along steep and winding California roads. Poignantly, Joe Dallesandro of Andy Warhol's 'Factory' plays a slow-witted and extremely violent gun for hire, Little Joe. Known for his substance abuse and brushes with the law in the 1960s, Dallesandro's presence represents perhaps the most realistic possible alternative of what could have been if Warhol and Morrissey had not channelled his aggression and looks into art, which gave him the confidence to land a role in classics such as Schlesinger's *Midnight Cowboy* (1969). Parallels here can be made to the life of Ian Hendry, whom Hodges had originally envisaged as Jack Carter, yet who ended up in the role of Carter's archenemy, Erick Paice. In *Get Carter*, Paice is forced to drink whiskey on the beach before Carter then smashes his head with a rifle. This provides a fitting ending for the real-life alcoholic whose antics on the set and jealousy of Caine's stardom added an extra edge and authenticity to the two characters' on-screen animosity (Chibnall 2003: 37–38). Both Dallesandro's and Hendry's characters and real-life biographies intertwine and reveal how, while the 1960s could provide a liberating force for some, others were lost to substance abuse, sometimes without return. Finally, we have Lesley Ann Warren as Elaine, a has-been who now gives acting lessons and, despite a sense of emptiness in her own career and romantic life, becomes a moral compass of the film without bitterness or attitude. Warren was associated with saccharine roles in Disney musicals in the 1960s, such as *The Happiest Millionaire* (Tokar, 1967) and *The One and Only, Genuine, Original Family Band* (O'Herlihy, 1968), but then struggled for many years to offload that image. Her delicate yet powerful presence becomes an antidote to the otherwise completely male world of noir. Bringing reason and compassion to the table, she accompanies the protagonist on his quest, becoming a second sidekick alongside Ed (Luis Guzán), and triggers his capacity for empathy and forgiveness.

However, casting, although vital, is not the only element that ties the film to its past and contributes towards its unofficial classification as the remake/sequel of *Get Carter*, since the scriptwriter and the director also included many other cross-cultural references. Dobbs – whose own roots are bicultural, having been born in Oxford in 1958 and grown up in England before then relocating to the US – infused the screenplay with humour based on transatlantic linguistic variations and misunderstandings. According to Wood, these 'highly amusing cross-cultural references regarding Britain and America' (2002: 64) must have appealed to Soderbergh alongside Wilson's Cockney slang, such as 'tea leaves' for 'thieves', 'china plate' for 'mate', 'butcher's hook' for 'look', which the hero must then translate for his confused American interlocutors. 'Limey' itself is an old American slang term, often pejorative, which originally referred to British sailors. In the original *Get Carter*, Londoners look down on working-class Geordies and make jokes about the lack of culture in Newcastle. In *The Limey*, however, Californians mock England as a 'rinky-dink country half the size of Wyoming' where cops do not even carry guns. Thus, unlike in Hodges' film, Wilson's glamorous London origins no longer impress anyone. LA now stands for the place of perceived development and cultural power. However, just as with the supposed modern Londoners in the original *Get Carter*, the viewer quickly sees through all this façade, realising that the wealthy Californians' present lifestyle is only sustainable thanks to criminal activities.

The idea of in-betweenness that pervades the film, with its main character trapped between two cultures as well as between past and present, is captured through the film's disjointed editing style and non-linear structure. The film follows a basic cause-and-effect structure, but the shots are often repeated, and scenes arranged in a non-linear order, which the viewer is able to navigate through and piece together thanks to familiar generic tropes and star iconography. When Soderbergh shows the same scene a few times, such as Wilson's determined walk in slow motion, he not only traps his character in a virtual loop but also alludes to the first official neo-noir, *Point Blank* (Boorman, 1967). There, the vigilante's characteristic reverberating footsteps equally mark the urgency of his revenge, reminding us how '[t]he single man walking [. . .] is just as iconic and has just as long a history as the male group walking' (Bruzzi 2013: 135–36) and how he is 'lonelier but also more self-sufficient' (2013: 136). Throughout the film, we keep on seeing close-ups of Wilson's face on a plane, but it is difficult to establish whether they are flashbacks or flashforwards, whether he is going to Los Angeles or returning to London. It is only upon a second viewing that we realise that the whole film is in fact an extended flashback and that all the shots of Wilson on the plane come from the moment after he has found his redemption and is on his way home, ready to continue with his life. This strategy recalls similar ones used in *Vanishing Point* or *Point Blank*, where the entire stories might be interpreted as their protagonists' extended flashbacks.

As Wilson moves along the curvature of the narrative towards its final resolution, each recurring flashback acquires a new significance, affecting his interpretation of the past events he thought he knew and understood. His journey down memory lane, however, also embodies the viewer's experience of *The Limey* as the film that extends its source, or a few of its sources, bringing back memories of characters, scenes and motifs that Soderbergh sampled from other films. *The Limey* becomes a literal representation of how 'the remake calls us actively to mediate the past with the present' (Lukas and Marmysz 2009: 13). It approximates our own experience of watching adaptations, identifying repetitions, variations and changes, as each moment in the film is brought into contact with its double, disrupting 'the linear unfolding of the text impelling the reader toward a non-linear (tabular) intertextual reading' (Verevis 2004:

94–95). Watching *The Limey*, one cannot help but meander between this film and its numerous inspirations. In this way, it 'recapitulates features of an "original", but additionally offers something new to its source', by advancing 'an exploration of alternatives, differences, and reenactments that are discretely charged with the various ways in which we may reread, remember, or return to a source' (Jess-Cooke and Verevis 2010: 5).

This book began by examining Hollywood remakes of iconic British films in terms of international business arrangements, then zoomed in close on the nuts and bolts and mechanics of cross-cultural remakes through identifying adaptation strategies, and finally provided an alternative to show how remakes can represent a director's personal journey to help them elucidate and understand their own cultural heritage. The creative potential to write, produce and film future remakes can draw on any or all of these factors and motivations. As Scott A. Lukas and John Marmysz observe, '[w]hile some may succeed and others may fail aesthetically and politically, they always, nonetheless, say something about the culture in which, and for which, they are produced' (2009: 2). Jennifer Forrest and Leonard R. Koos elaborate on that point further, claiming that all remakes, whether successful or not, are 'interesting for what they reveal, either about different cultures, about different directorial styles and aesthetic orientations, about class or gender perceptions, about different social-historical periods and changing audience expectations, about the dynamics of the genre film, or simply about the evolution of economic practices in the industry' (2002: 4–5). The true surprise, however, is that, while most remakes update class and gender conflicts of the original films to connect with a contemporary audience, *The Limey* delivers it by placing the character from the original in a similar situation a few decades later and observing how his values clash with those around him. This in the process forces Soderbergh, and the viewer, to re-assess the 1960s and possibly re-emerge from under their long shadow.

NOTES

1. Soderbergh's website, 'Extension 765' (2013–), whose name in a typical movie-geek fashion refers to yet another classic of the period, Francis Ford Coppola's *The Conversation* (1974), features, among others, 'seen, read' lists ordered by each year and month. These reveal his fascination with 1960s and 1970s American and British cinema.
2. The further irony is that Stamp's brother, Chris Stamp, was actually a British music producer and manager of such 1960s/70s bands as The Who or Jimi Hendrix.
3. A similar idea occurred to Sam Mendes, who used The Who's 'The Seeker' to comment on his protagonist's (Kevin Spacey) situation in *American Beauty*, released the same year.
4. The film was remade for TV in 1997.

References

adamblake77 (2005), 'Rejoice! Rejoice! It's out on DVD as of This Week!', *IMDB*, 31 July, <https://www.imdb.com/review/rw1139298/?ref_=tt_urv>.
Aldgate, Anthony and Jeffrey Richards (eds) (1999), *Best of British: Cinema and Society from 1930 to the Present*, London, New York: I. B. Tauris.
Allen, Michael (2003), *Contemporary US Cinema*, Harlow: Pearson Education Limited.
Alter, Ethan (2006), '*The Wicker Man*', *Film Journal International*, 109:10, (October), 50.
angelynx-2 (2000), 'Dry and Thoughtful Comedy', *IMDB*, 27 September 2000, <https://www.imdb.com/review/rw0096390/?ref_=tt_urv>.
Archer, Neil (2017), *Beyond a Joke: Parody in English Film and Television*, London: I. B. Tauris.
Asma, Stephen T. (2009), *On Monsters: An Unnatural History of Our Worst Fears*, Oxford and New York: Oxford University Press.
Aulert, Bob (n. d.), 'Review of *Bedazzled*', *Culture Vulture*, <https://culturevulture.net/film/bedazzled/>.
Baker, Aaron (2011), 'Remade by Steven Soderbergh', in R. Barton Palmer and Steven M. Sanders (eds), *The Philosophy of Steven Soderbergh*, Lexington: The University Press of Kentucky, pp. 121–42.
Bartholomew, David (1977), '*The Wicker Man*', *Cinefantastique*, 6:3.
Bell, Emma and Neil Mitchell (eds) (2012), *Directory of World Cinema: Britain*, Bristol: Intellect.
Bennett, Peter, Andrew Hickman and Peter Wall (eds) (2007), *Film Studies: The Essential Resource*, London and New York: Routledge.
Berardinelli, James (2007), 'Review of *Sleuth*', *ReelViews*, <http://www.reelviews.net/reelviews/sleuth>.
Bigsby, C. W. E. (2007), *Neil LaBute: Stage and Cinema*, Cambridge: Cambridge University Press.
Billington, Michael (1997), *The Life and Work of Harold Pinter*, London: Faber and Faber.
Bould, Mark, Kathrina Glitre and Greg Tuck (eds) (2009), 'Parallel Views: An Introduction', *Neo-Noir*, London and New York: Wallflower Press, pp. 1–10.
Bradshaw, Peter (2007), 'Review of *Sleuth*', *The Guardian*, 27 November, <https://www.theguardian.com/film/2007/nov/23/thriller>.
Bradshaw, Peter (2006), 'Review of *The Ipcress File*', *The Guardian*, 13 January, <https://www.theguardian.com/culture/2006/jan/13/lendeighton>.

Brashinsky, Michael (1998), 'The Spring, Defiled: Ingmar Bergman's *Virgin Spring* and Wes Craven's *Last House on the Left*', in Andrew Horton and Stuart Y. McDougal (eds), *Play It Again, Sam: Retakes on Remakes*, Berkeley, CA: University of California Press, pp. 162–71.

Braudy, Leo (1998), 'Afterword: Rethinking Remakes', in Andrew Horton and Stuart Y. McDougal (eds), *Play It Again, Sam: Retakes on Remakes*, Berkeley, CA: University of California Press, pp. 327–34.

Bray, Christopher (2006), *Michael Caine: A Class Act*, London: Faber and Faber.

Brickman, Barbara et al. (eds) (2021), *Love Across the Atlantic: US-UK Romance in Popular Culture*, Edinburgh: Edinburgh University Press.

'British Cinema' (2007), in Peter Bennett, Andrew Hickman and Peter Wall (eds), *Film Studies: The Essential Resource*, London and New York: Routledge, pp. 344–67.

Brown, Allan (2000), *Inside 'The Wicker Man': The Morbid Ingenuities*, London: Sidgwick & Jackson Ltd.

Bruzzi, Stella (2013), *Men's Cinema: Masculinity and Mise en Scène in Hollywood*, Edinburgh: Edinburgh University Press.

Burton, Alan and Steve Chibnall (2013), *Historical Dictionary of British Cinema*, Lanham: Scarecrow Press.

'Cage to Rekindle *Wicker Man* Remake' (2005), *The Guardian*, 4 March, <https://www.theguardian.com/film/2005/mar/04/news>.

Canby, Vincent (1969), '"Italian Job" and "Ace-High": Double Bill of Imports in Local Theatres', *New York Times*, 9 October, <https://www.nytimes.com/1969/10/09/archives/italian-job-and-ace-highdouble-bill-of-imports-at-local-theaters.html>.

Cashmore, E. Ellis (1989), *United Kingdom? Class, Race and Gender Since the War*, London: Unwin Hyman.

Catterall, Ali and Simon Wells (2002), *Your Face Here: British Cult Movies Since the Sixties*, London: Fourth Estate.

Chan, Kenneth (2017), 'The Chinese Cinematic Remake as Transnational Appeal: Zhang Yimou's *A Woman, A Gun, and A Noodle Shop*', in Constantine Verevis and Iain Robert Smith (eds), *Transnational Film Remakes*, Edinburgh: Edinburgh University Press, pp. 87–102.

Chapman, James (2000), *Licence to Thrill: A Cultural History of the James Bond Films*, New York: Columbia University Press.

Chibnall, Steve (2009), 'Travels in Ladland: The British Gangster Film Cycle, 1998–2001', in Robert Murphy (ed.), *The British Cinema Book*, 3rd edn, London: British Film Institute and Palgrave Macmillan, pp. 375–86.

Chibnall, Steve (2005), '*The Italian Job*', in Brian McFarlane (ed.), *The Cinema of Britain and Ireland*, London and New York: Wallflower Press, pp. 145–53.

Chibnall, Steve (2003), *Get Carter: The British Film Guide 6*, London: I. B. Tauris.

Chibnall, Steve and Julian Petley (eds) (2002), *British Horror Cinema*, London and New York: Routledge.

Chibnall, Steve and Robert Murphy (eds) (1999), *British Crime Cinema*, London and New York: Routledge.

Ciment, Michel (2008), 'An Interview with Joseph L. Mankiewicz', in Brian Dauth (ed.), *Joseph L. Mankiewicz: Interviews*, Jackson: University Press of Mississippi, pp. 125–43.

Claydon, Anna E. (2010), 'Masculinity and Deviance in British Cinema of the 1970s: Sex, Drugs and Rock 'n' Roll in *The Wicker Man*, *Tommy* and *The Rocky Horror Picture Show*', in Paul Newland (ed.), *Don't Look Now: British Cinema in the 1970s*, Bristol: Intellect Books, pp. 131–42.

Clover, Carol J. (2000), 'Her Body/Himself: Gender in the Slasher Film', in Stephen Prince (ed.), *Screening Violence*, London: The Athlone Press, pp. 125–73.

Clover, Carol J. ([1992] 2015), *Men, Women, and Chain Saws: Gender in the Modern Horror Film*, Princeton and Oxford: Princeton University Press.
Collins, J., H. Radner and A. Preacher Collins (eds) (1993), *Film Theory Goes to the Movies*, New York and London: Routledge.
Cook, Lez (2007), *Troy Kennedy Martin*, Manchester: Manchester University Press.
Cook, William (2014), *One Leg Too Few: The Adventures of Peter Cook and Dudley Moore*, London: Random House UK.
Cook, William (2005), 'The Legacy of *Bedazzled*', *New Statesman*, 25 July, 40–42.
Cook, William (2002), *Tragically I Was an Only Twin*, Century: London.
Corrigan, Timothy (2012), *American Cinema of the 2000s: Themes and Variations*, New Brunswick: Rutgers University Press.
Constandinides, Costas (2010), *From Film Adaptation to Post-Celluloid Adaptation: Rethinking the Transition of Popular Narratives and Characters Across Old and New Media*, New York: Continuum.
Crawford, Chelsey (2016), 'Familiar Otherness: On the Contemporary Cross-Cultural Remake', in Amanda Ann Klein and R. Barton Palmer (eds), *Multiplicities in Film and Television*, Austin: University of Texas Press, pp. 112–29.
Cronin, James E. (2014), *Global Rules: America, Britain and a Disordered World*, New Haven and London: Yale University Press.
Crowther, Bosley (1967), 'The Screen: Son of Seven Deadly Sins: *Bedazzled* by Moore and Cook at Plaza', *New York Times*, 11 December, <https://www.nytimes.com/1967/12/11/archives/the-screen-son-of-seven-deadly-sinsbedazzled-by-moore-and-cook-at.html>.
Cuelenaere, Eduard et al. (eds) (2021), *European Film Remakes*, Edinburgh: Edinburgh University Press.
DarekH (2006), 'Worst Movie I Have Ever Seen', *IMDB*, 6 April, <https://www.imdb.com/review/rw1334667/?ref_=tt_urv>.
Dargis, Manohla (2007), 'A Dance of Two Men, Twisting and Turning with a Gun That's More Than a Gun', *New York Times*, 12 October, <https://www.nytimes.com/2007/10/12/movies/12sleu.html>.
DaveNoodles (2006), 'Not Any Good', *IMDB*, 9 January, <https://www.imdb.com/review/rw1260292/?ref_=tt_urv>.
Dave-1511 (2004), 'Searching for Bedazzled (1967)', *IMDB*, 30 December, <https://www.imdb.com/review/rw0988324/?ref_=tt_urv>.
Davies, Hugh (2004), 'America Will Fall for Jude Law's Alfie, Predicts Michael Caine', *The Telegraph*, 23 August, <https://www.telegraph.co.uk/news/uknews/1469976/America-will-fall-for-Jude-Laws-Alfie-predicts-Michael-Caine.html>.
Deeley, Michael (2008), *Blade Runners, Deer Hunters, and Blowing the Bloody Doors Off: My Life in Cult Movies*, London: Faber and Faber.
deWaard, Andrew and R. Colin Tait (2013), *The Cinema of Steven Soderbergh*, London and New York: Wallflower Press.
Dilley, Ryan (1999), '*Italian Job* Goes for Gold', *BBC News Online*, 9 September, <http://news.bbc.co.uk/2/hi/entertainment/440991.stm>.
Divine, Christian (2000), 'Script Comments on *Get Carter*', *Creative Screenwriting*, 7:5, (September-October), 18–19.
Druxman, Michael, B. (1975), *Make It Again, Sam: A Survey of Movie Remakes*, Cranbury, NJ: A. S. Barnes.
Durham, Carolyn A. (1998), *Double Takes: Culture and Gender in French Films and Their American Remakes*, Dartmouth: University Press of New England.
Ebert, Roger (2007), 'Not with My Wife, You Don't', *Roger Ebert*, 18 October, <https://www.rogerebert.com/reviews/sleuth>.

Ebert, Roger (1999), 'Review of *The Limey*', *Roger Ebert*, 8 October, <https://www.rogerebert.com/reviews/the-limey-1999>.
Ebert, Roger (1982), 'Review of *Deathtrap*', *Roger Ebert*, 1 January, <https://www.rogerebert.com/reviews/deathtrap-1982>.
Ebert, Roger (1972), 'Review of *Sleuth*', *Roger Ebert*, 1 January, <https://www.rogerebert.com/reviews/sleuth-1972>.
Ebert, Roger (1967), 'Review of *Bedazzled*', *Roger Ebert*, 30 January, <https://www.rogerebert.com/reviews/bedazzled-1968>.
Ede, Laurie N. (2012), 'British Film Design in the 1970s', in Sue Harper and Justin Smith (eds), *British Film Culture in the 1970s: The Boundaries of Pleasure*, Edinburgh: Edinburgh University Press, pp. 50–61.
Edelman, Lee (2004), *No Future: Queer Theory and the Death Drive*, Durham, NC: Duke University Press.
Ellis, John (1992), *Visible Fictions: Cinema: Television: Video*, rev. edn, London: Routledge.
Errigo, Angie (2000), '*The Ipcress File* Review', *Empire*, 1 January, <https://www.empireonline.com/movies/ipcress-file/review/>.
Fahlenbrach, Kathrin (2014), 'Utopia and Dystopia in Science Fiction Films around 1968', in Timothy Scott Brown and Andrew Lison (eds), *The Global Sixties in Sound and Vision: Media, Counterculture, Revolt*, New York: Palgrave Macmillan, pp. 82–100.
Field, Matthew (2001), *The Making of 'The Italian Job'*, London: B. T. Batsford.
Forrest, Jennifer (2020), 'Gender, Genre and the Reboot: From *Ocean's 11/Eleven* to *Ocean's 8/Eight*', in Daniel Herbert and Constantine Verevis (eds), *Film Reboots*, Edinburgh: Edinburgh University Press, pp. 81–95.
Forrest, Jennifer and Leonard R. Koos (2002), 'Reviewing Remakes: An Introduction', in Jennifer Forrest and Leonard R. Koos (eds), *Dead Ringers: The Remake in Theory and Practice*, Albany, NY: SUNY Press, pp. 1–36.
Franks, Benjamin (2005), 'Demotic Possession: The Hierarchic and Anarchic in *The Wicker Man*', in J. Murray et al. (eds), *Constructing 'The Wicker Man': Film and Cultural Studies Perspectives*, Glasgow: University of Glasgow, Crichton Publications, pp. 63–78.
Friedman, Lester (2006), 'The Empire Strikes Out: An American Perspective on the British Film Industry', in Lester Friedman (ed.), *Fires Were Started: British Cinema and Thatcherism*, London and New York: Wallflower Press: pp. 1–11.
Fuchs, Cynthia (2004), 'Review of *Alfie*', *PopMatters*, 5 November, <https://www.popmatters.com/alfie-2004-2496220138.html>.
Fuchs, Cynthia (2003), 'Review of *The Italian Job*', *PopMatters*, 29 August, <https://www.popmatters.com/italian-job2-2496248652.html>.
Fuller, Graham (2000), '*Get Carter* 2000', *Film Comment*, (September-October), 35–37.
Gallagher, Mark (2013a), 'Discerning Independents: Steven Soderbergh and Transhistorical Taste Cultures', in Geoff King et al. (eds), *American Independent Cinema: Indie, Indiewood and Beyond*, London and New York: Routledge, pp. 83–95.
Gallagher, Mark (2013b), 'Male Style and Race in the Neoretro Heist Film', in Timothy Shary (ed.), *Millennial Masculinity: Men in Contemporary American Cinema*, Detroit: Wayne State University Press, pp. 265–87.
Games, Alexander (2012), *Pete and Dud*, [n. p.], Rocket 88.
Geraghty, Christine (2007), *Now a Major Motion Picture: Film Adaptations of Literature and Drama*, Lanham: Rowman & Littlefield.
Germaine Buckley, Chloé (2019), 'Witches, "Bitches" or Feminist Trailblazers? The Witch in Folk Horror Cinema', *Revenant: Creative and Critical Studies of the Supernatural*, 4, 22–42.
'*Get Carter* Director Deems Remake out of Shape' (2002), *The Guardian*, 16 October, <https://www.theguardian.com/film/2000/oct/16/news1>.

Gibson, Marion (2012), 'Wicker Men and *Straw Dogs*: Internal Colonialism in Celtic Novels and Films, 1968–1978', *National Identities*, 15:2, <https://www.tandfonline.com/eprint/ZQEit7FHCPPS8gqk8RIU/full>.

Gibson, Pamela Church (2017), 'The Fashioning of Julie Christie and the Mythologizing of "Swinging London": Changing Images in Sixties Britain', in Eugenia Paulicelli et al. (eds), *Film, Fashion, and the 1960s*, Bloomington: Indiana University Press, pp. 135–48.

Gibson, Pamela Church and Andrew Hill (2009), '"Tuute e marchio": Excess, Masquerade and Performativity in 70s Cinema', in Robert Murphy (ed.), *The British Cinema Book*, 3rd edn, London: British Film Institute and Palgrave Macmillan, pp. 333–40.

Gilbey, Ryan (2004), 'Dangerous Dandies', *The Independent*, 3 May, <https://www.independent.co.uk/arts-entertainment/films/features/dangerous-dandies-58700.html>.

Glancy, Mark (1999), *When Hollywood Loved Britain: The Hollywood 'British' Films 1939–1945*, Manchester: Manchester University Press.

Graham, Bob (2000), '*Get Carter* Takes Aim and Misfires', *SFGate*, 7 October, <https://www.sfgate.com/movies/article/Get-Carter-Takes-Aim-and-Misfires-3238232.php>.

Grant, Catherine (2002), 'Recognising *Billy Budd* in *Beau Travail*: Epistemology and Hermeneutics of Auteurist "Free" Adaptation', *Screen*, 43:1, 57–73.

Gray, Jonathan (2010), *Show Sold Separately: Promos, Spoilers, and Other Media Paratexts*, New York: New York University Press.

Grusin, Richard (2006), 'DVDs, Video Games, and the Cinema of Interactions', *Ilha Do Desterro*, 51, 69–91.

Hall, Lesley A. (2000), *Sex, Gender and Social Change in Britain since 1880*, Basingstoke: Palgrave.

Hamilton, Jack (2016), *Just Around Midnight: Rock and Roll and the Racial Imagination*, Cambridge, MA: Harvard University Press.

Harper, Stephen (2012), '*The Wicker Man*', in Emma Bell and Neil Mitchell (eds), *Directory of World Cinema: Britain*, Bristol: Intellect, pp. 154–56.

Harper, Sue and Justin Smith (eds) (2012), *British Film Culture in the 1970s: The Boundaries of Pleasure*, Edinburgh: Edinburgh University Press.

Hedges, Inez (2005), *Framing Faust: Twentieth-Century Cultural Struggles*, Carbondale: Southern Illinois University Press.

Henderson, Stuart (2014), *The Hollywood Sequel: History & Form, 1911–2010*, London: British Film Institute.

Herbert, Daniel and Constantine Verevis (eds) (2020), *Film Reboots*, Edinburgh: Edinburgh University Press.

Herbert, Daniel (2009), 'Trading Spaces: Transnational Dislocations in *Insomnia/Insomnia* and *Ju-on/The Grudge*', in John Marmysz and Scott A. Lucas (eds), *Fear, Cultural Anxiety, and Transformation: Horror, Science Fiction, and Fantasy Films Remade*, Lanham, MD: Lexington Books, pp. 143–64.

Higson, Andrew (2011), *Film England: Culturally English Filmmaking since the 1990s*, London and New York: I. B. Tauris.

Higson, Andrew (2002), 'The Concept of National Cinema', in Alan Williams (ed.), *Film and Nationalism*, New Brunswick, New Jersey and London: Rutgers University Press, pp. 52–67.

Hill, John (2016), 'Living with Hollywood: British Film Policy and the Definition of "Nationality"', *International Journal of Cultural Policy*, 22:5 (November), 706–23.

Hill, John (2001), 'Contemporary British Cinema: Industry, Policy, Identity', *Cineaste*, 26:4, 34–37.

Hill, John (1995), *Sex, Class and Realism: British Cinema, 1956–1963*, London: British Film Institute.

Hines, Claire (2018), *The Playboy and James Bond: 007, Ian Fleming and Playboy Magazine*, Manchester: Manchester University Press.

Hodges, Mike (2009), 'Forward: "If Only My Leg Didn't Itch"', in Mark Bould et al. (eds), *Neo-Noir*, London and New York: Wallflower Press, pp. ix–x.

Holden, Stephen (2006), 'Film Review: Rocky Balboa: Return of that Fighter with a Soft Heart inside a Hard Body', *New York Times*, 20 December, <https://www.nytimes.com/2006/12/20/movies/20rock.html>.

Holden, Stephen (2003), 'Film Review: Once Again, It Takes a Thief to Catch a Thief', *The New York Times*, 30 May, <https://www.nytimes.com/2003/05/30/movies/film-review-once-again-it-takes-a-thief-to-catch-a-thief.html>.

Holmlund, Chris (2014), 'Introduction: Presenting Stallone/Stallone Presents', in Chris Holmlund (ed.), *The Ultimate Stallone Reader: Sylvester Stallone as Star, Icon, Auteur*, London and New York: Wallflower Press, pp. 1–25.

Horton, Andrew and Stuart Y. McDougal (eds) (1998), *Play It Again, Sam: Retakes on Remakes*, Berkeley, CA: University of California Press.

Horwath, A. et al. (eds) (2004), *The Last Great American Picture Show: New Hollywood Cinema in the 1970s*, Amsterdam: Amsterdam University Press.

Howe, Desson (2000), 'Get Lost, Carter', *The Washington Post*, 6 October, <https://www.washingtonpost.com/wp-srv/entertainment/movies/reviews/getcarterhowe.htm>.

Hoxna, Timothy M. (2011), 'The Masculinity of James Bonds: Sexism, Misogyny, Racism, and the Female Character', in Jack Becker et al. (eds), *James Bond in World and Popular Culture: The Films Are Not Enough*, Newcastle Upon Tyne: Cambridge Scholars Publishing, pp. 193–205.

Hughs, Alan (2017), 'Looking West, not South: The Anglo-American Films Agreement and the North on Film, 1948–1958', in Ewa Mazierska (ed), *Heading North: The North of England in Film and Television*, Basingstoke and New York: Palgrave Macmillan, pp. 215–34.

Hunt, Leon (2002), 'Necromancy in the UK: Witchcraft and the Occult in British Horror', in Steve Chibnall and Julian Petley (eds), *British Horror Cinema*, London and New York: Routledge, pp. 82–98.

Hutcheon, Linda (2006), *A Theory of Adaptation*, New York: Routledge.

Hutchings, Peter (2015), '10 Great British Rural Horror Films', *British Film Institute*, 21 August, <https://www2.bfi.org.uk/news/10-great-british-rural-horror-films>.

Idle, Eric (2011), 'Forward', in Rena Fruchter, *Dudley Moore: An Intimate Portrait*, [n. p.], Ebury Digital.

'In Brief: Cage in The Wicker Man' (2002), *The Guardian*, 22 March, <https://www.theguardian.com/film/2002/mar/22/news2>.

James, Nick (2001), 'They Think It's All Over: British Cinema's US Surrender', in Robert Murphy (ed), *The British Cinema Book*, 2nd edn, London: British Film Institute, pp. 301–17.

Jeffords, Susan (1994), *Hard Bodies: Hollywood Masculinity in the Reagan Era*, New Brunswick, NJ: Rutgers University Press.

Jeffords, Susan (1993), 'The Big Switch: Hollywood Masculinity in the Nineties', in J. Collins et al. (eds), *Film Theory Goes to the Movies*, New York and London: Routledge, pp. 196–208.

Jenkins, Henry (2006), *Convergence Culture: Where Old and New Media Collide*, New York and London: New York University Press.

Jenkins, Henry (1992), *Textual Poachers: Television Fans & Participatory Culture*, New York: Routledge.

Jess-Cooke, Carolyn and Constantine Verevis (eds) (2010), *Second Takes: Critical Approaches to the Film Sequel*, Albany, NY: SUNY Press.

Jess-Cooke, Carolyn (2009), *Film Sequels: Theory and Practice from Hollywood to Bollywood*, Edinburgh: Edinburgh University Press.

Keen, Andrew (2007), *The Cult of the Amateur: How Today's Internet is Killing Our Culture*, New York: Doubleday.

Kelleter, Frank and Kathleen Loock (2017), 'Hollywood Remaking as Second-Order Serialization', in Frank Kelleter (ed.), *Media of Serial Narrative*, Columbus, OH: Ohio State University Press, pp. 112–33.
Kellner, Douglas (2010), *Cinema Wars: Hollywood Film and Politics in the Bush-Cheney Era*, Oxford: Wiley-Blackwell.
King, Geoff et al. (eds) (2013), *American Independent Cinema: Indie, Indiewood and Beyond*, London and New York: Routledge.
Klein, Amanda Ann and R. Barton Palmer (eds) (2016), *Cycles, Sequels, Spin-Offs, Remakes, and Reboots: Multiplicities in Film and Television*, Austin, TX: University of Texas Press.
Klinger, Barbara (2006), *Beyond the Multiplex Cinema: New Technologies and the Home*, Berkeley, CA: University of California Press.
Krzywinska, Tanya (2000), *A Skin for Dancing In: Possession, Witchcraft and Voodoo in Film*, Trowbridge: Flicks Books.
Laverty, Christopher (2011), 'Michael Caine in *Get Carter*: Killer Suit', <https://clothesonfilm.com/michael-caine-in-get-carter-killer-suit/>.
Lay, Samantha (2002), *British Social Realism: From Documentary to Brit Grit*, London and New York: Wallflower.
Leach, Jim (2004), *British Film*, Cambridge: Cambridge University Press.
Leadbeater, Charles (2008), *We-Think: Mass Innovation, Not Mass Production*, London: Profile Books.
Lee, Daryl (2014), *The Heist Film: Stealing with Style*, London and New York: Wallflower.
Leitch, Luke (2004), 'Alfie Revisited', *The Evening Standard*, 7 October, <https://www.standard.co.uk/showbiz/alfie-revisited-7227727.html>.
Leitch, Thomas (2003), 'Hitchcock Without Hitchcock', *Literature/Film Quarterly*, 31:4, 248–59.
Leitch, Thomas (2002), 'Twice-Told Tales: Disavowal and the Rhetoric of the Remake', in Jennifer Forrest and Leonard R. Koos (eds), *Dead Ringers: The Remake in Theory and Practice*, Albany NY: SUNY Press, pp. 37–62.
LennyRenquist (2003), 'Italian Whatnow?', *IMDB*, 18 August, <https://www.imdb.com/review/rw0872231/?ref_=tt_urv>.
Levy, Ariel (2004), 'The Pretty-Boy Syndrome', *New York Magazine*, 15 October, <http://nymag.com/nymetro/news/people/features/10120/index1.html>.
Leydon, Joe (2006), '*The Wicker Man*', *Daily Variety*, 5 September, 8, 14.
Leydon, Joe (2000), 'Review of *Bedazzled*', *Variety*, 16 October, <https://variety.com/2000/film/reviews/bedazzled-2-1200464798/>.
Lippe, Adam (2009), 'Can You Get a Stuntman for My Dialogue Too?' *A Regrettable Moment of Sincerity*, 18 January, <https://regrettablesincerity.com/?p=82>.
littlemartinarocena (2007), 'Sleuth According to Harold Pinter', *IMDB*, 17 November, <https://www.imdb.com/review/rw1765068/?ref_=rw_urv>.
livewire-6 (2004), 'What's It All for?', *IMDB*, 11 November, <https://www.imdb.com/review/rw0960873/?ref_=tt_urv>.
Loock, Kathleen (2020), 'Reboot, Requel, Legacyquel: *Jurassic World* and the Nostalgia Franchise', in Daniel Herbert and Constantine Verevis (eds), *Film Reboots*, Edinburgh: Edinburgh University Press, pp. 173–88.
Loock, Kathleen and Constantine Verevis (2012), 'Introduction: Remake-Remodel', in Kathleen Loock and Constantine Verevis (eds), *Film Remakes, Adaptations and Fan Productions: Remake-Remodel*, Basingstoke: Palgrave Macmillan, pp. 1–15.
Lovell, Alan (2009), 'The British Cinema: The Known Cinema?' in Robert Murphy (ed.), *The British Cinema Book*, 3rd edn, London: British Film Institute and Palgrave, pp. 5–12.
Lukas, Scott A. and John Marmysz (2009), 'Horror, Science Fiction, and Fantasy Films Remade', in John Marmysz and Scott A. Lucas (eds), *Fear, Cultural Anxiety, and*

Transformation: Horror, Science Fiction, and Fantasy Films Remade, Lanham, MD: Lexington Books, pp. 1–20.

Lyons, Charles (2006), 'Remake "The Wicker Man"? Now That's Scary?', *The New York Times*, 6 August, <https://www.nytimes.com/2006/08/06/movies/06lyon.html?mtrref=www.google.pl&gwh=2C0C6AB6FD35DE7D27B29F664205E764&gwt=pay&assetType=REGIWALL>.

majikstl, (2007), 'Criminal Intent', *IMDB*, 9 December, <https://www.imdb.com/review/rw1777909/?ref_=rw_urv>.

Maslin, Janet (1999), '*The Talented Mr. Ripley:* Carnal, Glamorous and Worth the Price', *The New York Times*, 24 December, <https://archive.nytimes.com/www.nytimes.com/library/film/122499ripley-film-review.html>.

Maslin, Janet (1982), 'Film: *Deathtrap* with Michael Caine', *The New York Times*, 19 March, <https://www.nytimes.com/1982/03/19/movies/film-deathtrap-with-michael-caine.html>.

Matties25 (2004), 'A Castrated Version of the Classic Original', *IMDB*, 15 October, <https://www.imdb.com/review/rw0948113/?ref_=tt_urv>.

Mazdon, Lucy (2000), *Encore Hollywood: Remaking French Cinema*, London: British Film Institute.

McCarthy, Todd (2000), 'Review of *Get Carter*', *Variety*, 5 October, <https://variety.com/2000/film/reviews/get-carter-2-1200464985/>.

McDearmont, Ryan (2018), '*The Wicker Man*: The Eye of the Beholder', *Bee Culture* (June), 65–67.

McDonald, Paul (2014), 'Stallone's Stomach: *Cop Land* and the Weight of Actorly Legitimisation', in Chris Holmlund (ed.), *The Ultimate Stallone Reader: Sylvester Stallone as Star, Icon, Auteur*, London and New York: Wallflower Press, pp. 147–70.

McDonnell, Jenny (2006), 'Year of the Remake: *The Omen 666* and *The Wicker Man*', *The Irish Journal of Gothic and Horror Studies*, 1 (October), 117–23.

McElvoy, Anne (2016), 'Real Life Has Turned into a Remake of *The Italian Job*', *The Guardian*, 21 October, <https://www.theguardian.com/commentisfree/2016/oct/21/italian-job-brexit-vote>.

McFarlane, Brian and A. Slide (2013), *The Encyclopedia of British Film: Fourth Edition*, Manchester: Manchester University Press.

McFarlane, Brian (2009), 'The More Things Change . . . British Cinema in the 90s', in Robert Murphy (ed.), *The British Cinema Book*, 3rd edn, London: British Film Institute and Palgrave Macmillan, pp. 366–74.

Medhurst, Andy (2007), *Popular Comedy and English National Identities*, London and New York: Routledge.

Melis, Behlil (2016), *Hollywood Is Everywhere: Global Directors in the Blockbuster Era*, Amsterdam: Amsterdam University Press.

'Mike Hodges Discusses *Get Carter* with NFT audience, 23 September 1997' (1999), in Steve Chibnall and Robert Murphy (eds), *British Crime Cinema*, London and New York: Routledge, pp. 120–26.

Miller, Jeffrey S. (2000), *Something Completely Different: British Television and American Culture*, Minneapolis and London: University of Minnesota Press.

Miller, Toby et al. (eds) (2006), *Global Hollywood 2*, London: British Film Institute.

Mitchell, Elvis (2000), 'Film Review: Slimline Stallone, with a Bruising Touch and a Gentle Mutter', *The New York Times*, 7 October, <https://www.nytimes.com/2000/10/07/movies/film-review-slimline-stallone-with-a-bruising-touch-and-a-gentle-mutter.html>.

Monk, Claire (1999), 'From Underworld to Underclass: Crime and British Cinema in the 1990s', in Steve Chibnall and Robert Murphy (eds), *British Crime Cinema*, London and New York: Routledge, pp. 177–93.

Morgan, Kim (2017), 'Neil LaBute: *The Wicker Man* Interview', *Beverly Cinema*, 24 April, <https://thenewbev.com/blog/2017/04/neil-labute-the-wicker-man/>.
Moses, Michael Valdez (2011), '*Solaris*, Cinema, and Simulacra', in R. Barton Palmer and Steven M. Sanders (eds), *The Philosophy of Steven Soderbergh*, Lexington: The University Press of Kentucky, pp. 281–303.
Mottram, James (2004), 'Review of *Alfie*', *Film Review*, (November), 102.
Murphy, Bernice M. (2013), *The Rural Gothic in American Popular Culture: Backwoods Horror and Terror in the Wilderness*, New York: Palgrave Macmillan.
Murphy, Robert (2009), 'Strange Days: British Cinema in the Late 1960s', in Robert Murphy (ed.), *The British Cinema Book*, 3rd edn, London: British Film Institute/Palgrave, pp. 321–32.
Murphy, Robert ([1992] 2008), *Sixties British Cinema*, London: British Film Institute.
Murphy, Robert (1999), 'A Revenger's Tragedy–*Get Carter*', in Steve Chibnall and Robert Murphy (eds), *British Crime Cinema*, London and New York: Routledge, pp. 123–33.
Murray, J. et al. (eds) (2005), *Constructing 'The Wicker Man': Film and Cultural Studies Perspectives*, Glasgow: University of Glasgow and Crichton Publications.
Naremore, James (1999–2000), 'Remaking *Psycho*', in *Hitchcock Annual*, pp. 3–12.
Nathan, Ian (2004), '*Alfie* Review', *Empire Online*, 22 October, <https://www.empireonline.com/movies/alfie-2/review/>.
Naughton, Bill ([1966] 2012), *Alfie*, London: Allison and Busby Limited.
Newland, Paul (2013), *British Films of the 1970s*, Manchester: Manchester University Press.
Newland, Paul (ed.) (2010), *Don't Look Now: British Cinema in the 1970s*, Bristol: Intellect Books.
Newland, Paul (2008), 'Folksploitation: Charting the Horrors of the British Folk Music Tradition in *The Wicker Man*', in Robert Shail (ed.), *Seventies British Cinema*, London: Palgrave Macmillan, pp. 119–28.
Orr, John (2010), *Romantics and Modernists in British Cinema*, Edinburgh: Edinburgh University Press.
O'Toole, Fintan (2018), 'Brexit Was Only Supposed to Blow the Bloody Doors Off', *The Irish Times*, 2 January, <https://www.irishtimes.com/opinion/fintan-o-toole-brexit-was-only-supposed-to-blow-the-bloody-doors-off-1.3342337>.
Palmer, R. Barton (2011), 'Alain Resnais Meets Film Noir in *The Underneath* and *The Limey*', in R. Barton Palmer and Steven M. Sanders (eds), *The Philosophy of Steven Soderbergh*, Lexington: The University Press of Kentucky, pp. 69–90.
Palmer, R. Barton (2001), 'Literary Adaptations', in Cheryl Bray Lower and R. Barton Palmer, *Joseph L. Mankiewicz: Critical Essays and an Annotated Bibliography and Filmography*, Jefferson, NC, and London: McFarland & Company, pp. 141–72.
Papamichael, Stella (2003), 'Review of *The Italian Job*', *BBC*, 4 October, <http://www.bbc.co.uk/films/2003/09/04/the_italian_job_2003_review.shtml>.
penseur (2004), 'Please Don't Let Hollywood Massacre This One', *IMDB*, 22 January, <https://www.imdb.com/review/rw0132778/?ref_=tt_urv>.
Perkins, Claire (2020), 'Ghost Girls: *Ghostbusters*, Popular Feminism and the Gender-Swap Reboot', in Daniel Herbert and Constantine Verevis (eds), *Film Reboots*, Edinburgh: Edinburgh University Press, pp. 157–70.
Perkins, Claire and Constantine Verevis (eds) (2012), *Film Trilogies: New Critical Approaches*, Basingstoke: Palgrave Macmillan.
philip-63 (2004), 'Toothless Remake, a Missed Opportunity', *IMDB*, 21 October, <https://www.imdb.com/review/rw0950001/?ref_=tt_urv>.
Porton, Richard (2004), 'The Character Actor as Movie Star: An Interview with Michael Caine', *Cineaste*, 29:2, 4–7.

Pratt, Vic (2016), 'Long Arm of the Lore: Robin Hardy on *The Wicker Man*', *British Film Institute*, 4 July, <https://www2.bfi.org.uk/news-opinion/sight-sound-magazine/features/long-arm-lore-robin-hardy-wicker-man>.

primodanielelori (2007), 'The Darker Side of a Darkish Comedy', 18 November, *IMDB*, <https://www.imdb.com/review/rw1765550/?ref_=tt_urv>.

Proctor, William (2012), 'Regeneration and Rebirth: Anatomy of the Franchise Reboot', *Scope: An Online Journal of Film and Television Studies*, 22 (February), 1–19

Quaresima, Leonardo (2002), 'Loving Texts Two at a Time: The Film Remake', *Cinémas*, 12:3 (Printemps), 73–84.

Rasmus, Agnieszka (2013), '"I know where I've seen you before!" Remaking Gender, Class, Nationality and Politics from *The Lady Vanishes* (1938) to *Flightplan* (2005)', *Ekphrasis. Images, Cinema, Theatre, Media*, 10:1, 26–38.

'Reboot Definition' (2010), *Computer Hope*, <http://www.computerhope.com/jargon/r/reboot.htm>.

Rehling, Nicola (2009), *Extra-Ordinary Men: White Heterosexual Masculinity and Contemporary Popular Cinema*, Lanham, MD: Lexington Books.

Reynolds, David (2006), *From World War to Cold War: Churchill, Roosevelt, and the International History of the 1940s*, Oxford: Oxford University Press.

Richards, Jeffrey (1999), 'The Revolt of the Young: *If* . . .', in Anthony Aldgate and Jeffrey Richards (eds), *Best of British: Cinema and Society from 1930 to the Present*, London and New York: I. B. Tauris, pp. 203–18.

Richards, Jeffrey (1997), *Film and British National Identity*, Manchester and New York: Manchester University Press.

Ross, Deborah (2007), 'Botched Job', *The Spectator*, 21 November, <https://www.spectator.co.uk/2007/11/botched-job/>.

Scovell, Adam (2017), 'Brexit-Is-Iccumen-In: The Wicker Man and Britain Today', *The Quietus*, 10 March, <https://thequietus.com/articles/21954-wicker-man-article>.

Self, Will (2004), 'What's It All About, Jude?', *Evening Standard*, 21 October, <https://www.standard.co.uk/go/london/film/whats-it-all-about-jude-7382675.html>.

Shaffer, Anthony ([1970] 2004), *Sleuth: A Play*, London and New York: Marion Boyars.

Shail, Robert, (2019), 'Reframing the British Tough Guy: Jason Statham as Postmodern Hero', in Robert Shail and Steven Gerrard (eds), *Crank it Up – Jason Statham: Star!* Manchester: Manchester University Press, pp. 15–28.

Shail, Robert (2008), 'More, Much More . . . Roger Moore': A New Bond for a New Decade', in Robert Shail (ed.), *Seventies British Cinema*, London: Palgrave Macmillan, pp. 150–58.

Shail, Robert (ed.) (2008), *Seventies British Cinema*, London: Palgrave Macmillan.

Shail, Robert (2004), 'Masculinity and Class: Michael Caine as "Working-Class Hero"', in Phil Powrie et al. (eds), *The Trouble with Men: Masculinities in European and Hollywood Cinema*, London: Wallflower Press, pp. 66–76.

'Shelley Winters, Two-Time Academy Award Winner, Dies at 85' (2006), *New York Times*, 14 July 2006, <https://www.nytimes.com/2006/01/14/arts/shelley-winters-twotime-academy-award-winner-dies-at-85.html>.

Shreve, Ivan G. (2014), '1967 in Film Blogathon: *Bedazzled*', *Thrilling Days of Yesteryear*, 20 June, <http://thrillingdaysofyesteryear.blogspot.com/2014/06/1967-in-film-blogathon-bedazzled.html>.

Simpson, Mark (2002), 'Meet the Metrosexual', *Salon*, 22 July, <https://www.salon.com/2002/07/22/metrosexual/>.

Singer, Matt (2015), 'Welcome to the Age of the Legacyquel', *Screen Crush*, 23 November, <https://screencrush.com/the-age-of-legacyquels/>.

'*Sleuth:* Sir Michael Caine Interview' (n. d.), *IndieLondon*, <http://www.indielondon.co.uk/Film-Review/sleuth-sir-michael-caine-interview>.
Smith, Iain Robert and Constantine Verevis (eds) (2017), *Transnational Film Remakes*, Edinburgh: Edinburgh University Press.
Smith, Iain Robert (2016), *The Hollywood Meme: Transnational Adaptations in World Cinema*, Edinburgh: Edinburgh University Press.
Smith, Justin (2010), *With Nail and Us: Cult Films and Film Cults in British Cinema*, London and New York: I. B. Tauris.
Smith, Justin (2009), 'British Cult Cinema', in Robert Murphy (ed.), *The British Cinema Book*, 3rd edn, London: British Film Institute and Palgrave Macmillan, pp. 57–64.
Spelling, Ian (2000a), 'Review of *Bedazzled*', *Film Review*, (December), 22.
Spelling, Ian (2000b), 'The Devil's in the Details: Interview with Brendan Fraser and Frances O'Connor', *Film Review* (December), 63–4.
Spicer, Andrew (2010), *Historical Dictionary of Film Noir*, Lanham: Scarecrow Press.
Steenberg, Lindsay (2012a), 'Crime', in Emma Bell and Neil Mitchell (eds), *Directory of World Cinema: Britain*, Bristol: Intellect, pp. 86–89.
Steenberg, Lindsay (2012b), '*The Italian Job*', in Emma Bell and Neil Mitchell (eds), *Directory of World Cinema: Britain*, Bristol: Intellect, [n. p.].
Street, Sarah (2002), *Transatlantic Crossings: British Feature Films in the USA*, New York and London: Continuum.
Street, Sarah (1997), *British National Cinema*, London and New York: Routledge.
Stubbs, Jonathan (2002), *Sleeping with the Hegemony: British Cinema and Hollywood in the 1990s*, unpublished Master's thesis, The University of British Columbia.
Taylor, Ella (2007), '*Sleuth*: Jude Law Embraces Homophobia and Misogyny', *The Seattle Weekly*, 23 October, <https://www.seattleweekly.com/film/sleuth-jude-law-embraces-homophobia-and-misogyny/>.
'The Total Film Interview – Jude Law' (2004), *Total Film*, 1 November, <https://www.gamesradar.com/the-total-film-interview-jude-law/>.
tober (2001), 'Not That Bad a Remake Considering . . .', *IMDB*, 20 March, <https://www.imdb.com/review/rw0664266/?ref_=tt_urv>.
Tobin, Patrick (2012), '*Get Carter*', in Emma Bell and Neil Mitchell (eds), *Directory of World Cinema: Britain*, Bristol: Intellect, pp. 101–2.
Trumpbour, John (2007), *Selling Hollywood to the World: U.S. and European Struggles for Mastery of the Global Film Industry, 1920–1950*, Cambridge and New York: Cambridge University Press.
Tryon, Chuck (2009), *Reinventing Cinema: Movies in the Age of Media Convergence*, New Brunswick, NJ: Rutgers University Press.
Verevis, Constantine (2017), 'New Millennial Remakes', in Frank Kelleter (ed.), *Media of Serial Narrative*, Columbus, OH: Ohio State University Press, pp. 148–66.
Verevis, Constantine (2010), 'Redefining the Sequel: The Case of the (Living) Dead', in Carolyn Jess-Cooke and Constantine Verevis (eds), *Second Takes: Critical Approaches to the Film Sequel*, Albany, NY: SUNY Press, pp. 11–29.
Verevis, Constantine (2006a), *Film Remakes*, Edinburgh: Edinburgh University Press.
Verevis, Constantine (2006b), 'For Ever Hitchcock: *Psycho* and Its Remakes', in David Boyd and R. Barton Palmer (eds), *After Hitchcock: Influence, Imitation, and Intertextuality*, Austin, TX: University of Texas Press, pp. 15–29.
Verevis, Constantine (2004), 'Remaking Film', *Film Studies*, 4:1 (Summer), 87–103.
Walker, Alexander ([1974] 2005), *Hollywood England: The British Film Industry in the Sixties*, London: Orion.
Wang, Yiman (2013), *Remaking Chinese Cinema: Through the Prism of Shanghai, Hong Kong, and Hollywood*, Hong Kong: Hong Kong University Press.

Warmoth, Brian (2009), 'Exclusive: Michael Caine Thinks Jude Law Should Be the Next Harry Palmer', *MTV News*, 4 August, <http://www.mtv.com/news/2431881/exclusive-michael-caine-thinks-jude-law-should-be-the-next-harry-palmer/>.
Wasko, Janet (2003), *How Hollywood Works*, London, Thousand Oaks, CA, and New Delhi: Sage.
Wayne, Mike (2006), 'Working Title II: A Critique of the Atlanticist Paradigm for British Cinema', *International Journal of Media and Cultural Politics*, 2:1 (January), 59–73.
Wee, Valerie (2013), *Japanese Horror Films and Their American Remakes: Translating Fear, Adapting Culture*, New York: Routledge.
Weintraub, Steve (2007), 'Michael Caine and Kenneth Branagh Interview – *SLEUTH*', *Collider*, 8 October, <https://collider.com/michael-caine-and-kenneth-branagh-interview-sleuth/>.
'We Polled the Public on the Best Ever British Films – Can You Guess the Winner?' (2007), *Vue*, 10 July, <http://www.myvue.com/news-competitions/we-polled-the-public-on-the-best-ever-british-films>.
Williams, Alan (ed.) (2002), *Film and Nationalism*, New Brunswick, NJ, and London: Rutgers University Press.
Wood, Jason (2002), *Steven Soderbergh: The Pocket Essential Guide*, Herts: Pocket Essentials.
Young, Rob (2015), 'Examining Hollywood Remakes: *Bedazzled*', *Cinelinx*, 28 December, <http://www.cinelinx.com/movie-news/movie-stuff/examining-hollywood-remakes-bedazzled/>.
Zanger, Anat (2006), *Film Remakes as Ritual and Disguise: From Carmen to Ripley*, Amsterdam: Amsterdam University Press.

Index

References to notes are indicated by n.

10 (Edwards, 1979), 108
1960s *see* 'Swinging London'

A. I. Artificial Intelligence (Spielberg, 2001), 75, 93
abortion, 9, 67, 78, 98n16
ABPC, 4
action genre, 53–4
adolescence, 109–10
Affleck, Ben, 17
age ratings, 36
Alderman, Naomi
  The Power, 126
Alfie (Gilbert, 1966), 2, 9, 11, 13, 14, 15, 22, 29n6
  and 'Best 100' list, 23
  and Caine, 30n8, 37
  and class, 65
  and cultural context, 66–70
  and DVD, 19
  and masculinity, 76
  and misogyny, 55
  and *Sleuth* (1972), 88
  and Stamp, 142
  and 'Swinging London,' 100
  and Winters, 72–3
  and women, 76–8

Alfie (Shyer, 2004), 2, 19, 23, 28, 29n6, 134–7
  and cross-culturalism, 25, 26
  and Law, 65, 70–2, 75–6, 95–6
  and masculinity, 76
  and metrosexuality, 73–4
  and women, 78–81
'Alfie' (song), 26
Alfie Darling (Hughes, 1975), 70
Alton Towers, 114
America *see* Anglo-American relations; Hollywood; United States of America
American Beauty (Mendes, 1999), 113, 114, 146n3
And Soon the Darkness (Fuest, 1970/ Efron, 2010), 29n6
Anderson, Lindsay, 133
Andrews, Julie, 103, 108
Angel Heart (Parker, 1987), 101, 140
Anglo-American Film Agreement (1948), 5, 7
Anglo-American relations, 2–3, 24–5, 71–3
Angry Young Men, 6
Antonioni, Michelangelo, 11, 16
Armchair Theatre (TV series), 6

art, 9
Asher, Jane, 79
Asian film industry, 16
Atwood, Margaret
  The Handmaid's Tale, 126
audiences, 16–17
Austin Powers: International Man of Mystery (Roach, 1997), 21
Avenging Angelo (Burke, 2002), 61

Bacharach, Burt, 26
Badalamenti, Angelo, 26
Bailey, David, 9, 66–7, 95, 96
Balcon, Michael, 3
Bale, Christian, 95
Bancroft, Anne, 104
Bandits (Levinson, 2003), 34
Bass, Alfie, 76
Bates, Alan, 82
Bates, Tyler, 26
Beahan, Kate, 122
Beatles, 8, 9, 11, 12, 21, 141
  and mania, 103, 104–5
Bedazzled (Donen, 1967), 2, 13, 14, 15, 22, 29n6
  and BFI, 30n8
  and class, 106–8
  and DVD, 17, 18–19
  and Faustian myth, 99–103
  and old order, 129
  and promotional material, 111
  and religion, 105–6, 130n7
  and screenplay, 103–5
Bedazzled (Ramis, 2000), 2, 28, 29n6, 99, 100, 134–7
  and adolescent theme, 108–10, 113–14
  and comedy, 130
  and cross-culturalism, 25
  and economics, 23
  and Hurley, 112–13, 129
  and plot, 110–12
bees, 124, 127
Bees in Paradise (Guest, 1944), 124
BFI (British Film Institute), 18, 23, 100, 114, 133–4

Billington, Keith, 108
Billy Liar (Schlesinger, 1963), 29n6, 77
Bindon, John, 143
Black, Cilla, 26, 30n10
Blair, Tony, 21
Blood on Satan's Claw (Haggard, 1971), 116
Blow-Up (Antonioni, 1967), 11, 51, 100
Blow-Up: Blow Out (De Palma, 1981), 16
Blur, 21
Blye, Maggie, 14, 38
Bond *see* James Bond film franchise
Bonnie and Clyde (Penn, 1967), 12
Boorman, John, 11, 50
Bowie, David, 21
Braine, John, 6
Branagh, Kenneth, 87, 88
Brexit, 33, 129
Britain *see* Great Britain
British film industry, 1–7, 13–15, 21, 133–6
  and 'Best 100' list, 23, 133–4
  and 'Swinging Sixties,' 7–13
British New Wave, 5–7, 8, 11, 69, 77
  and *Get Carter*, 51, 52
Bron, Eleanor, 30n8, 100, 101, 104, 130n3
Brosnan, Pierce, 95
brutality *see* violence
Budd, Roy, 26
Bulgakov, Mikhail
  The Master and Margarita, 106
Bunny Lake is Missing (Preminger, 1965), 29n1
'Burn the Witch' (video), 114
Burning Man Festival, 114
Burstyn, Ellen, 100, 124
Burton, Richard, 48, 103
Bush, George H. W., 58

Cage, Nicolas, 20, 114–15, 122, 123–4
Caine, Michael, 21–2, 25, 31, 37–8, 63
  and class, 40
  and *Get Carter* (1971), 49, 52–3, 55, 61
  and *The Ipcress File*, 75–6
  and *The Italian Job* (1969), 32, 33, 44

and Law, 65, 70, 71, 96, 134
and *The Limey*, 139, 142
and masculinity, 41–2, 93–4, 95
and *Sleuth* (1972), 82, 85–6, 94–5
and *Sleuth* (2007), 19, 28, 87, 88
and *Zulu*, 98n18
see also Alfie (Gilbert, 1966)
California Suite (Ross, 1978), 93
cameos, 36, 44, 52–3, 134
capital punishment, 9
casting, 2, 3, 14, 27–8, 134–5
  and *Bedazzled* (2000), 108–9
  and British actors, 113
  and *Get Carter* (1971), 51–2
  and *The Italian Job* (1969), 42
  and *The Limey*, 142–4
Catch Us If You Can (Boorman, 1965), 11
censorship, 9, 27
CGI, 15
Chandler, Raymond
  Farewell, My Lovely, 50
Chapman, Graham, 108
Cher, 26
China, 14
Christie, Agatha, 82
Christie, Julie, 11, 29n6, 77, 98n13
cinemas, 4
cinematography, 51
Circus (Walker, 2000), 22
class, 2, 27, 65, 99
  and *Alfie* (1966), 65, 68
  and *Bedazzled* (1967), 103, 105, 106–8
  and English accent, 113
  and *The Italian Job* (1969), 40–1, 43
  and *Sleuth* (1972), 81–2, 83–6
  and *The Wicker Man* (1973), 116, 120, 129
  see also working classes
classical Greece, 125
Cleese, John, 108
clichés, 113, 126, 135, 136
Clinton, Hillary, 128
Clooney, George, 17
clothing, 8, 9, 21, 73–4, 105, 112–13
  and *Sleuth* (2007), 91–2, 93
Cockney slang, 144

Cold Mountain (Minghella, 2003), 72
Cold War, 5
Collection, The (Pinter), 91–2
Collector, The (Wyler, 1965), 29n1
Collins, Joan, 113, 135
Collinson, Peter, 35, 44, 133
Columbine massacre (1999), 109
comedy, 31, 35–6, 67, 108, 130, 137
  and *The Wicker Man* (2006), 124, 127, 128
comic books, 53
Compson, Betty, 3
Connery, Sean, 9, 11, 68, 95
consumerism, 68–9, 76
Conversation, The (Coppola, 1974), 16, 146n1
Cook, Peter, 18, 25, 30n8, 99–100, 101
  and class, 106–7
  and screenplay, 103, 104–5
'Cool Britannia,' 20–1, 33
Cop Land (Mangold, 1997), 54, 61, 135
Coppola, Francis Ford, 16
Corman, Roger, 19
counterculture, 99, 100, 106, 143
  and *The Wicker Man* (1973), 115, 116, 119–20
Courtenay, Tom, 6–7
Coward, Noël, 32, 40
Cox, Alex, 22, 29n7
Creed (Coogler, 2015), 86
crime genre, 31
criminal underworld, 143–4; *see also* Kray brothers
cross-culturalism, 23–9, 134, 136, 144–5
cross-pollination, 14

D-Tox (Gillespie, 2002), 61
Dallesandro, Joe, 144
Damn Yankees (Donen, 1958), 101, 105
Darling (Schlesinger, 1965), 100
Dave Clark Five, 11
David, Hal, 26
Day of the Jackal, The (Zinnemann, 1973), 29n6
De Niro, Robert, 54
De Palma, Brian, 16

Death at a Funeral (Oz, 2007/LaBute, 2010), 29n5
Deathtrap (Lumet, 1982), 88, 93
Deeley, Michael, 13, 33, 34, 36, 42
Deep End (Skolimowski, 1970), 11
Delaney, Shelagh, 6
design, 51
detective genre, 82, 84, 115, 116
Devil *see* Faust legend; religion
Devil's Advocate, The (Hackford, 1997), 101
Did You Hear About The Morgans (Lawrence, 2009), 71
digital era, 15–20, 60–1
direct address to camera, 66, 74, 79
directors, 10
directors' cuts, 19–20
Dirty Harry (Siegel, 1971), 50
Dirty Rotten Scoundrels (Oz, 1988), 99
divorce, 9
Dobbs, Lem, 139, 142, 144
documentaries, 6, 51
Donen, Stanley, 10, 13, 14, 29n1, 101
Don't Look Now (Roeg, 1973), 25, 29n6, 37, 122
Dr. No (Young, 1962), 68
Dracula (Browning, 1931), 105
Dracula (Fisher, 1958), 105
DVDs, 15–16, 17–20
Dylan, Bob, 141
Dynasty (TV series), 113

Eady Levy, 11
Easy Rider (Hopper, 1969), 12, 143
economics, 23–4
editing, 145
education, 9
Edwards, Blake, 108
Ekland, Britt, 55, 118
Elstree Studios, 4
England *see* London; Northern England
Englishness, 71–2
Epps, Omar, 76
Equal Pay Act (1970), 9
Escape (Mankiewicz, 1948), 29n4
Escape! (Dean, 1930), 29n4

Exorcist, The (Friedkin, 1973), 124
Eye of the Devil (Thompson, 1967), 119
Eyes Wide Shut (Kubrick, 1999), 29n1

fantasies, 100, 129
fashion *see* clothing
Faust myth, 99–100, 101–3, 106
female characters *see* women
feminism, 21; *see also* post-feminism
Ferris Bueller's Day Off (Hughes, 1986), 74
Field, Shirley Anne, 77
film geeks, 16–17
film noir, 7, 14
Finney, Albert, 6–7, 9, 69
F.I.S.T. (Jewison, 1978), 53
flashbacks, 145
Flightplan (Schwentke, 2005), 29n1
Fonda, Peter, 25, 140, 143
Force Awakens, The (Abrams, 2015), 86
Four Weddings and a Funeral (Newell, 1994), 21, 24, 71, 112
Franco, James, 127
Fraser, Brendan, 25, 100, 105, 108–9, 110
Frazer, Sir James George
 The Golden Bough: A Study in Comparative Religion, 116
French film industry, 6, 16
Frenzy (Hitchcock, 1972), 82
From Russia with Love (Young, 1963), 68
Full Fidelity (Frears, 2000), 74
Full Monty, The (Cattaneo, 1997), 21, 34, 97n6
funding, 11

Gaghan, Stephen, 76
Gair, Erika-Shaye, 122
Gallagher, Liam, 21
Gambit (Neame, 1966), 32
gambling, 9
gangster genre, 22, 31, 45; see also *Get Carter*
Gangster No. 1 (McGuigan, 2000), 22

Gaskin, Stephen, 120
Gatiss, Mark, 116
gay culture, 73, 74–5, 76; *see also* homosexuality
gender, 2, 89–94, 121–2, 124
  and swapping, 99–100, 129, 130n1
  and updating, 27, 28
  see also men; women
genre, 2, 7, 32, 53–4, 89; *see also* detective genre; gangster genre; heist genre; horror genre; neo-noir; romantic comedy genre; westerns
George, Melissa, 140
Get Carter (Hodges, 1971), 2, 13, 14, 15, 29n6
  and 'Best 100' list, 23
  and Caine, 30n8
  and casting, 51–2
  and filmmakers, 22
  and genre, 31, 50–1
  and Hendry, 144
  and journey, 58–60
  and *Moviedrome*, 29n7
  and original idea, 47–8
  and plot, 48–9
  and poster, 64n1
  and restored print, 18
  and violence, 49–50
  and women, 55–6, 57, 62
  see also *Limey, The*
Get Carter (Kay, 2000), 2, 28, 29n6, 63, 134–7
  and Caine, 52–3, 142
  and cross-culturalism, 25, 26
  and economics, 23
  and journey, 60–1
  and morality, 56–8
  and Stallone, 54–5, 61–2
Ghost Rider (Johnson, 2007), 101
Ghostbusters (Feigs, 2016), 99
Gilbert, Lewis, 11, 133
Giovanni, Paul, 26
Girl with the Dragon Tattoo, The (Oplev, 2009/Fincher, 2011), 29n5
Gish, Dorothy, 3

Goethe, Johann Wolfgang von
  Faust, 101
Goldfinger (Hamilton, 1964), 68
Gorton, Asheton, 51
Graduate, The (Nichols, 1967), 12, 103–4
Grant, Hugh, 71, 97n6, 112
Gray, F. Gary, 42
Great Britain, 11–12, 20–1, 48, 67–8, 129; see also Anglo-American relations; British film industry; London; Northern England; Scotland
Green, Seth, 44
Guzán, Luis, 144

Haggard, Piers, 116
Handl, Irene, 36
Happiest Millionaire, The (Tokar, 1967), 144
Hard Day's Night, A (Lester, 1964), 8, 21
Hardy, Robin, 114
Hardy, Thomas, 133
Harris, Richard, 6–7
Heist (Mamet, 2003), 34
heist genre, 32–3, 34, 36, 45
Hendrix, Jimi, 146n2
Hendry, Ian, 144
heroism, 27
Hill, Benny, 36, 44
Hill, The (Lumet, 1965), 29n1
hippie movements, 103, 115, 119, 120
History of Horror, A (documentary), 116
Hit Man (Armitage, 1972), 47
Hitchcock, Alfred, 10, 16, 29n1, 123, 137
Hodges, Mike, 51–2, 53, 55, 133
Hollies, The, 141
Hollywood, 7, 23
  and British film industry, 1–6, 13–15, 133–7
  and 'Swinging London', 7–8, 9–11
homosexuality, 9, 105, 82, 86, 89–94
horror genre, 121, 122, 124, 135; *see also* rural horror genre

Hot Fuzz (Wright, 2007), 114
housing, 9
Houston, Whitney, 26
How to Kill Your Neighbor's Dog (Kalesniko, 2000), 97n6
Human Traffic (Kerrigan, 1999), 97n6
Hurley, Elizabeth, 25, 100, 108–9, 111–13, 135
Hustle, The (Addison, 2019), 99

iconic British films, 13–15
identity, 6
Idle, Eric, 103
Insomnia (Nolan, 2002), 122–3
interaction, 16–17
internationalism, 11
Internet Movie Database (IMDb), 16, 17, 18
intertextuality, 27, 53
Into Thin Air (Hitchcock, 1955), 29n1
Invasion, The (Hirschbiegel, 2007), 130n1
Ipcress File, The (Furie, 1965), 9, 32, 75–6, 97n10
Iron Maiden, 114
Italian Job, The (Collinson, 1969), 2, 13, 14, 15, 29n6
  and 'Best 100' list, 23
  and Caine, 30n8
  and class, 40–1
  and cliff-hanger, 45–6, 64n2
  and DVD, 17–18
  and genre, 31
  and *Get Carter* (1971), 52
  and masculinity, 41–2
  and plot, 34–5
  and poster, 64n1
  and Ritchie, 22
  and script, 32–3, 35–6
  and success, 33–4
  and women, 37, 38, *39*, 44, 55, 62
Italian Job, The (Gray, 2003), 2, 17–18, 28, 29n6, 34, 63, 134–7
  and British references, 46–7
  and cross-culturalism, 25

  and economics, 23
  and love story, 42–3
  and masculinity, 44–5
  and plot, 36–7
  and Wahlberg, 43–4
  and women, 38–40, *41*

Jackal (Caton-Jones, 1997), 29n6
Jagger, Mick, 26
James Bond film franchise, 11, 12, 68, 69, 77, 97n10
Jones, Quincy, 14, 33

Kay, Stephen, 47, 52–3, 61
Keitel, Harvey, 54, 55
Kennedy, Jackie, 103
Kennedy, John F., 10
Kennedy Martin, Troy, 32–3, 35–6, 38
Kensit, Patsy, 21
Kermode, Mark, 20
Kidman, Nicole, 130n1
King, Stephen
  Children of the Corn, 121
Kinks, The, 21
'kitchen sink' drama, 6, 25–6, 66, 68
Knack… and How to Get It, The (Lester, 1965), 100, 103
Korda, Alexander, 4
Krakowski, Jane, 78
Kray brothers, 9, 48
Kubrick, Stanley, 10, 29n1, 133

LaBute, Neil, 100, 121, 122, 123, 124–9, 136–7
Lad culture, 14, 21–2, 33, 45, 49
Lady Vanishes, The (Hitchcock, 1939), 29n1
Ladykillers, The (Mackendrick, 1955), 29n5, 32
Ladykillers, The (Cohen brothers, 2004), 29n5
Latessa, Dick, 81
Lavender Hill Mob (Crichton, 1951), 32
Law, Jude, 19, 25, 28, 65, 70–2, 81
  and Caine, 75–6
  and metrosexuality, 73–5, 92, 94, 95

and 'Sexiest Man Alive' award, 97n9
and *Sleuth* (2007), 86–7
and *The Third Day*, 114
League of Gentlemen, The (TV series), 114
Leary, Timothy, 141
Lee, Christopher, 20, 100, 105, 115, 117, 120
legacyquels, 86, 94
Lennon, John, 9, 104–5
Lester, Richard, 8, 133, 138
Levin, Ira, 88
Lewis, Ted
 Jack's Return Home, 48
lighting, 138
Limey, The (Soderbergh, 1999), 2, 22, 28–9, 29n6, 47
 and analysis, 137–47
 and cross-culturalism, 25–6
 and economics, 23
literature, 6
Loach, Ken, 25–6, 133, 139
location, 51, 52, 138
Lock, Stock and Two Smoking Barrels (Ritchie, 1998), 21, 22, 44–5
Lodger, The (Hitchcock, 1927/Brahm, 1944), 29n4
Lolita (Kubrick, 1963), 29n1
London, 7–13, 48–9, 50, 144–5; *see also* 'Swinging London'
Long, Nia, 79
Look Back in Anger (Osborne), 52
Look Back in Anger (Richardson, 1958), 6, 103
Lord of the Flies (Brook, 1963/Hook, 1990), 29n4
Losey, Joseph, 133
Love Actually (Curtis, 2003), 34
Love, Honour and Obey (Burdis and Anciano, 2000), 22
Lucifer (TV series), 113
Lugosi, Bela, 105
Lumet, Sidney, 10, 29n1

McCartney, Paul, 9, 79, 104
MacDowell, Andie, 71
McGrath, Joe, 106

McGregor, Ewan, 95
Man Who Knew Too Much, The (Hitchcock, 1934/1956), 16
Mankiewicz, Joseph, 10, 14, 29n1, 85
Manson murders, 120
Marlowe, Christopher
 Doctor Faustus, 101
Marsh, Mae, 3
Martin, Millicent, 66
Marvin, Lee, 11
masculinity, 9, 14, 21, 134
 and *Alfie* (1966), 68–70, 76
 and Caine, 93–4, 95
 and *Get Carter* (1971), 49
 and *The Italian Job* (2003), 41–2, 43, 44–5
 see also metrosexuality
mash-up videos, 136
May, Theresa, 128
Melvin, Murray, 76
men, 9, 62, 97n6, 113–14, 132n22;
 see also masculinity
Mendes, Sam, 146n3
Mephisto (Szabó, 1981), 101
Merchant, Vivien, 67
metrosexuality, 73–5, 94
MGM Studios, 13, 47–8
Mickey Blue Eyes (Makin, 1999), 71
Midnight Cowboy (Schlesinger, 1969), 12, 144
Miller, Arthur, 6
Miller, Jonathan, 107
Miller, Sienna, 25, 79
Mini Cooper cars, 22, 25, 32, 35, 36, 42, 46–7
mise-en-scène, 51, 88
Misery (Reiner, 1990), 123
misogyny, 6, 49, 55, 62, 77
 and *Alfie* (1966), 66
 and *The Wicker Man* (2006), 127–9
Monthy Python, 103
Moore, Dudley, 18, 99–100, 101, 106–7, 108
 and screenplay, 103, 104–5
morality, 50, 55, 56–8
Mormonism, 121

Moss, Kate, 21
motifs, 139
Motion Picture Association of America (MPAA), 4
Motown Records, 12
Moviedrome (TV series), 22, 29n7
Murder, My Sweet (Dmytryk, 1944), 50
music, 8, 9, 12, 21, 114
   and cross-culturalism, 26
   and *The Limey*, 141–2
   see also soundtracks
Music and Lyrics (Lawrence, 2007), 71

narrative, 134, 137
Naughton, Bill, 72
neo-noir, 31, 48, 50, 140, 145
New Wave *see* British New Wave
Newcastle, 50–1, 52, 58–60
Newman, Barry, 143–4
Newman, Sydney, 6
Nine Months (Columbus, 1995), 71
noir *see* film noir; neo-noir
Northern England, 6–7, 8, 50–1, 52, 58–60, 69–70
Norton, Edward, 44
nostalgia, 21, 33, 49
Not Only But Also (TV show), 104, 105, 106
Notting Hill (Michell, 1999), 1, 3, 21, 24, 71

Oasis, 21
Ocean's 8 (Ross, 2018), 99
Ocean's Eleven (Soderbergh, 2001), 34
O'Connor, Frances, 25, 110
'Old Habits Die Hard' (song), 26
Oldman, Gary, 21, 95
Olivier, Sir Laurence, 65, 82, 85–6, 94–5
Omen, The (Donner, 1976/Moore, 2006), 29n6
One and Only, Genuine, Original Family Band, The (O'Herlihy, 1968), 144
online content, 136
Osborne, John, 6, 51–2, 143
O'Toole, Fintan, 33
Owen, Clive, 95

paganism, 114, 116, 124–7, 129, 131n16
Palomar Pictures International, 13
Paramount Studios, 13, 14, 17, 19, 33
patriarchy, 62, 136
peace movements, 103
Peckinpah, Sam, 10, 29n1
Performance (Cammell/Roeg, 1969), 48, 141, 143
Phantom of the Paradise (De Palma, 1974), 101
Pinewood Studios, 4, 11
Pinner, David
   Ritual, 116
Pinter, Harold, 86–8, 89
Point Blank (Boorman, 1967), 11, 50, 145
Polanski, Roman, 11
politics, 3, 11, 33, 35, 103, 129
Poor Cow (Loach, 1967), 26, 139, 143
Pop art, 8, 9
pop music *see* music
Pope, Elaine, 75, 76, 78
post-feminism, 128
posters, 21, 50, 52, 64n1, 111
   and *The Italian Job* (1969), 33, 38
   and *The Wicker Man* (2006), 121, 132n21
Powers, Donna and Wayne, 36
Preminger, Otto, 10, 29n1
Private Life of Henry VIII (Korda, 1933), 4
production facilities, 11
promiscuity, 77, 104, 129
Psycho (Hitchcock, 1960), 137
Psycho (Van Sant, 1998), 137–8
Psychomania (Sharp, 1973), 131n16

Quale, Anthony, 82
Quant, Mary, 9
Quota Act (1927), 3
quotability, 25, 34, 55

race, 12, 64n6, 79
Radiohead, 114
Rambo film series, 53, 55, 58
Ramis, Harold, 100, 108, 109–10, 137

Rancid Aluminium (Thomas, 2000), 22
Rank, 4
re-adaptations, 87, 135
Reagan, Ronald, 58
Real Blonde, The (DiCillo, 1998), 97n6
reboots, 53–5, 61–2, 94, 135
Redford, Robert, 14, 42
Reed, Oliver, 21
regionalism, 6–7, 14, 138
Reisz, Karel, 133
religion, 100, 104–6, 122, 130n7
   and *Bedazzled* (2000), 111, 113
   and *The Wicker Man* (1973), 131n15, 131n18
   see also paganism
remakes, 22, 15–20, 133–7, 138–9
   and cross-cultural, 23–9
   and gender-switching, 99–100
Repulsion (Polanski, 1965), 11
Resnais, Alain, 138
Rewrite, The (Lawrence, 2014), 71
Richardson, Tony, 133
Richardson gang, 48
Rise and Rise of Michael Rimmer, The (Billington, 1971), 108
Ritchie, Guy, 22, 44–5
Ritt, Martin, 10, 29n1
Road to Perdition (Mendes, 2002), 72
Rocky film series, 53, 55, 58, 62
Roeg, Nicolas, 133
Rolling Stones, 9, 12, 106; *see also* Jagger, Mick
Rollins, Sonny, 26
romantic comedy genre, 1, 71, 72, 81, 96, 135
   and *Bedazzled* (2000), 100, 109, 129
Room, The (Wiseau, 2003), 130
Room at The Top (Clayton, 1959), 6
Roth, Tim, 95
rural horror genre, 115–16

Sarandon, Susan, 25, 78, 79
Sassoon, Vidal, 9, 84
Saturday Night and Sunday Morning (Reisz, 1960), 6, 69
Schlesinger, John, 11, 133

School for Scoundrels (Hamer, 1960/ Phillips, 2006), 29n6
Score, The (Oz, 2003), 34
Scotland, 115, 116
secularism, 103
'Self-Preservation Society, The' (song), 14
sequels, 66, 70, 135, 139
Servant, The (Losey, 1963), 88, 92, 93
sex, 6, 27, 62
sexism, 21
sexual revolution, 9, 59, 77, 103
sexuality, 88, 129, 111–12; *see also* homosexuality; women
Shaffer, Anthony, 82–2, 86, 88, 116
Shakespeare, William
   Macbeth, 123
Shyer, Charles, 72, 75, 81
Sillitoe, Alan, 6
Skolimowski, Jerzy, 11
Sleuth (Branagh, 2007), 19, 28, 29n6, 134–7
   and Caine, 142
   and cross-culturalism, 27
   and economics, 24
   and homo-eroticism, 89–94
   and influences, 88–9
   and Law, 65, 95–6
   and re-adapation, 86–8
Sleuth (Mankiewicz, 1972), 13, 14, 15, 22, 29n6
   and Caine, 30n8, 94–5
   and class, 65, 81–2, 83–6
   and DVD, 19
   and remake, 87–8, 89
Sleuth (Shaffer), 82, 87, 89
slum clearances, 9
Snatch (Ritchie, 2000), 44
Sobieski, Leelee, 127
social-realism, 6–7
Soderbergh, Steven *see Limey, The*
soundtracks, 14, 26, 33, 68, 104
'special relationship,' 2–3, 5, 24–5
Spice Girls, 21
Spies, Johann
   Historia von D. Johann Fausten, 101

Spy Who Came In from the Cold, The (Ritt, 1965), 29n1
Stallone, Sylvester, 18, 25, 28, 52–3, 63
   and rebooting, 53–5, 61–2
Stamp, Chris, 146n2
Stamp, Terence, 9, 25, 29n1, 38, 139, 142–3
Star Wars (Lucas, 1977), 11
Stark, Graham, 76
Statham, Jason, 25, 44–5, 134
Stepford Wives (Forbes, 1974), 13
Stepford Wives, The (Oz, 2007), 130n1
Stewart, David A., 26
Storey, David, 6
Straw Dogs (Lurie, 2011), 29n6
Straw Dogs (Peckinpah, 1971), 29n1, 29n6
Streisand, Barbra, 26
structure, 145
substance abuse, 144
Superman (Donner, 1978), 11
supernatural, 99, 105
Suschitzky, Wolfgang, 51
Sutherland, Donald, 37, 44
'Swinging London,' 7–13, 21, 42, 58–60, 100
   and *The Italian Job* (1969), 32, 33

taglines, 37
Talented Mr Ripley, The (Minghella, 1999), 72, 74
Tarantino, Quentin, 22
Taste of Honey, A (Richardson, 1961), 76
taxation, 4
television, 12
Terminator: Genisys (Taylor, 2015), 86
theatre, 6, 9, 52, 82
Theron, Charlize, 32, 38–9
Third Day, The (TV series), 114
thriller genre, 89
Thunderball (Young, 1965), 11, 68, 97n10
Tom Jones (Richardson, 1963), 8
Tomei, Marisa, 25, 76
tone, 35–6
Trainspotting (Boyle, 1996), 21, 34
transnationalism, 2–4, 11, 14, 24, 50, 136

Truffaut, François, 11
Tushingham, Rita, 6–7, 103
Twiggy, 21
Two Weeks Notice (Lawrence, 2002), 71

Union Jack flag, 21
United States of America (USA), 7, 11–12, 21, 33, 144–5; *see also* Anglo-American relations; Hollywood

vampires, 105
Van Sant, Gus, 137
Vanishing Point (Sarafian, 1971), 143, 145
VHS, 16, 17
Village of the Damned, The (Rilla, 1960/ Carpenter, 1995), 29n6, 121
Villain (Tuchner, 1971), 48
violence, 35–6, 49–50, 57–8

Wahlberg, Mark, 25, 28, 39, 42–4, 63
Walker, Alexander, 66–7, 68, 70
   Hollywood England, 8
Warhol, Andy, 144
Warner Bros Studios, 18, 19–20, 121–2
Warren, Lesley Ann, 144
Warwick, Dionne, 26
Watanabe, Gedde, 80
Web 2.0, 16
Welch, Raquel, 14, 103, 111
welfare state, 9
westerns, 7, 14, 50–1, 123
Whisky Galore! (Mackendrick, 1949/ Mackinnon, 2016), 29n4
Who, The, 141, 146n2–3
Wicker Man, The (Hardy, 1973), 13, 15, 22, 29n6, 100
   and 'Best 100' list, 23
   and cult status, 114
   and DVD, 19–20
   and genre, 115–16
   and *Moviedrome*, 29n7
   and plot, 116–20
   and Shaffer, 82
   and women, 129

Wicker Man, The (LaBute, 2006), 28, 29n6, 99, 100, 114–15, 134–7
  and comedy, 130
  and cross-culturalism, 25, 26, 27
  and economics, 23–4
  and gender, 121–2, 124–9
  and Lee, 142
  and plot, 122–4
'Wicker Man, The' (song), 114
Wilcox, Herbert, 3
Williams, Tennessee, 6
Williams, Vanessa, 26
Wilson, Harold, 21
Winters, Shelley, 14, 72–3
witchcraft, 123, 126
Witchfinder General (Reeves, 1968), 116
women, 6, 27, 62, 64n4, 136
  and *Alfie* (1966), 66, 67, 76–8
  and *Alfie* (2004), 78–81
  and *Bedazzled* (2000), 111–12
  and *Get Carter* (1971), 55–7, 59
  and Hitchcock, 123
  and *The Italian Job* (1969), 32, 37, 38–40, 42–3, 47
  and male fantasies, 102
  and rights, 9
  and *The Wicker Man* (1973), 122
  and *The Wicker Man* (2006), 124–9
  see also feminism; misogyny
Wonder, Stevie, 12, 26
Woodward, Edward, 116
working classes, 6–7, 9, 14, 28, 69
  and *Get Carter* (1971), 51, 52
World Trade Center (Stone, 2006), 124
World War II, 68
Wyler, William, 10, 29n1

youth, 9
YouTube, 127

Zeitgeist, 13, 22, 33, 66, 142
Zulu (Endfield, 1964), 34, 40, 98n18

EU representative:
Easy Access System Europe
Mustamäe tee 50, 10621 Tallinn, Estonia
Gpsr.requests@easproject.com

www.ingramcontent.com/pod-product-compliance
Lightning Source LLC
Chambersburg PA
CBHW071847230426
43671CB00012B/2091